"Namedropper" is published by :

Trinity Mirror NW²

Trinity Mirror North West & North Wales
PO Box 48
Old Hall Street,
Liverpool L69 3EB

Trinity Mirror Sport Media. Executive Editor:
Ken Rogers

Design / production:
Daisy Dutton, Jonathan Low, Emma Smart

Cover image:
Adam Yaffé

ISBN 978 1 905266 41 8

PETE PRICE
namedropper

with
Adrian Butler

Foreword
by Paul O'Grady

In the days of the early 70's, a time when I was living at home with my parents in Birkenhead, life was still relatively simple. My only worries and concerns back then were getting a ticket to see T Rex at The Liverpool Stadium and whether or not my dad would lend me thirty bob towards a gingham Ben Sherman shirt that I'd coveted since the day I'd clapped eyes on it in the window of 'the Gear Box' on Borough Road. I was working as a clerical assistant at the time, in the D.H.S.S in the now demolished Steers House on Canning Place.

I was paid eight quid a week plus luncheon vouchers. To brighten our social lives the Civil Service saw fit to inflict upon us a sports and social club run by a very outgoing president – an enthusiastic woman called Doreen who chivvied and bossed us into taking part in the numerous after work activities that she'd carefully planned to broaden our minds and bond the staff of Steers House together.

She was a very persuasive woman this Doreen, to be honest she was a pain in the bloody neck but her persistence eventually wore me down and I found myself horse riding on a cold Sunday morning in the grounds of a convent in Childwall and then traipsing around Speke Hall in the afternoon with a pack of brownies who Doreen 'Brown-Owled" in what little spare time she had.

She also organised trips to the theatre and it was on one of

these that I first encountered Pete Price. Somehow I was shanghaied into joining a party of women and one pasty faced youth, a peculiar individual who had boils on the back of his neck and rarely spoke. He was known as 'Lurch' due to his uncanny resemblance to the butler in The Addams Family.

They were off to see Soloman King, whose hit record was She Wears My Ring, a singer who was appearing at the Shakespeare Club, a former theatre that sadly burned down in 1976. The 'Shakey' had been turned into a very smart club, all red plush and mood lighting with scampi and chips in baskets and big international names appearing on the bill each week. Pete was resident compere and mine host. It was the era of the night club, an exciting time.

Now in those days, believe or not, I was still comparatively innocent (it was a long time ago). I must have been breast fed chlorophyll I was so green. Pete's act was a revelation. He strutted around the stage like an arrogant turkey-cock, baiting the audience, abusing them, sending them up and ruthlessly taking the piss. He was lewd, rude, bawdy but above all, I thought, extremely brave as proudly and unashamedly he flirted with the male punters, making no bones about his sexuality, defying the audience of mainly gangsters and their molls not to like him. The crowd loved him. Pete Price WAS the Shakespeare. His name was synonymous with the place.

Like a latter day Texas Guinan he controlled the crowd with the effortless ease of a seasoned lion tamer. He was as flamboyant off stage as he was on. There used to be a club in Wood Street called 'The Bar Royale' known universally as 'Sadie's' after the club's owner, a malevolent old queen with the profile of a gargoyle and the misdemeanour of a Doberman Pinscher with toothache.

It was into Sadie's Pete would sweep with a retinue of followers. Talk about the circus arriving in town. He was quite a sight – not camp at all – three-inch platform shoes peeping out from under the hem of a pair of white flares, a pink paisley patterned shirt, unbuttoned to the waist revealing a deeply tanned chest, festooned with an assortment of gold chains and medallions. Startlingly large diamond rings adorned each finger and a pair of enormous (and I daresay highly expensive) designer sunglasses were perched on top of his peroxide blonde head. To complete this modest ensemble he sported a full length wolf fur coat, casually draped over his shoulders.

He could've been the lovechild of Dick Emery and Cruella De Vil. He made Liberace look like a member of the Amish.

I'd never seen anything like it. I was part fascinated, part terrified.

Our paths didn't cross until many years later. The clerical assistant had by now emerged from his chrysalis and become Lily Savage and was returning home to play a few nights at The Neptune Theatre. It was my first proper tour: I was still relatively unknown to a mainstream audience and I needed all the publicity I could get if I was to sell tickets, however, producers and bookers were very wary. No matter how many times I tried I couldn't get a spot on This Morning, which was then still broadcasting from Albert Dock. Richard and Judy were more than a little apprehensive at the idea of having a drag queen with a dubious reputation on their sofa. The Big Breakfast wouldn't touch me with a barge pole and even Granada Reports were reticent to have anything to do with me. Then Pete came to the rescue and invited me on to his radio show, generously letting me burble on for three hours. Result? House Sold Out.

I've been burbling on Pete's show regularly now for years, not necessarily just to plug a new project, but because I enjoy doing it, and I'm not the only one. It's a great show and Pete is very good at his job, as his many listeners who tune in and phone in each night will testify. There he sits in his ivory tower night after night, surveying the city below that he loves so much, inviting its night owls to "give us a call". Pete can be funny, bitchy, annoying, interesting, provocative and, on those poignant occasions, incredibly understanding as he provides the only ear willing to listen to a lonely little voice in the wee small hours of the morning. He's part DJ, part counsellor, and should be put on the payroll of Liverpool Social Services.

His energy knows no bounds, he thinks nothing of doing two shows a day in panto, popping into a children's ward with some of the cast between the matinee and evening performance to cheer the kids up, and then driving to the studio when the curtain comes down to present three hours of radio stopping off en route to do a spot in a club.

He drives up and down the length and breadth of the motorway, on his own, week in, week out to perform 'the act' in various venues: clubs, holiday camps, care-homes, mortuaries, hospital wards for the bewildered – you name it, he plays 'em all, managing to remain stoic and optimistic in the face of it at all times. He's a survivor, an eternal optimist and is what's known in the trade as a trouper. I salute him.

And just in case you're thinking it… no, he hasn't had a leg-over with me in the back of his car on Otterspool Prom.

Sonia was mine and Lily's love child

Peter has been a close and treasured friend of mine since I was a teenager.

We first became friends when he had the first ever karaoke night in Southport where on a weekly basis we would belt out the duet "Love Lifts Us Up Where We Belong" (Peter as macho as possible).

Not only has Peter been a great support throughout my career he's been a true and valued friend (Peter you talked me into doing my album when I had doubts and I thank you for that).

Peter has made me, his listeners and many others LAUGH over the years (especially at the Grand National, our annual day out).

But there is also a very caring and sensitive side to Peter which I have witnessed first hand, with his dedicated commitment and ongoing support to Claire House Children's Hospice.

Peter, not only are you a survivor, a brilliant entertainer, and a credit to Liverpool, Tony and I feel very blessed to have you in our lives.

We love you dearly and wish you every success and happiness.

Claire Sweeney

PS You can sleep in our office anytime.

PPS Stop stalking Shirley BASSEYYYYYY!

God I wish I was straight!

CHAPTER ONE

£300
for a fur coat

"YOU soft get!" I shrieked. "How could you believe that?"

I'd just told someone the story of how my mum got me – the story she told me when I was a little boy. It was a little white lie to make me feel good about my background as I grew up. And he'd believed it!

Let me explain. I was adopted when I was three months old, and my mum was determined I would know about it straight away – before I grew up and the nose grew big enough to give it away. She used a little bit of poetic licence. It doesn't involve the stork dropping me in the window, or dad finding me in the vegetable garden, but it isn't far off. Want to hear it? Well, here it is.

In May 1946, the story went, Hilda May Price set off from the two-bed semi-detached house where she lived with her husband David. She caught a train at West Kirby station which took her across Wirral, under the River Mersey, and out into Liverpool Central Station. Hilda, a quiet, pretty 32-year-old, was nervously carrying a thick pile of banknotes in her coat pocket. David had given her £300 in cash – about £7,000 today, but it doesn't really matter – and she was going to buy a fur coat.

Hilda, however, never got that far. On the way to look around George Henry Lee's or one of the posh boutiques that would have sold her the coat, she walked past a little shop window. Her eye caught a baby sitting there, watching the people walk by.

She stopped and looked at the baby. It was about three months old, and starting to get the blond curls she would let grow like all the mums did in those days, making him look like a little girl. And, like someone who spots the perfect pair of shoes and walks in a trance to buy them, she went inside and asked if she could have the baby. They got me off the shelves, packaged me up and she took me home. I was what you call an impulse purchase.

That's the story – see what I mean? Who on earth would actually think they'd put a baby in a shop window, not to mention let someone who'd just walked off the street buy one? It sounds like something from Oliver Twist.

Then I realised something: It must have been the way I told the story.

Because, to me, it's more than a story; it's something I've been telling all my life to people who ask where I came from. Everyone I've met knows it.

And the reason why? I don't actually know much more than that. I don't know how many forms she had to fill in, how long her and my dad had to wait patiently for the telephone call or the letter in the post or the man in a suit calling at their house. Until the day she died, I never managed to get more than that story out of my mum.

Whenever I brought it up, I would never get anywhere. She would look hurt, start crying, or go into one of the long sulks that could last for days. She had been desperate for a child for years. I've no idea why she couldn't have one – do you think I was going to ask her that? – but I think it might have been something hereditary, as there were a few of us on her side of the family who were adopted. One of my cousins had real problems dealing with the idea, and would later die in a motorcycle accident.

And the story of the baby in the window, if I'm honest, helped me a bit as well. Although I had the most loving mother anyone could wish for, I spent my whole childhood feeling insecure. I remember once I had done something naughty – she'd given me money for something and I'd spent it on grapes, which were expensive then. I'd eaten them all myself, not keeping any for her – typical.

I got back and when she asked for her change I'd lied, and told her I had put the money down for a Christmas present for her. "I don't want the Christmas present," she said. "I need the money back. Go back to the shop and cancel it."

I broke down in tears and told her the truth. She was furious and started slapping the back of my legs. "I didn't tell you because I was worried you'd send me back to the adoption agency!" I told her.

When I said that, she stopped, stared at me, and started slapping me again. "Don't ever say that!" she cried. She was devastated I could even think she'd do something like that.

And as I grew up, she didn't just drum in that I wasn't going to be sent back anywhere. She made proud of the fact I was adopted.

"Remember," she'd say to me, "I chose you. Everyone else's parents didn't have a choice. But I did, and you were the one I picked." When I remembered this, all through my life, I always saw the image of a little baby sitting like a hat or a gas cooker in the shop window. It helped me when, years later, I was appearing in a show and mum was telling my horrible cousin John she was looking forward to seeing me.

"Why are you bothering?" he sneered. "He's only adopted – it's not as if he's even your real son." Maybe not, but to this woman, I was more important than any child on earth, and saying that was like putting a knife into her heart.

So what sort of family was I adopted into? Well, mum had fallen for dad after he moved to Merseyside from the South Wales mining town of Merthyr Tydfil where he grew up in a strict Welsh church background. The fruit seller's son wasn't the best looking in the world – he was small and bald and nondescript looking – but he was an outgoing, jokey, popular man and everyone loved him around the local pubs.

They were married in February 1938 in the Presbyterian Church on Meols Drive, West Kirby: dad was 25 and working as a joiner; mum was 26. Who'd have thought all those years later I'd have had her funeral there.

Then there was a six-year wait until I came along. Mum must have been heartbroken when she found out she couldn't have children. But somehow, in April 1946 (as Britain's Labour government was nationalising the coal mines) she got me.

I wonder what this quiet, middle class couple would have said if someone had told them how their son would grow up? How I'd discover I was gay, and go through hell to try and change it. How I'd train as a chef, get a job at a nightclub and then find myself on the stage. How I'd spend more than 40 years in showbusiness, going through the excitement, the glory and later, the heartbreak and suicidal thoughts when things didn't go right. How I'd tour the world, playing to audiences in Las Vegas, Hollywood and South Africa. How, five times a week, I'd spend the hours of 10pm to 2am listening to anyone in the North West who was up at that time and wanted a chat – a lot of interesting people who want to get their views across, and dozens of drunks, drug addicts, prats, pranksters and suicides.

How, after the late-night phone-in show had become a place all sorts of people turned to for company, I would twice drop the phone and rush out of the studio after getting worried about a caller. Once I would be in time; the other I wouldn't.

You WILL like me!

And how, more than 50 years later, I would solve the mystery of who my parents were. Plus, of course, how I'd become the biggest namedropper on the planet. "Oh, you've dropped a name," my friends say to me when I mention yet another famous person. "Shall I pick it up for you?"

"Pricey's off again.
You'd actually spoken for five minutes
without namedropping till now."

Because namedropping, for me, is like a disease. I've seen George Michael naked (before everyone knew he was gay), and been suspected of dating Olivia Newton-John (before everyone knew I was gay). I've gone on stage with Tommy Cooper and been Bob Monkhouse's double in Barbados, even though I look nothing like him. But don't get me started on the namedropping. There'll be plenty of that later in the book.

It's an odd life story, isn't it? And it certainly isn't for the faint-hearted, I'll warn you now. I have no idea what Hilda Price, this modest woman, who shied away from all sort of fuss, would have done back in 1946 if she knew her son Peter Lloyd Price would grow up to be, well, Pete Price. But as the years went on, after she had finished telling the story about buying me, she would joke: "I went into town for a fur coat and I brought you home. And to this day, I wish I'd got that fur coat." At least I know that was only a joke.

CHAPTER TWO

the key in the door

IT'S not your ideal first memory of this world, seeing a dog being led through a front door into a van to be put down. But I'm stuck with it.

The dog in question was Pal, our pet Labrador, and the front door belonged to our house in Granger Avenue. It was in West Kirby on the top left-hand corner of Wirral, by the coast. I must have been about three years old, so it would have been 1949. Poor old Pal had gone blind. He didn't know what was happening but three-year-old Peter Price did, and he was stood there in his shorts crying his eyes out.

Don't worry, it wasn't all that miserable. You'll have to bear with me because my memories are so patchy, but from what I can remember of the rest of my childhood, it was fairly happy.

In fact, over the years when things haven't been going well or I'm in a mood, I'll get in the car and drive around the area I grew up in to cheer myself up. It only takes a few minutes to see the whole thing, and I still see the same faces of people who I grew up with. My work car – one of those little Smart cars – has my name all over it so people will often come up and say hello. The older ones will tell me they remember me going for piano lessons or delivering orders to their house.

Don't you just hate school photos?

As a child at the time, that corner of Wirral seemed like a miniature country, surrounded by water.

On sunny days, we'd walk up Grange Hill, marked out with a big war memorial. From our dens at the top you could see for miles down to the sea at Hoylake and West Kirby and across the peninsula. We'd sit there and dream of wealth and fame.

Living in Wirral, you're never far from a beach, and huge groups of 50 or 60 of us would go down to the coast. Every boy dreams of exploring his own island, and off the coast of West Kirby beach there's a small one, Hilbre, you can walk across the beach to when the tide is out. I still go there when I've got something important to think through. But in those days it wasn't quite as safe as it is now.

In the days when there weren't safely marked paths, I remember one boy got stuck in the sand and was left paralyzed. Its geography makes it a sun-trap and another two girls died when their bathing costumes melted into their bodies. The ambulance driver who was trying to rescue them nearly died himself when his vehicle got stuck in the water.

Ask anyone in Wirral and they'll tell you it can be a bit of a snobby place. I tell them: "Try living there when I was growing up."

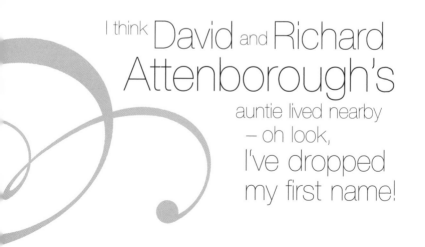

I think David and Richard Attenborough's auntie lived nearby – oh look, I've dropped my first name!

I'd grown up in Granger Avenue, in a road of two-bed semis. As soon as I was able to, I got little jobs, helping my dad and working at a local pig farm. After working there I'd have to strip off and be hosed down with water in the garden.

I may have had lots of jobs, but I wasn't a particularly tough child. Like everyone in those days I was in the cubs – just like I went to Sunday school – and aged about eight, I went on my first camp. But I got so homesick I spent the whole time bawling my eyes out.

The leaders must not have known what to make of me – we were only in the field opposite my house.

Dad had set up a company making concrete paving stones and, as World War II finished and a building boom started, they must have become that season's must-have item. And when he'd sold so many he had cash to spare, the three of us went up in the world.

We all packed up and moved a few streets away to detached Vine Cottage on Darmond's Green. It wasn't a huge house – about four bedrooms – but it was a beautiful historic property, set in about an acre of land with an orchard. There were gooseberry bushes, plum trees and apple trees, and I went round showing off to everyone that we lived there.

But then disaster struck. Dad may have been good at selling paving stones, but he was also good at drinking in the Dee Hotel Pub nearby, and bad at gambling. And one day he lost everything.

How did it happen? I don't think I'll ever find out the truth. But for our family there was one terrible consequence. We had to move out.

So it was another trip in a removal van – one you could walk in a few minutes but which, in Wirral, might as well have been miles away.

Mum would just have soldiered on with it, but for her adopted son it was a complete humiliation.

Mum and dad didn't need the hassle – things were already going wrong between them. From other parts of the house I'd hear their voices start to raise in one of the rows that were becoming more and more frequent. One afternoon I was downstairs and I heard another argument start up. "Oh blimey," I thought.

Then, out of the corner of my eye, I saw something flying through the air, coming down the stairs. It was mum, and she landed awkwardly with a thump at the bottom. She got up quickly, wincing silently and told me she had fallen.

So my dad was a wife-beater. Every now and then on my radio show I get letters and calls from women like my mum. They tell me there's one little sound that scares them more than anything else on earth – the sound of a key sliding into the lock of a front door. That sound makes them wonder what's in store for them. Has his team won? Has he been drinking? Is he in a good mood?

From now on, I was mum's support in the house, and she was mine. We would do anything for each other, and our love for one another meant everything. And that's how it would stay from then on.

I don't know how many other times dad got violent with mum, but he never touched me. The only time I remember him shouting at me was once when I'd stood on a nail that went through my foot at his concrete works, and after I did it again in the same place with a piece of glass at the beach. I think he loved me in his own way – he'd wanted a child just like mum had – but we were never close.

Anyway, my newly broke parents put the house up for sale and found somewhere smaller for us. It was a three-bed terraced house in Bridge Road. Mum and dad would take in lodgers to make ends meet, they told me.

I had loved the house's huge gardens, telling friends I lived there and repeating the address – Vine Cottage on Darmond's Green – to people who asked me where I lived. Now I was devastated.

So the night before we moved, I had one last party in the garden. It was autumn, and I invited all the kids I knew round. Together, we climbed up the fruit trees with our baskets and ate everything there was. It took hours, but between us we managed it.

The next morning, mum went out into the garden and saw what we'd all done. She went absolutely mad, smacking me and smacking me.

I found out the person who had bought the house liked it because he wanted to bottle his own fruit as a hobby, and now there was nothing for him to take.

I imagine they probably had to give him back some of the money they had been banking on to keep us afloat. The combination of having to move and doing this to my parents was too much and I broke down sobbing.

Still in disgrace, I settled down in the new house. Things didn't get off to a good start. My room was at the top at the front, looking onto the street.

One day I'd been to see a film that had a man with no face, and it had terrified me. That night, the small nightlight in my room blew out while I was still awake. So it's that room I have to thank for the fact that, even though I go to the cinema most weeks, I haven't seen a horror movie in 50 years.

Now I didn't want anyone to know our family had been forced to move to Bridge Road. I'd lie, telling friends we still lived in the cottage. I'd even get dropped off at the old house, walk round to the back while the car was pulling away, then run through the garden, hop over the fence, and take the back route to our new house. It was a ridiculous lie to try to pull off. I was ashamed – and I was ashamed of being ashamed.

To make matters worse, mum had to get any work she could find with dad out of business, working all the hours God sent to pay off his debts. When she took a job cleaning at the Ring 'o' Bells pub, our family's humiliation was complete.

So from then on, there would never be enough money to go round. The other children had brand new bikes, but I had one from the Army and Navy store. It was a khaki-coloured, revolting-looking thing, went slower than all the others, and came in two pieces, bolted together.

The other children thought this was hilarious and took the mickey. One day I was riding down Grange Hill when, suddenly, the bike started going out of control.

I looked down and instead of one bike there were two. Someone had made sure I wasn't looking and taken out the screw that connected this bit of World War Two kit. There was blood everywhere.

But mum must have been under huge pressure to get everything I wanted. Later she told me that during that period, when she was working all hours and trying to look after her ungrateful son, she had wanted to give up and commit suicide.

Once a group of us decided we'd walk across the lake at West Kirby. Wearing my Sunday best, I got stuck, and some firemen had to come and get me out. But the shoes stayed in there – they're probably still there today. Mum smacked me and smacked me – she would have saved for weeks to buy those shoes.

At the age of about seven, I had my first introduction to show business, on stage at primary school. I sang a song called Tiddly Winky, with two dancing girls. Goodness knows what I looked and sounded like. But after I'd finished and the audience started clapping, I thought: "If this is what show business is like, it's for me. I've got a career here." And I can still remember all the words.

Soon afterwards, I got my first look at a real celebrity. With his sharp suits, top hats and canes, I'd idolised the singer Frankie Vaughan. Born locally in Liverpool, he was now a big name, about go to America to appear in movies with film stars such as Marilyn Monroe.

He had been involved in boys' clubs, and was making a guest appearance at West Kirby YMCA. Everyone had gone to get a look at him and the police had to block off traffic in the streets around to protect him from the crowds of people.

Years later when I met him and we became friends, I'd tellhim how I was one of the thousands who mobbed him that afternoon. From then on, I'd say, that was it. I was absolutely hooked.

I loved my school, Orisdale Road primary, and I didn't want to leave. I remember saving up pocket money to buy a teapot for my teacher, Miss Owen. It had a strawberry on the lid – how tasteful. I had failed my 11-plus, and suffered the shame of seeing my friends go off to Caldy Grammar while I had to start at Hoylake Parade Secondary Modern.

Then, around the age of 12 I realised I was different from my friends. Well, I was different in quite a few ways. I liked to dress up

– in fact, I'd get into my three-piece suit and go and sit in Whiteley's fish and chip shop, pretending I was in a posh restaurant like the French restaurant in the Adelphi Hotel, Liverpool, dreaming of being rich and famous.

I wanted to join the West Kirby Yachting Club – I saw the people out on their boats and thought they looked amazingly glamorous. Driving past it today, it just looks a bit naff.

There was one difference that was bothering me though. A lot of other gay people tell me they started thinking the same thing at the same age. We'd all started mucking around together, experimenting and playing doctors and nurses. In the scouts we'd get up to stuff late at night or round the back of the hut. It wasn't that I hated the girls – I had been crazy about three girls by then. I just couldn't understand why I had a crush on the lads as well.

Aged 12 with no one to talk to about what I was feeling, I came to a decision. I was ill, and needed professional help. Our family GP, Dr Lansley, was handsome, well-spoken and always immaculately dressed – he looked like an American film star, like Errol Flynn. If anyone could help me, I thought, it was him. I had made an appointment to see him, hoping he could tell me what was wrong, and if there was a cure.

But it was at that time something else happened which would change things forever. I was walking over the bridge by West Kirby station, possibly coming back from school, when I saw a familiar sight. I could tell my dad by the same clothes he always wore – the suit and tie with the overcoat on top and the same hat. This time, though, he was carrying a suitcase.

Thinking about it now, my most vivid memory of dad in my life was when he left it that day.

One day, years later, I'd run into him and not recognise him at first. Many years later still I'd go looking for him among the audience when I was appearing on stage somewhere. But we would never spend any more time together.

Since that day I'd seen mum fly down the stairs, dad had been around the house less and less. I remember not seeing him, and not understanding why he wasn't there. Because of his background, they never divorced, and when the two of us went to Wales to meet my grandmother for the first time we were carefully chaperoned around.

"What are you doing, dad?"
I asked him.
"I'm just going
on holiday
for the
weekend,"
he said.

So that was it. Mum didn't have to worry about the sound of the key in the door any more. She'd stood up to the man that had battered her, and thrown him out. And there he was, about to get on a train to a new life. It must have taken incredible guts for her to do that, and I bet she didn't regret it for a day.

I went home, and waited for mum to get in. From then on – and for 20 years after that – it would just be just me and her. And that was all we needed.

CHAPTER THREE
The unexploded

I SAT down in Dr Lansley's surgery

"Well what seems to be the problem?" he asked. I came out with what I'd been saying over in my head. This man, with the film-star looks and the smart suits, was the first person I had told in my life.

"I…I think I'm a homosexual."

Dr Lansley looked at me and frowned. I froze. What was he going to do? In the playground the others would talk about "shirt lifters" and "queers", and I'd heard homosexuals could be sent to prison – was this going to happen to me?

Finally, he spoke. "Don't be stupid," he said. "You're 12 years old. How could you possibly know?" He smiled. "You'll grow out of it."

And that was it. Counselling, 1958-style. I still get angry when people ring up my radio show and tell me how gay people have it easy and shouldn't complain so much. This was all the help I had for now, and when I did get involved with doctors in a few years, what they would do would scar me for life.

I left the surgery utterly miserable, and went home. Now there was nobody I could tell – certainly not mum.

For one thing, she would have been even more clueless than me. She wasn't a worldly person and, even though we were close, we would never talk about such things. Even worse, though, I couldn't tell her because I was terrified of losing her.

One mum had already abandoned me and I couldn't get it out of my mind that she could do the same.

All children get a fear of their parents dying at some stage. But for me it had become an obsession. When I got in late at night I'd go upstairs and creep into her room, just to check she was still alive. If I couldn't see hear breathing, I'd put my face close to hers until I could feel it. Once, she woke up and saw a face inches away from hers. She screamed and jumped.

"Peter! What are you doing there, I thought someone had got in!"

"I was just checking you were still alive."

"Soft sod," she replied. "Get to bed."

Of course, sometimes she'd get in a mood with me. To say mum had a talent for sulking wasn't the half of it – she could win a sulking contest against anybody out there.

Usually every morning she'd wake me up by gently shaking me, putting a cup of tea next to my bed and opening up the curtains.

But when she was in a mood, everything changed. Then, I'd get woken up by a sharp poke, and the tea would be banged down. I'd dread that poke coming.

That evening at dinner, she'd sit silently. And the only way to get her to say something was to copy her, and just sit there. After a while, with my plate of lamb chops or chicken still untouched, she'd say: "Why aren't you eating?"

"I thought you weren't talking to me."

"I'm not. Why aren't you eating your tea?" she'd say.

"But you just spoke to me."

"No I didn't."

With dad gone, mum had been doing every odd job she could to stay afloat, still taking in lodgers and setting herself a tight budget. Whenever I was on the phone to friends she'd be there, rattling a tin next to my ear until I paid up. Every month I'd get a big tin of Smith's Crisps – my special treat – that I had to make last. When I got my own key at 12 years old, mum said: "If you abuse that, that's it. You'll never get another one." I never did – it was so special that she'd let me have a key to the door at that age. She trusted me, and I would never betray it.

All her spare money went on me. I got a piano, and one of the rooms in the house became my music room. I went to a music teacher who had nine cats. While I was playing, she would stand next to me and play the violin, and if I made a mistake, she'd whack me across the hands with her bow. A combination of her and me meant I never got much better – I've had 12 years of lessons and I'm still crap.

Mum would still pull out all the stops at birthdays and Christmas though. One year, I remember waking up at 4am on December 25. I had got so bored, I'd ate all the mince pies I'd left out for Father Christmas.

"Is he here yet?" I'd keep asking. Then, five minutes later, "Is he here yet?"

"Go to sleep."

"But he must have come by now."

I kept pestering mum for hours, and finally, she gave up. "Go on, open your presents," she said, handing me a parcel.

I tore into my present, pulling off the wrapping paper. To my shock and horror I found a school satchel. I remember crying myself back to sleep. "How dare she?" I thought. "That's something for school, not a real present." What a little brat I was.

Back to bed I went, sulking. So that was Christmas over for the year – nothing to look forward to now until my birthday. At 10am I woke up and stomped into the toilet. There was something sitting on the seat. What was it? I went to have a look, and my face lit up. Sitting on the loo was a record player – the one I'd wanted. She wasn't going to give me that at 4am. No way.

Mum and I would go out and have fun together, getting dressed up to go to modern sequence dancing, accompanied by my auntie Jean on the piano. The family would have sing-songs round the piano at my Auntie Mac's (one of those pretend aunts you have when you're a kid.) I'd play and we'd all sing "He's Got The Whole World In His Hands."

She had been doing all the work she could to make enough

Hello, big boy!

for us, but suddenly mum's luck changed. My great aunt Florrie died and left her some money.

She scraped together enough to buy a shop at 5a Bridge Road. We moved to live there. It was a chandler's shop, packed with everything you could think of, like Arkwright's in Open All Hours. There was china, vinegar, sandpaper, paint, soap powder – an absolute Aladdin's cave. We had a pet cat and budgie. Mum standing there in her apron and breathing in the smell of paraffin, wood, soap powder and firelighters is the most vivid memory of my childhood.

It was just an old-fashioned chandler's – mum would put a saucer of milk out for the cats and a bowl of water for the dogs and sit there, drinking tea out of a Pyrex cup while the teabag floated round.

Having a 13-year-old behind the counter didn't always work. Women would regularly come in for one item we sold, and the conversation would go like this.

"Have you got any mmm-mmms?" they would mutter.

"What?" I would say, and they would look embarrassed and point at a shelf above my head.

"Any, hmmm mmms?"

"MUM!" I'd shout upstairs. "SHE WANTS SANITARY TOWELS!"

"Shut up, you little..." she'd say, running down the stairs to clip me round the ear.

Once, a batch had got wet and,
thinking of a way to make some money,
I put up a huge sign:
"Soggy STs for sale
– half price".

That didn't
go down well.

Our shop was by a baker and dairy, greengrocer, butcher and a sweet shop, as well as the chippy next door. The shopkeepers respected each other and no one would ever muscle in on the other's business – old-fashioned values. I get so angry today when I hear about people abusing their corner shops. The workers put in ridiculous hours to try and make the most of their tiny profit margins, putting up with gangs of kids hanging around trying to steal things.

If mum was alive today, the supermarket culture we have now would break her heart – her chandler's wouldn't have a cat in hell's chance of surviving.

Customers had credit accounts we'd write in the book. Everyone in the neighborhood would stop by, although mum once banned a pair of Welsh women who would come in and refuse to speak English. Maybe they reminded her of dad's Welsh roots.

Looking back on it, it's a wonder I'm still here as the place was a bomb waiting to go off in the middle of West Kirby.

Out the back was a huge drum of paraffin – about 2,000 gallons – for people's heaters. I had the job of carrying buckets of it back and forth through the shop to fill the tank inside. So I'd fill two five-gallon drums, stagger into the kitchen, slopping some on the carpet as the containers wobbled, and fill the tank up. In the winter, we'd sell so much paraffin I'd have to make the trip three times a day.

If you think that was a fire risk, you should have seen what mum kept by the paraffin tank. On one side were the fire lighters, on the other were the bags of wood – and my bedroom was on top. Oh yes, and there was also the chippy next door.

On Bonfire night, we'd stay up all night with buckets of water in case anything happened, walking round to check it every few minutes. These days mum would probably have been locked up by health and safety officers – and they'd have thrown away the key.

For years, I worked and worked in that shop. I did it because I loved her. My dad had lost everything, and that made me want to work harder. Every six months without fail, she'd do a stock take, counting every button and pin. When she got bored of our tea service, she'd quietly swap it with one on sale, and when we were short of a bit of bleach, she'd pour it out of a bottle from the shop. Mum's money was always right, to the penny. So once I was confused when I found a little box with some coins in. I asked her what it was for.

"When I've cashed up, if the money's over I put it in the box. And if it is short I take some money out."

"What do you do with the money that's left?" I asked.

"At the end of the week, I buy myself a box of cream cakes."

I never saw dad again growing up. Except once, when I was walking along West Kirby beach and a man came up to me. I didn't recognise him at first.

"Give this to your mother," he said, and put something in my hand. Then he walked off. It was a matchbox, with a £5 note in it. Big deal. Mum was so disgusted and angry she ripped it up. Luckily I managed to keep the pieces and tape it together, so I did well with my pocket money that week.

Meanwhile, my friends and I were turning into teenagers and getting up to all the things teenage boys do. We'd take it in turns to go a shop and buy dirty magazines, looking around as we dashed onto the street, carrying them in a plain paper bag. Once it had been my turn. But this time, when we started looking through it, I got the shock of my life.

There, looking out from the pages, staring to the right in a way that made her look a bit shifty, was my auntie Dot.

She was even named as Dorothy from West Kirby, 36"/26"/36", 26, 5ft 6ins. She had some sort of fur covering her, but by the standards of the time, it was quite racy – I swear you could see a nipple.

The caption read: "Some husbands are very lucky!"

"Can we go round and see your auntie?" My friends would ask me. "Does your auntie want any jobs doing round the house? Can I borrow that picture of your auntie Dot?" (Oh and by the way, I've kept the photo).

Even for someone whose auntie was a glamour model, it was still an amazing time to be a teenager living near Liverpool. A whole generation of people who'd go on to be huge stars were a couple of years older than us: the Beatles, Gerry Marsden, the Big Three, the Undertakers, the Escorts. We would queue up outside Hoylake YMCA to see them: The club held dances on Wednesdays and Saturdays until 10.30pm and it was a shilling to get in.

Opposite was the Lantern Coffee Bar, where a new generation of teenagers would go to get a trendy "frothy coffee in a glass mug". We'd try and make the drinks last as long as we could before the cry went up of: "Oi, you! Half an hour you've been there with that coffee. There's a limit, you know."

We'd still go swimming in the baths on sunny days, but now we'd all go to the pictures on Saturday mornings. Everyone else wanted to be cowboys, but I wanted to be a pirate – they were better dressed and more glamorous, you see. Back when I was dressing up in my suit to go to the café in the back of the chippy I had started becoming a clothes horse. But now it got ridiculous. I had a jacket with "PP" on the pockets in gold, and a matching gold cummerbund. There was also the mauve polo neck jumper with matching trousers and big black belt, and the imitation snakeskin winkle-pickers. There's a word for what I looked like, and it isn't a very long word.

Mum didn't get any of the signals – she just thought I was eccentric. And among my friends I was known as a sex maniac, because I was always around girls. But inside I was still frightened and confused. Nothing was talked about in those days. You would see the camp man who lived down the road and you weren't too sure of him, or the two women who lived together in the next street and hear whispers about them. In Liverpool, there was "Sadie the queer", a bar owner who was openly gay, but I hadn't met him yet. Me and my friends would get up to stuff behind the bike sheds – I'll touch yours if you touch mine,

that sort of thing. But I was secretly crazy about the other boys.

It was time, I thought, to try Dr Lansley again.

Two years ago I'd been turned away but this time they had to take me seriously, I thought. I acted old for my age, dressed older than I was and one day desperately wanted a family. I wanted, more than anything, to be respectable. Surely they could help me?

This time I walked out of the surgery with something – a prescription for some valium. "Take these tablets," Dr Lansley told me. "You'll be all right."

Well, surprise surprise, the tablets didn't work. In fact, they made things even harder as I was terrified of mum finding them and scared about how they were making me feel. Once, after checking mum was out, I poured them all out of the bottle and flushed them down the toilet.

Then things got worse still. I got into a fight with another boy, and – I can't remember the exact details – I think I pushed him when he was standing in the toilet. We were caught and one of the teachers gave us some sort of lecture about being homosexual. Did I need any more convincing that what I was feeling was wrong?

Alone and confused, I worked myself up into a right state. The doctor wouldn't take me seriously and there was no one else to talk to. Being how I was, I decided, I couldn't go on living.

I got ready for bed, then went into the medicine cabinet and took out a bottle of aspirins. I had probably seen someone use them to kill themselves in one of our Saturday morning films. Down went about half the bottle. Then I got into bed next to my mum, because I thought I was going to die and I wanted to be with her, and I went to sleep.

· "Wake up darling," I heard mum say the next morning, as she put a cup of tea next to the bed as usual. I had a thumping headache and, as I woke up, I remembered what had happened last night. But as I gave mum a cuddle, it felt good to be alive.

PETE PRICE

The aspirins, you see, had only been the children's variety – orange flavour – so the dose must not have been high enough. I got up and went to school as normal, relieved it hadn't worked.

Oddly enough, the very next weekend, I had another brush with death. It was Sunday morning and mum was in bed reading her Daily Sketch. I got in next to her, sucking on a gobstopper as big as a golf ball. In those days you'd get one and save it for days, taking it out and putting it back in again. As I lay down, it got stuck in the back of my throat.

I tried to yell and waved my arms, and mum started banging me on the back. I was starting to feel faint when she hit me extra hard and it flew across the room.

Part of what was making me so depressed was that school wasn't exactly going well. After I'd failed my 11+, things didn't improve. Socially, I was old for my age, just like I looked and dressed older. And bits of school were fun – we'd play on the beach at lunch, and because I was quick at cracking jokes I was never badly bullied. But I didn't really like games after I had run up to vault over a horse and fell awkwardly on my back, laying me up in bed for weeks.

And I was never academic. In science I blew up a Bunsen burner, and the rest of the chemistry lab almost went up with it. Another teacher threw a blackboard duster at me for messing around. I was always up to no good and I was caned regularly. Many years later I'd find out I was dyslexic, not just terrible at spelling; but by then it was too late. For years afterwards I would try to avoid writing anything down because I was so worried about how it would look.

There was, however, one subject I loved. It was cookery or, as we called it at school, domestic science. At home I'd make egg and bacon pie and fairy cakes, and at school I was learning to make new things. Unsurprisingly, I was the only boy who chose to do the subject – everyone else did metalwork – so it was me and a class of girls.

No, it is not Fanny Craddock

These were my favourite lessons, mucking about with food in the school kitchens and bringing home what I'd made to show mum.

Unfortunately, word got round about my cooking skills. Walking home from school, I got jumped by the other boys who robbed my sausage rolls. After a while it got so bad I had to start thinking about what I made – "Try and steal that," I'd say, walking along the street brandishing a casserole.

As school was about to end, we all went to a careers fair. I'd spoken to mum about wanting to go into show business, and she'd told me "Get a trade first." But what trade? At the moment, there were two I was weighing up – hairdressing and cookery. I had idolised a hairdresser called Paul Raymond, known as Mr Teasy-Weasy. He was on TV on a show called Quite Contrary, where he would show off his super-camp, elaborate hairdos, talking in a fake French accent with a cigarette holder in his hand. Off screen, his clients included movie stars like Vivien Leigh, and he taught Vidal Sassoon. His super-glamorous world was fascinating to the 11-year-old Pete Price.

But cookery was the winner. I signed up at Birkenhead Technical College. I was going to be a chef – the best there was, at a college where nobody nicked your sausage rolls. Looking back on it, it was a decision that would change my life.

CHAPTER FOUR

sieve it and
serve it

It's 1962 on the 8am train from West Kirby to Birkenhead and a smartly dressed man in a trilby is getting on. He's dressed in a perfectly pressed suit and his face looks like nothing could make him smile.

There's a seat waiting for him, as there always is – he sits in the same place every day, and the rest of the train knows to keep it free. He folds up his coat to sit down.

Prrrrrrrrrp!

Opposite him, a group of lads aged 15 and 16 all start cracking up. Then the rest of the train wakes up and joins in.

Without a hint of a smile crossing his face, the man lifts up the cushion on his seat and pulls it out – a red rubber whoopee cushion. Holding it by his fingertips, he picks it up, opens the train window and flings it out. Then he sits down, still with the same expression, as if nothing has happened, and unfolds his paper.

The lads – including a young trainee chef – were travelling to Birkenhead Technical College (Birkenhead Tec) for another day's lessons.

Well, a young slightly overweight trainee chef if I'm honest. Because by now, the 15-year-old Peter Price had fallen in love with food. I'd make myself a washing-up bowl full of chips, smothered in my own curry sauce, and wash it down with a bucket of ice-cream. Apart from tripe, there was absolutely nothing I wouldn't eat.

So here I was, learning to cook. Mum had helped me buy the essentials every chef had to own before he could start work. I had chef's whites, checks (which is what we called the trousers) and a set of knives. I still use my filleting knife now, with my name scratched in it, 45 years on. It's incredible to think I walked through the streets each day with these huge knives – now I'd be stopped by the police and given an asbo.

I was taking City and Guilds 150, 151 and Waiting Intermediate, which covered cooking and silver service.

If cooking in a restaurant nowadays seems straightforward, it wasn't then. The biggest hotels and restaurants would do everything from scratch. They had an in-house butcher, patisserie and bakery – and we were expected to know how to do it all.

A young Hazel Collinge at her charity barbecue with Nancy and Mervyn Kieron

Once we were all cleaning out chickens and I got my hand stuck inside. I could feel something and I knew what it was – there was an egg, and it was a bad egg. I was stuck there smelling the stench and not knowing what to do. And don't even ask me about jugging a hare – there was a lot of blood involved. We went on a trip to an abattoir, down the road from Fairfield, and I still remember seeing the animals' expressions as they were about to be killed. It never put me off eating meat, though.

We were learning the classic French techniques that all the best restaurants practiced. We even had to learn "catering

French" and I'd never spoken a word of it in my life. There was so much to take in, and I'd never been the brightest spark at school. Our teachers were old professionals with years in the business – one was a gold medal chef.

I'd try my recipes out on mum, who must have had to scrimp and save to kit me out.

She'd always been a straightforward, chops and mash kind of cook and she was amazed by the kinds of things I was doing in the kitchen.

Then we would test our recipes out on members of the public at the college's own restaurant, taking it in turns to cook and wait tables.

Us chefs were in a funny situation at Birkenhead Tec. Working in a world of five-star hotels and expensive restaurants we thought we were above the people doing building or engineering – and they weren't too keen on us.

Downstairs there was a disco where the other boys would stand around at the sides.

Mr Sex Maniac, as I was known, was the only one who'd want to get up and dance.

Meanwhile, life was busy outside college. I was still working all hours helping mum in the shop. And I'd got myself another job, in a hair salon, to keep my options open in case I wanted to switch jobs and become the next Teasy-Weasy.

I had got a Saturday job working for Peter Collinge in his salon in West Kirby. His son Andrew is now a hairdresser with an international reputation. But back then, his dad ran the hairdressing empire from the Cooper's building in Church Street. He would do incredible things with people's hair, like comb it into a birdcage shape and then put two model birds in it.

Of course, they wouldn't let me near a pair of scissors. It was strictly washing customers' hair and sweeping up. And it didn't go particularly well. One day I was sent home for being outrageously dressed – can you imagine that happening to a hairdresser now? From memory, I was wearing powder blue corduroy trousers, my artificial snakeskin winkle-pickers and a pink lace shirt with pink cuffs.

Another time I was washing an old lady's hair when I forgot myself and got a bit carried away. You see, these old ladies would sit there yapping for hours and hours, and it would get on my nerves. The woman called the manager over.

"Would you ask this young man why he washed my ears?" she said furiously.

"Why did you wash this lady's ears?"

"Because they were dirty," I said. I was sent home again and told I couldn't talk to the customers like that.

But I carried on going every weekend, in case something happened and the cookery didn't work out. I suppose I'm doing the same thing nowadays with the amount of different jobs I do – flying out for gigs, appearing in panto, all on top of my radio show. I've always worked my arse off.

I became friends with Peter and his wife Hazel and would visit their beautiful house on Bidston Hill. When one of these visits was coming close, I'd read up on things like art and current affairs so I'd have something to say to them. I'd got the job thanks to a new friend – someone who became very important in my life when I was growing up. Margaret Ward was the wife of Tommy, a successful entrepreneur born in Scotland Road, Liverpool, who would install the first computer system at Littlewoods. His son went on to found the company Ocean Software.

Margaret Ward: The first woman I ever saw naked

I knew about the couple by reputation – I knew that they were the sort of people who can help make you with their connections. I had become friends with their children Dave, Johnny and Kate, and we all hung around in a group.

But the first time I met Mrs Ward, I knew she wasn't exactly going to be what you would expect.

I'd arranged to come round to talk about catering for a dinner party they were having. Nervously I knocked on the front door and opened it. Standing at the top of the stairs was a naked woman. Naked, that is, apart from a towel the size of a face flannel she was using to cover herself.

"You must be Peter!" she squeaked. "I've just got out of the shower, but if you go and sit down I'll be down in a minute."

Then she turned round and walked off across the landing – still without a stitch on. I had just seen my first naked woman. Where I grew up you'd never have done that, I thought. I had never seen my own mother naked. These people were going to be fun.

With my new-found cookery skills, I became a regular visitor to their huge house in Caldy. It was one of those open houses, where everybody just seems to congregate. The Wards were great fun to know, although you disturbed Tommy when Everton were playing at your peril.

Together, Mrs Ward and I came up with incredible recipes to dazzle their dinner guests. One summer we cooked a whole wild boar in the garden on banana leaves. I'd do petits pois a la Francaise, stuffed lamb, freshly baked bread, and prawn cocktail with proper sauce Marie-Rose – well, it was the 60s.

They were untidy and – even aged 15 – I was a cleaning fanatic. I loved their house so much I'd throw them out and scrub their floor for them.

I was taking any catering gigs I could, and I would spend days working on elaborate buffets and icing cakes. But I would often stand next to my handiwork and wish I could eat it all myself.

For one dinner party at the Wards, I'd written them a menu with the long list of things I'd prepared. A few days later, some snotty woman they'd invited wrote to thank them, but pointed out that I'd made a mistake on the menu. Right at the top in big writing, I'd put: "Welcome to are house". I hated putting anything on paper and it really embarrassed me. But Mrs Ward pointed out that the woman who had written had made some basic mistakes too, which made me feel better about it – after all, she was a professional woman.

On Tuesdays, I'd make every cauliflower recipe in the book for Mrs Ward. There was one with a fish sauce, cauliflower cheese (quite a novelty back then) and my favourite recipe, with golden breadcrumbs, egg whites chopped up, yolks and parsley. And when I'd finished going through the book, I made a few up myself.

I'd go for long walks with Mrs Ward and pour my heart out to her about everything that was happening to me. And, after I'd got to know her, I decided to tell her the big secret – the one only Dr Lansley knew.

Once again, I built it up and built it up before I did it. We were walking to Hilbre Island and, passing the strange houses without any toilets, seeing the flocks of birds on the rocks, I felt like I could confess everything to her. This was like my Narnia, far away from everything, and it was a beautiful day.

Mrs Ward didn't really react at all, just took it in her stride, gave me a hug and a kiss and carried on talking as if nothing had happened. I think she'd already guessed – could the camp clothes have been a giveaway? She didn't give me any advice, but it helped just to know someone else knew about me.

Seeing her son spending so much time with these rich families must have been hard on mum, who would have never tried to speak to people like the Wards and the Collinges. One day she asked me: "Why do you mix with people who are better than you?" At the time I thought it was a stupid thing to say – I was mixing with them because I enjoyed their company. But it must have hurt her to see her son trying to climb up a rank while she was selling paraffin out of a tank to make ends meet.

Meanwhile, as I started going to these glamorous parties, something was happening to me – things were going well at college for the first time. I had finally found a subject I really liked, and I began to shine. I've still got a book on French cooking I won in an ice-cream-making competition back then.

But passing the course wouldn't be much use if I didn't have a job to go to and for that, you needed experience. In the summer holiday after the first year of the course, everyone had to go and do a placement in a proper kitchen. What everyone wanted was a summer season in a posh hotel, and I'd applied for lots of jobs to be on the safe side.

I managed to get one – mum's friend Mrs McGreavy had family down in Eastbourne on the Sussex coast who I would be staying with. It was my first job in catering, and I'd be earning just over £5 a week.

I would be spending the summer at the Cavendish Hotel. Nowadays Eastbourne has a reputation as "God's waiting room", full of old people sitting on hotel porches staring out to sea. But back then, although it still wasn't the raciest destination, it was quite an upmarket place to go on holiday, and the Cavendish was one of the huge, five-star hotels that used to be dotted all around the coast.

The other passengers on the endless, 10-shilling train journey from West Kirby to Eastbourne must have wondered why there was a teenage boy sitting there in a straw trilby, raincoat, gloves and scarf. But I was going to do this in style.

Leafing through the postcards I've kept of the Cavendish, it just looks like a very 60s dining room with a lot of brown paint. But when I walked through the doors of the kitchen, my jaw dropped. It was like another world – all the stuff we'd learnt at catering college but on a much, much larger scale. There were huge teams of chefs in each department – pastry, meat, grilling – and food was made in huge vats for the hundreds of guests. The larder on its own seemed to be the size of our house.

The 15-shilling lunch had all the things posh people were eating at the time – fois gras, caviar – alongside traditional dishes like whole roast chicken for two and roast beef.

Chefs do the longest hours of almost anyone out there and I was worked hard at the Cavendish. And not everyone there was very nice.

Anyone who's worked in a kitchen will tell you stories about the sort of things chefs get up to, but now I was seeing it at first hand. Once, me and another chef had to carry a huge iron pan of leek and potato soup from the main kitchen into a function room, to heat up for a wedding. One of us stumbled and it crashed on the floor, splashing soup everywhere.

"What the hell are we going to do?" I said. "We can't just go back to the kitchen and tell them it's all gone."

"No, we can't." the other bloke said. "Get a ladle and a sieve."

"What?"

"Get a ladle and a sieve. We'll sieve it and serve it."

And we did – we scooped it off the floor and carried it into the room to be heated up – a slightly different shade of grey. Those poor people got married and never knew.

I'd sit by the bandstand on sunny days and send home postcards to mum telling her about what I'd been up to and how homesick I was, while the brass band played in the background.

But the most exciting thing to happen to me was meeting an actor I had idolised, who was staying in the hotel. Ian Carmichael was a regular in films of the time and I was thrilled to spot him at the hotel – it reignited my passion for showbusiness. On one night off I paid a fortune to see Max Bygraves down the road in Brighton, getiing another dose of the glitzy world I was obsessed with.

September came, the season ended and I went back to West Kirby. Now we had to prepare for the exams at the end of the course, and I was getting nervous. Everything was going well, but would my habit of failing things let me down at the last minute?

In the middle of one exam, I lost it and started to panic. I had to make a roux – a basic sauce made of flour, milk and butter – and it had gone wrong. I must have been distracted because it had stuck to the pan and burnt. I knew that this could spell the end of my catering career.

One of my teachers – he said never to tell anyone so I won't tell you his name – switched it for me. He believed in me and said I had a gift for cooking. He realised I hadn't done myself justice by botching up this simple sauce. Most of the other tests had gone well but I was paranoid I had messed something up. I waited weeks for the results, still doing catering jobs, still helping mum in the shop.

Then one day, I'd been out and I was walking back home. Coming over the bridge where dad had left us, I saw mum waiting for me, beaming and waving the envelope in the air. I had passed the City and Guilds 150, 151 and Waiting Intermediate. It was a better feeling than I could have imagined.

So it was catering for me. I started applying for jobs and it didn't take me long to get one. It involved travelling back down to Eastbourne, but I didn't mind very much – I had happy memories of my summer in this posh resort. I would be running a tea shop for Forte's, a company that at the time owned hundreds of shops across the country. I'd talked it over with Mrs Ward, and it seemed like a good start in a big organisation.

Mum was devastated when I told her I could be leaving forever.

She threw a party for me and I remember singing "I'll see you again when spring breaks through again" and playing the piano as she stood there, sobbing. I was such a drama queen.

Coming out (catering college). Here I am with mum in her beautiful yellow dress

Two weeks later, I was back. It hadn't worked out. They'd sent me down the road to Worthing – a place that made Eastbourne look like New York. I was running the Fullers Tea Shop, part of Rocco Forte's hotel and restaurant empire, but there was a big problem. Across the road was a rival Lyons tea shop.

Managing a tea shop sounds classy, but it was a bit like being a McDonald's manager today. And the worst thing about it was the other tea shop paid better wages, so no one wanted to work for me. I was running around trying to keep the thing going single-handed. The whole thing was no fun, so I quit.

Mum was pleased to see me – she still hadn't finished up the food from my leaving party. And I knew what I was going to do next. There was another catering job I wanted – one which would take me around the world.

CHAPTER FIVE

2,000 fried eggs

THE bank of the Mersey was packed with excitement on April 20, 1964 – a cruise liner was setting off across the Atlantic.

On the jetty by the Liver Building, crowds of people had gathered to wave off their families and friends. Some of them would be emigrating for good, and streamers were flying through the air. Those streamers were lifelines, and when they snapped the lifeline was broken. The boat would be spending 19 days at sea, before arriving in Quebec and Montreal, Canada.

Among the crowds, one teenager stood out. He was slightly overweight with a face older than his years. Waving at the crowd with his hankerchief, he sobbed theatrically at the emotion of it all, even though he didn't have a clue who any of the people were.

For the 17-year-old Peter Price, this was a dream come true. I'd always wanted to go to sea and as a trained chef, this was the way to do it. Who'd want to serve cakes to old ladies in Eastbourne when you could see the world like this?

I was going to be a trainee chef – part of the first batch the Canadian Pacific Company who ran the boat had ever taken on out of catering college. All the other chefs on board would have had to work their way up to our level and, surprise surprise, I thought I was something pretty special for getting the job.

My tears were partly out of relief that I'd got there at all.

My friend Frank Gaskin had borrowed my Honda scooter to impress a girl the night before, and had got a puncture. I had to be on the boat early to sail down the river from Bootle docks – the passengers got on in Liverpool after everything was loaded. I remember running all around Wirral to find a puncture kit on the one day I didn't want to be late.

But now I was on, complete with new set of whites, and dreams of a glamorous journey, dazzling everyone with my cookery like I had at the Wards' and the Collinges' dinner parties. Oh, I was so wrong, as I was about to find out.

Just before I left, mum and me had been on holiday. The holiday from hell, to be precise.

My nan – dad's mum – had written to mum. She wanted to see her grandson and her daughter-in-law. Remember, mum and dad never divorced because of his strict Welsh Chapel upbringing. Mum had been putting this off and she wasn't happy about it, but we decided to get it over with.

Dad's family lived in Georgetown, Merthyr Tydfil. I'm sure the residents of Merthyr Tydfil won't get too angry if I say it isn't the most glamorous place. Well, 45 years ago it certainly wasn't.

The train journey, involving a change at Bristol and hours on freezing platforms, was miserable. It seemed to stop at every station, and for part of it we shared our carriage with a woman and her four chickens. But we finally arrived in the early hours of the morning. We got the works when we arrived, Merthyr-style. Dad's brother, a milkman, picked us up in one of the only cars in the town. In great style, he introduced us to my nan, a tiny, shrivelled woman who looked like a dwarf – all that was missing was the gnome's hat. She would blow her nose on her pinny, then she'd wipe an apple on it and give it to me.

There were no guestrooms for me and mum. In fact, there wasn't even one spare room, but there was an outside lavvy. Everybody squashed in, like the family in Charlie and the

Chocolate Factory. I was put in a bed with a 40-year-old uncle I'd never met before in my life. I'd caught my nan peeling a banana for him earlier so I think he was a bit soft. My auntie Mary had slept with her mother in a room with an iron bedhead, while Mum had a bed of her own in a bit of room screened off by a curtain. Except the curtain didn't stretch as far as it should.

"Mum!" I hissed as she got changed. "Everyone can see!"

What seemed like 10 minutes later, everyone was up – it was a mining town. At 6am, we sat there like zombies, eating our breakfast as everyone else hurried to get out of the house. "Tonight," nan told us, "We are all going to sit down and have a family meal. Do you like chicken?" I nodded.

When it arrived at the table, it was the size of an anorexic quail. Mum and I ate it, then sneaked out to a Chinese restaurant because we were starving.

Of course, if people had known David Lloyd Price's wife was in town, the gossips would have gone mad, so there was no way we were meeting anyone else. We were shepherded around like fugitives and not allowed to go out unless it was under cover of darkness.

After three days of this, mum and I lost patience with it all, and cut short our seven-day stay.

But as the ship pulled away, it all became a distant memory. I may not be in first class, but now I was travelling on a bang-up-to-date, luxury liner I'd read about in the newspapers. As Liverpool vanished on the horizon, my head was buzzing and I went down to look for the other chefs, and saw one of my bosses.

"Hello Mr Price. Where have you been?" he asked, smiling.

"I've just been to see everyone off," I said.

"That's lovely, isn't it? Can I get you a coffee? Get to work, you twat!" he yelled.

I spent the rest of the day cooking, and that night I fell straight asleep. The next morning I was still exhausted and overslept in my bunk bed. I went down to breakfast to see the same man there, with the same sarcastic grin.

"Mr Price! Would you like to sit down? Fry eggs. Now, please."

I reached for a small frying pan, started to heat the oil and carefully chose a couple of eggs.

"NOT THERE YOU DOZY LITTLE FUCKER," he yelled. "Over there."

Over there was the biggest frying pan I had ever seen, and a mountain of eggs. It was like a railway station, with people shouting: "Come in number four! Come in number four!"

We must have cooked 2,000 eggs a day, every day. It was catering on a huge scale, and even in the Cavendish I had never seen anything like it.

There was a huge amount to learn. It wasn't the recipes – compared to some of the advanced stuff I'd done it wasn't that bad. It was how you behaved at work. The kitchen, as I was discovering, ran on an intricate system of little payments and bribes. At the end of the cruise when a waiter was tipped, he didn't just pocket it. He had to give some to the chef, the pot washer and the silver man. And if you didn't remember everyone, they'd stop doing things for you and the passengers would suffer. They reckon there's a million pounds' worth of

silverware in the ocean thanks to washers who were in a bad mood and couldn't be bothered washing it. The whole system was incredible to see in action – waiters who played the game didn't have any problems and others would be blacklisted because they hadn't passed money on.

Once I was sitting in the dispensary and a fat, greasy-looking fish chef called Joe pushed in front of me to get a pint of shandy.

"Excuse me, I was first," I piped up. "You didn't serve me, but you served that lout?"

Joe turned round, took one look at me, and started pummeling me with his fish-stained hands, yelling: "Who do you think you are, you no-mark? You're only a trainee chef you little scumbag."

He picked me up, carried me across the kitchen and threw me in a sink the size of a swimming pool. It was caked in grease and slime by that point of the night, and stank of all the rubbish in the world.

Lying in there waiting for the laughter to stop, I thought: "Peter, you're going to have to get your head around this."

Unfortunately, that wasn't the first cock up. I had a taste for the high life that wouldn't go away. So one evening when I had a night off, I decided to go to the first class bar. I put on my best suit – an expensive black one I loved, and went for a drink. Some friends of mum's were on the boat and I was sitting with them sipping a large cocktail.

The captain was doing the rounds chatting to passengers, and he reached our group. This was more like it, I thought.

"And who are you?" he said to me. "I've never seen you on board before."

"No, that's because I work in the galley," I blurted out. His face froze.

"Can we have a private word?" he asked, and pulled me to one side. "What do you think you're doing down here?" he hissed.

I'd had a few drinks, and I blurted out: "Well, you don't think I'm going to drink down there with those louts, do you?" I said. The next morning at 9am I got a written warning. I started to realise this wasn't a game. This was a job. I always say my time at sea taught me two important lessons – don't muck around with people and do the job you're there for. The next few days were difficult, but I tried hard to fit in with the rest of the crew and started to make a few friends.

There was, however, another problem. Going over the ferry to France as a child I'd been badly seasick, but I thought it was something that would wear off. It didn't. I threw up and threw up. Picturing a cruise in my head, I hadn't imagined the Atlantic Ocean in late winter. It was like the Poseidon adventure, with waves lashing over the funnels.

Once I even threw up in a big vat of soup, felt too ill to tell anyone about it, and it was served. I suppose those were the days when, if you gave the waiter any abuse, he'd do something terrible to your gravy.

But when we got to Canada, the most incredible sight I had ever seen suddenly appeared. We went down the St Lawrence Seaway from the mouth at the Atlantic to the source at Montreal. At its narrowest, the huge ship seemed to be inches from the land. I saw packs of dogs pulling sleighs, the famous 365 churches. I remember the ship turning round the corner and suddenly seeing the Chateau Fontenac, which looked like Cinderella's palace.

Getting off the boat at Quebec, I was amazed at the height of the skyscrapers and stood there with my camera looking up and taking photos to take home.

All this time, I hadn't really had a chance to think about my sexuality. I'd heard the usual references and nicknames. You'd hear camp voices around the ship sometimes, visiting other people's bunks in the small hours. But I'd been too busy to worry about anything like that.

But one night when I was ashore something happened which drummed it home to me how dangerous being a homosexual could be. It's something I've always been ashamed of, and have only told a few friends until now.

I was on a night out in Montreal and a group of people asked me to join them to try and pull some local girls. I said that would be good.

Later that night, though, one of the lads patted me on the back and said something that made me shiver. "We're a bit short of money, he whispered. "So let's go queer-bashing."

I didn't understand what they meant. Were they really going to do something so calculated and cruel? And I'd never been in a fight in my life – I didn't stand a chance. But we carried on drinking, and I carried on following them.

I followed them into a bar where homosexuals went. I had a few more drinks. We got talking to some men, then someone I was with suggested we all go back to one of their flats. The man who agreed was quiet and skinny, and wore glasses.

He lived in a high-rise apartment building and when we got inside he offered us a drink. As soon as the last one in shut the door, they flew at him. The gang punched and kicked him and snatched his wallet.

I just watched, then ran out of the flat.

I arrived back in England on May 9, just as it was getting warmer. I was glad to get off that first crossing, even though I couldn't walk properly for few days as I still had my sea legs. But the day we arrived back in Liverpool, I witnessed the biggest fiddle I have ever seen in my life.

For £2 you got what was called a shore box. This was made up entirely of things that the crew had nicked from the ship. But the system was so well-organised, you actually got it delivered to your door!

Your money bought you booze, cigarettes and all the meat you could eat – ham, beef, lamb, the lot. The money went on bribes to every official you passed and towards paying the delivery man. It was described as a perk of the job. You'd pay the policeman at the port half a crown per delivery and there was talk of one who was so weighed down with bribes in his pockets, his braces snapped.

Then, a few days later, the delivery van would call at your house and you'd get your stuff. Some people had made off with so much meat they had it delivered to their own cold storage facility.

When I got home from my second crossing on May 29, mum had bad news for me. She showed me a copy of the paper and I couldn't believe what I was reading.

One of my friends, Chris Mole, had died in a horrific car crash aged just 18. Mum passed me this report from one of the local papers:

Chris Mole

"A West Kirby youth was killed and four others injured last night when a car left a Wirral road, shot across a grass verge, went through a barbed wire fence and overturned in a field."

Chris was a beautiful, beautiful person – he had been one of my friends for years.

Thankfully, the rest of the people in the car had survived and the next day, there was a light-hearted follow-up story about how Julia Skelly and Jean Farnie got a surprise visit from the Rolling Stones in hospital. They didn't seem too bothered by it – they were grieving – but the group got their picture in the paper.

I kept thinking: he was sitting in my seat. If I hadn't been in Canada, it would have been me instead of him.

I went on another crossing, and realised life as a ship's cook was never going to be for me. The problem was, I just couldn't stop being sick, and I didn't think I was ever going to snap out of it. I didn't want to quit another job, but I did.

My final crossing sailed from Liverpool on June 2, and on June 23, I walked off the ship for the last time, with all the chops, Guinness, whisky and fags £2 could get me.

Back to the shop in West Kirby, and back looking for work. There were the summer barbecues to come, all the other catering bits and bobs and helping mum in the shop, so I knew I wouldn't starve.

And, I didn't know it yet,
but I was about to get another
job – the happiest I had ever been.
In fact, the job that would lead
to me stumbling accidentally into

showbusiness.

CHAPTER SIX

I made ❧
the prawn cocktail

THE Magic Clock. Sounds like a children's TV show, doesn't it? But the very mention of the words in one of my Liverpool Echo columns brought phone calls from people I hadn't seen for years.

Drop it into a conversation with a gay Scouser of a certain age, and just watch their eyes light up.

At 18 I was off the boats and back at my mum's – she had been overjoyed when I'd told her I was quitting. And I was making the most of living near Liverpool by becoming a fully paid-up member of the city's fledgling gay community (although, as I have to keep reminding myself, it wasn't called gay in those days).

Visit Liverpool now and you can't see where the gay pubs used to be. They've moved a few streets north, near the solicitors' offices and estate agents. The square where they used to be, by the Royal Court Theatre, is now a load of bus stops and a Marriott hotel.

But go back 45 years and it was a completely different place. By day, the square held a huge market where another generation of barrow boys and girls, with weathered faces and dressed in hats and shawls, sold fruit and veg. But after they had all locked up and gone home, the lights would come on in five or six little pubs, dotted discreetly around the squares by the Royal Court and Playhouse theatres and the Stork hotel.

Because the Magic Clock was opposite the Royal Court, you had to be careful when you went in. You didn't want to let your mum's friends catch a glimpse of you as they walked out of the theatre.

Inside, the pub was decorated plainly, with wood panels, little red lights, wall lamps and red leather bar stools. The police tolerated us, but it was an uneasy relationship. If we had been caught inside we would have been thrown out for being underage, although the bar would not have been shut down because at the time it was a grey area. But we weren't liked, and if the police had wanted to make trouble for us, they could have done.

After all, for the next three years until the House of Commons voted to decriminalise homosexuality, being gay could still land you in prison. The year 1967 is set in the minds of my generation, because it meant the end of frightened men being taken from their homes and locked up, reported in the papers and disowned.

But most of the time in Liverpool you could have a good night out and meet other gay people in private. At the Magic Clock, people would light cigarettes in holders, wear their coats on their shoulders and drink large gin and tonics around the long bar.

I soon got to know and trust the people I'd meet in there.

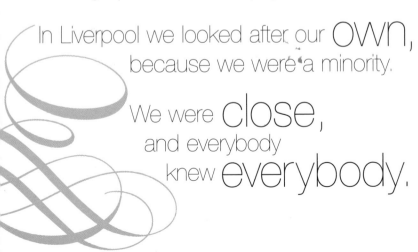

In Liverpool we looked after our OWN, because we were a minority.

We were close, and everybody knew everybody.

There was a bit of backbiting and bitching, but it wasn't as bad as the sort of thing you get in some gay communities today.

Sounds nice, wouldn't you say? Well it was, but that was only half the picture. I was still fighting hard against my sexuality, going out with girls and being seen in public with them. Oh, and I also

Sent to me just before she died

got engaged to one – almost forgot to mention that.

Her name was Vivienne, she had dark brown hair and I'd met her in a club. She worked for an aristocrat as a nanny to his children. We'd got on well – considering – and I'd proposed to her.

I don't know what would have happened if I'd gone through with marrying her, but thankfully it never happened. What finally put an end to it was when I went round to her family's house to surprise her. She raced to the back of the house and hid, mortified that her boyfriend with the flash clothes and big ambitions had seen where she came from.

"Why did you do that?" I asked her.

"I didn't want you to see me like this. I thought you wouldn't like it."

I had been in that position too, as a child. I had wanted everyone to think I still lived in the detached cottage with the orchards and got people to drop me off there. But I had learned to grow out of it. I was proud that mum had paid off dad's debts and was keeping going through her own hard work.

So seeing how she was made me worried. What if I never made it in show business, or as a top chef? Would she be ashamed of where I lived? I broke up with her, telling her I may never be able to give her what she wanted. And I was secretly relieved.

I kept the engagement ring. In my act I used to put it on and do this joke: "Do you like the ring? That was my mother-in-law's. She said, when I die, here's £500 get me a nice stone. I thought: 'Why wait?'"

By now I had got another catering job. My uncle lived next door to one of the owners of an up-and-coming nightclub in the centre of Liverpool called the Cabin – not the Cavern, the Cabin. The man, Ian Bell, was looking for an assistant chef for the club's restaurant and I nearly bit his hand off for the job.

I had heard stories about the exclusive set that ate at the Cabin, and it didn't disappoint. Walking in there for the first time, I breathed in the smell of prawn cocktail which brought back memories of parties at Mrs Ward's house. I saw one of the other owners polishing a grand piano, and I fell in love with the place.

The Cabin was incredibly sophisticated for the time in Liverpool. It had a bar where the bottles were lit up with fairy lights, and a glass dance floor with lights underneath. It had an in-house band, the Billy Ellis Trio, led by a blind piano player who played poker with Braille cards and had been known to cheat. Downstairs there was a tree growing – it died in the end, but you can still see the stump.

I learned a lot about the smart, Liverpool set who came to the Cabin. One day, I spotted a woman I recognised having dinner with a strange man. I turned to Colin, the other chef.

"Wasn't she in here yesterday, looking all lovey-dovey? I thought she'd just got married."

"That's nothing," Colin said. "Wait and see what happens tomorrow."

And sure enough, her husband would arrive, with another woman in tow. Everybody seemed to be at it. I became very disillusioned with marriage. Someone I worked with there – I'd better not be any more specific than that – was also playing around, and I went blabbing.

"I want to see you," he said to me, and I followed him into an office. "I'm not going to get you sacked because you're good at your job. I'm going to teach you a lesson," he said. "So I'm going to knock you out, and not speak to you for a year."

He did – another lesson learned the hard way. I never blabbed again.

The guests expected top-quality food at the Cabin and it was bloody hard work. But it wasn't bad compared to the cruise ships – nothing ever could be. We made shish kebabs for 6s 6d, curried prawns for 10s 6d. There was a special "Cabin Two Finger Menu" which inclued a James Bond themed dish, Goldfingers of Scampi in a basket and Whole Roast Liver Bird. Desserts included Pineapple in Kirsch and Pear Helene. When Tommy Steele was in town, I always remember he would eat a whole roast chicken, bones and all.

It was the only club around that didn't have a doorman. One of the owners, Mrs Windsor was on the door, and this women with a round face and glasses was more fearsome than any bouncer. She turned away Paul McCartney once because he didn't meet the dress code.

"Don't you know who that was?" I asked in disbelief as McCartney and his friends walked off.

"I don't care, scruffy little oik," she said.

But when one of Paul's bandmates got let into the club, I became totally star-struck. It was February 1964, and the Beatle was George Harrison. He sat with the wife of club owner Ian. At that time he was one of the biggest stars in the country, and I managed to sneak up to him and get his autograph. Stuck in a scrapbook from the time is a picture of him sitting at a table there. I've drawn an arrow to his plate and proudly written the words: "I made the prawn cocktail." I spoke to a Beatles expert the other day, and he told me that piece of paper would be worth £1,300 today. That's more than I made in a year back then.

The day after George's visit, though, I couldn't believe what I read in the papers. The picture showed the back of Ian's wife's head, and everyone had a field day speculating who the new mystery woman was.

One paper invented these quotes for George: "She's a friend of the family. I like to take out various girlfriends on my nights off. This is one of them." What a load of rubbish.

I soon grew to love the Cabin even more. There was a regular gang of us, including Alfonso the restaurant manager, whom I had huge crush on, and Franco the barman, who I'm still friends with today. I saved up and bought my first car, one of those bubble cars. Well, I wasn't exactly going to get something normal like a Morris Minor, was I? My new bosses knew I was gay. They let me save up my days off so I could take long weekends away. And I used them to go and see the bars and clubs everyone was talking about.

Because in those days it was just the same as it is now – everyone in Liverpool moaned about how the gay scene was better in Manchester, and better still in London.

I decided I was going to see Soho for myself, so I got a long weekend off work, planned where I was going to stay and got on the train on Saturday. As it pulled through Crewe and Stafford I got changed. I'd been planning my outfit for weeks.

I was thrilled at the chance to be myself, meet new people and, of course, go on the pull.

Mum didn't know what I was doing – I'd told her I was going to see some friends I'd met. In the innocent belief that her son was just a bit eccentric, she'd started talking about grandchildren. But that was a problem I could deal with another day, I thought as the train arrived at Euston.

I was staying at the Regent Palace at Piccadilly Circus – the cheapest hotel I could find in London. But after I'd checked in, I didn't have a clue where to go.

People in Liverpool had mentioned a few names to me: the A&B and the Rockingham in Soho, and the Carousel Bar off Leicester Square. But the places weren't exactly going to advertise themselves, were they?

But in the end I managed to get there, and had one of the best weekends of my life. I was an 18-year-old lad out on the town, finally able to act naturally without looking over my shoulder. From the moment I left London, I was counting the days until I could go back.

Over the weeks, I'd go back and forth as much as I could. Here you could dance waltzes, quicksteps and jives with whoever you wanted and, although the clubs didn't get easier to find, I started to make friends down there. After getting to know one man called Michael, I'd stay with him, in a flat next to Harrods. When he took me to Danny La Rue's club I was completely star-struck. Princess Margaret and Shirley Bassey sat nearby, and there I was ordering champagne.

There had been one man down in London who had been writing to me regularly. I'd gone off him and he had taken it badly. He had sent me one letter threatening to kill himself if I started going out with someone else – typical drama queen stuff. I'd read it and hid it in my bureau as I was late in for work at the Cabin. But it must have slipped out as I closed the door behind me.

After work that night I got a lift back with Brian Gilbertson, another owner of the club. It was 3am on a Thursday morning after a busy night and I crept into the house. I was used to getting in late and silently going to bed without waking mum, but walking up the stairs I saw a light on. Thinking she hadn't been able to sleep, I went in to say goodnight.

Mum was white. In her hand was a sheet of paper, and she looked absolutely destroyed.

She silently handed the love letter to me. "What does this mean?" she asked.

I felt sick to my guts. The letter had fallen out where she could see it. Everything I had done flashed before me. I glanced at the letter again. Everything was there, plain as could be. Did I try and lie my way out of this? Did I tell her it was all right because I was bisexual, even though I knew I wasn't? It might soften the blow if she could think her son might still settle down and give her grandchildren. No, I thought, that would be another lie – and this has to stop now. I had gone through six years of lying to the person I loved most in the world, and it had been the most miserable experience of my life.

So I said:

"It's true, mum. I'm a homosexual."

She looked at me, then screamed:

"Get out of the house!"

Then she rushed to the toilet and I heard her throwing up as I ran down the stairs.

CHAPTER SEVEN
a crate of
Guinness

I wasn't standing outside the house for very long. Mum got me back inside.

"I'm so sorry," she said, her voice trembling "I should never have done that."

But that didn't mean she was feeling any better about it – in fact she was having a breakdown in front of me. I rang an ambulance and she went to hospital where they treated her for shock, keeping her in Clatterbridge overnight.

In the morning, after a sleepless night, she got out and I told her everything. How I'd been to Dr Lansley and tried to kill myself when he couldn't help. Why I preferred to go to pubs in Liverpool than have a pint at the Ring O'Bells. How those trips down to London weren't quite what they seemed. I had made that split decision not to lie to her, and now there was no going back. But for her it was the first time I'd broken her trust. We made a pact neither of us would tell anyone.

Like lots of parents in her position back then – and a few today – she blamed herself. Had she raised me badly, she said? Was it because I hadn't had a father in my life for the last six years? Was it because she had told me I was adopted instead of lying to me?

I tried to explain to her it was none of these things, and it was just how I was. I even sent off for a record I had heard about that explained that someone's sexuality was not a man-made thing. It was called Dr Murray Banks Speaks on the Drama of Sex ("Authentic! Non Technical!" it said on the back).

But none of it helped. She cried herself to sleep over it, and later told me she did the same thing every night for the next three years.

Every morning I would dread waking up and going downstairs to see her. I stopped going to London and stopped going to gay bars in Liverpool. It wasn't worth it, I thought. Nothing was worth it if mum was going to be hurt like this.

When teenagers come out to their parents these days it's often difficult, but there are positive role models out there, and most of Britain is a tolerant place. Back then, in the eyes of the law and of most right-thinking people, it was a disgusting crime.

Other people I've met who came out around that time were disowned, beaten to a pulp and thrown out of their homes.

Mum felt like she'd lost her son, and we were in the middle of a period of mourning.

Desperate to make things better, one day, in the middle of another fraught conversation, I made a new suggestion. "Maybe we could go and see Dr Lansley – together this time – and we could talk it over with him?" I said.

Mum looked up: "Do you think so?"

"Anything to make you happy."

"I think that would be a good idea," she said.

She may have thought that, but deep down, I didn't. Why would he be able to help me now if he had laughed at me the first time and given me useless pills the second? But I clung onto the idea there was some way out.

I remember sitting in the dingy waiting room thinking: "Whatever you do, don't look at the National Geographic. There might be naked men in there, and that's the last thing I need. As we were ushered into the surgery, all I could think about was how dashing Dr Lansley looked in his suit. That wasn't a good sign.

We sat down, and I could see mum was struggling to keep it together. She was always mortified by any talk of sex, so hearing about it must have put her through hell.

I remember Dr Lansley repeating the sort of things mum had said – that it could be her fault because I didn't have a man in my life. She said nothing, but I could see she was getting more and more distraught. Finally, she said: "I've failed you, it's all my fault."

Then Dr Lansley said something I wasn't expecting. He said he thought there was a cure.

I sat there, taken aback. On the one hand, I was desperate to make everything all right with mum. But, at the same time, I thought: "How could there be a cure?"

"Would you like to go and see a psychiatrist?" Dr Lansley asked me. Out of the corner of my eye I could see mum nodding. She desperately wanted me to agree. So I did.

I've tried to remember the next bit, but it's a blur. I remember being scared, and I remember thinking: "What are they going to do?" My subconscious must have blanked a lot of it out, but I suppose the psychiatrist will have asked me the same sorts of questions as Dr Lansley.

The next thing I remember I had agreed to be 'cured', it was a wet, miserable day and my friend was driving me – terrified – to a hospital in Chester. Except, as I waved him off and went inside, I realised this wasn't a hospital. It was a loony bin. A place they used to lock single women up just for being pregnant and keeping them there for 20 years or more. A place no human being deserves to be.

I hadn't told my friend what I was going to hospital for, and no one was to know Peter Price was here. In fact, even the hospital staff didn't know Peter Price was there – I had been checked in under an assumed name because in the law's eyes, I was a criminal. Nobody knew what that name was. I was completely in the hands of the National Health Service.

What I would be having, I later found out, was called aversion therapy – and at the time it was a big idea in the scientific community. It had developed from the famous Pavlov's dog experiment. Pavlov would flash a light whenever he gave a dog some food, making the dog salivate. After this had been done enough times, the dog would learn to associate the food with the light, and all Pavlov would need to do was flash his light to set the dog drooling. It must have seemed like a neat solution to solving problem behaviour, and scientists had been trying it since the 30s. It would be used for many years after that day in 1964, on hundreds of people around the world. In his history of lesbian and gay Britain in the 20th Century, Alkarim Jivani writes:

"In many cases gay men who came before the courts were advised by their defence counsel that if they elected to take a 'cure' they would be treated more leniently by the judges... Indeed, some gay men and lesbians volunteered themselves.

At a time when homosexuality was so stigmatized and the medical establishment had the kind of authority that it hadn't enjoyed before or since, it is easy to see how gay men and lesbians talked themselves into a form of torture."

I went to see a psychiatrist who told me what was going to happen. He didn't use the phrase aversion therapy, and made it sound like nothing to worry about.

But when I got back to my room, I became even more scared. I was surrounded by people who had been committed. There were bars on the window and everything was locked behind us, so there was no way out. I changed into my favourite red pyjamas and, as it became dark, around me people carried on chattering and laughing. Someone put a cigarette butt at the bottom of my bed, and someone brushed up against my face. It was terrifying – what the hell had I got myself into?

The next day, I sat down in the doctor's room. An old-fashioned Grundy TK 20 reel-to-reel tape recorder was sitting on his desk. He started to speak to me about sex acts between men in the gay community. His questions became more and more graphic, dirtier and dirtier, and it went on for an hour.

"Don't you feel degraded about what you are doing?" I remember him asking me.

Then he stopped the tape, and told me we would be starting the therapy the next day.

"You're going to have aversion therapy," he said. "We're going to try and put you off looking at men. By the end you will be turned off by seeing a male body."

As the chattering and screaming
started around me that night,
I thought about what he had said.

How would they manage to do it?
Were they going to torture me?
Was it going to work,

and what
if it didn't?

In the morning, I was shown into a windowless room. Inside was a male nurse, who I though was very attractive. Tucked up in a bed in my pyjamas, he asked me what I drank. I told him Guinness, and soon a crate arrived. I was also given a stack of dirty magazines showing body builders and men in bathing costumes – not the sort of thing that would have turned me on in a million years. Then he started playing a tape.

It was the tape of my conversation with the doctor from the day before. I sat and listened to this, flicking through the books with a pint of Guinness, not knowing what the hell was going on.

Then the male nurse asked me for my arm and gave me an injection. What he was giving me, I later learned, was amp morphine, a chemical that could react with the alcohol in my bloodstream to make me violently ill. It is thought to have killed at least one person.

Suddenly, I started feeling a bit sick, then very sick. I yelled

out: "I think I'm going to vomit. I need a basin"

The doctor smiled: "Then be sick."

"I think I'm going to go to the toilet."

"Just do it on the bed."

I have always been strict about cleanliness and quite prudish about my personal hygiene, and here I was sitting in my own mess, completely embarrassed.

I screamed: "You're joking!"

"No, just do it on the bed," he said calmly.

"Do you realise anal sex is vile?" the doctor's voice on the tape was saying, over and over. "Do you realise oral sex is vile? What you do is disgusting."

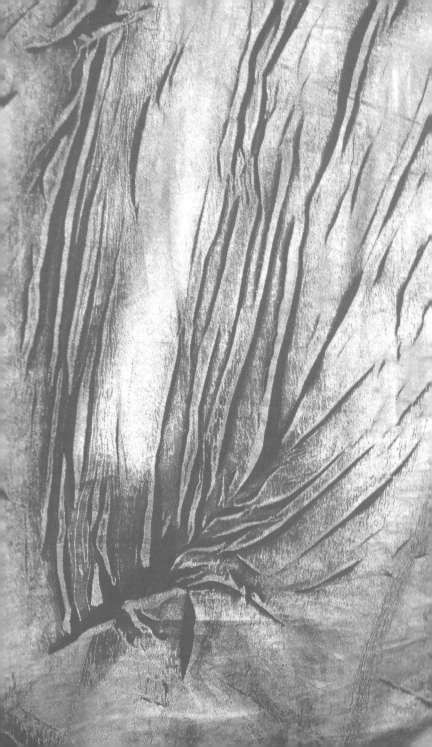

CHAPTER EIGHT
time for
the electrodes

WHAT the psychiatrist was trying to do to me was rewire my brain. So whenever I saw a naked man or thought about sex this is what I would think about – lying in my own mess in a loony bin feeling sick.

The idea was to make me feel as dirty and disgusted as possible. And doctors at the time actually claimed it worked. It was called the "slide and emetic" method, as most people had slides of naked men instead of the naff dirty books I was given. In the BBC's 1996 documentary Dark Secret: Sexual Aversion, which I was interviewed for, a doctor is shown in a piece of film from the time boasting about how good the treatment is.

"It does seem to work to a very satisfactory extent," he says. "The subject is sexually aroused by the opposite sex to a very normal extent."

The therapy continued for three whole days – 72 hours. I went through the same sequence again and again – the drink, the injections, the vomiting and excrement; drink, injections, vomiting, excrement – hour after hour after hour. I don't remember being given any food. Soon, there was nothing left to throw up.

I can't remember if I slept at all, and there was no difference between night and day. When the nurse went away, I was worried I would be able to hear the patients outside screaming and rattling the windows. But the nurse didn't leave me alone for long as he must have been worried I would kill myself. I had no concept of what day it was or how long I had been in there. And the nurse just stood there and watched me. Just putting this section together, in my clean flat in 2007, has made me start scratching myself.

For the last 12 hours all I could think was: "I want my mum. I don't think I'm going to get out of here alive." I could hardly get out of bed, I was so weak.

As I lay there sobbing, the psychiatrist came in. "Now you've got to have the electrodes," he said.

I looked up. "Electrodes?" I repeated in disbelief. This was One Flew Over the Cuckoo's Nest; the funny farm.

"What we are going to do is put electrodes on your penis. If you get an erection a jolt of electricity will go through you and stop you."

Was he serious? Which warped person had thought this up? Did he think I could get sexually excited lying in this bed terrified out of my skin? My strength came back to me as I started getting angrier and angrier.

"I want to go home," I shouted.

"But we haven't finished," he said calmly.

"I volunteered in here," I yelled. "I'm an experiment. If this is supposed to make me better I don't want to be better."

From the look in his eyes I thought they were going to put a straightjacket on me. "But we've still got two days to go. We need you for another two days. You've got to try the electrodes."

That was it. I went bananas, screaming the same things over and over at him. He sighed, realising he couldn't win now, and looked at me with pity.

"Then you're a failure."

What would have happened, had I stayed? Other people who had had their electric shocks said they were painful and frightening to go through – one man said it was like a sharp bolt of pain whooshing through the body. He said he thought he was about to be electrified. Then, at the end of the slide, he was rewarded by being shown a slide of a naked woman.

It completely screwed him up. Afterwards, he said, he tried to commit suicide. Then he was celibate for years, then married a woman because he felt he had to.

Under the disapproving glares of the hospital staff, I rang my friend to come and pick me up. I said nothing about what had happened to me.

In the car, I made the decision that I wouldn't tell mum. It would destroy her if she knew what I had been through. She wouldn't be able to forgive herself for letting her son sign himself up to be poisoned.

I went back to my friend's house, ran a bath, then got out, dried myself off and ran another. Then another, then another, over and over again. I scrubbed and scrubbed my hands until the skin hurt. Then I went home to mum.

"What are you doing back?" she said, looking surprised.

"I've left," I answered.

She looked angry. "I'm disappointed you haven't finished the treatment," she said quietly.

The doctor had called me a failure, and I felt like one. I felt I'd let everybody down. And I didn't know what the therapy had done to me. Was I still gay? Would I be attracted to anyone ever again? Dare I try having sex with anybody?

There was only one thing to do. I went to a gay bar. I needed to be wanted and feel human again, instead of degraded like the doctors had wanted. Mum was angry with me and I needed somebody to stay with me. I found someone I knew, and we spent the evening together, kissing and holding one another.

This story has a strange ending. A while later, and I'm at the Rockingham in Manchester. It was another gay club of its time.

They had a little bell, and when you rang it someone would come to the door. If you looked right, knew the secret knock or the password, they'd let you in. Even inside, you couldn't take any chances.

At one place, you wouldn't be allowed to dance properly until the last song of the night – the staff would actually go round separating you if you tried anything beforehand, as if you were 12-year-olds at a church disco. They were just like the old speakeasys they had in America when alcohol was banned, and that's exactly what they were like.

A group of about three of us were sitting there, surrounded by cigarette holders and customers dressed up to the nines, having a few drinks. While I was in the middle of a sentence, I noticed someone I recognised standing at the bar. But who was it?

Then it clicked – it was the psychiatrist.

I hadn't recognised his face at first because I'd been blanking out what had happened to try and deal with it. But now in my head I heard his voice again, saying: "Don't you realise what you do is disgusting, it's vile." It was him. Here, in a gay bar. He was gay all along.

I got up from my table, the anger building in me as I walked across the room. "Hello," I said, barely containing my utter rage.

"I'm sorry," he said. "Do I know you?"

"Yes you fucking do," I yelled, and straight away I went like a banshee, screaming and punching him. I've only been in three fights in my life, but I wanted him dead. How could he say those things to me when he was in here?

The rest of the bar flew into a panic, and the doormen rushed to help him. It took three of them to pull me off him, yelling and lunging at him.

Once it calmed down they asked him if he wanted to press charges against me. He said he didn't want any trouble. I left, making up some story explaining why I'd reacted like that. I couldn't tell anyone.

I wonder if he got off on me being punished? Did he enjoy the dirty talk, the tear-choked confessions from frightened teenage boys? I wonder if he wanted to go through the "cure" himself, after seeing what it had done to other people?

Well, I believe what he did to me has left me scarred. In gay clubs, I find myself lecturing people when they boast about some of the things they get up to. I have never had a long-lasting sexual relationship, something which upsets me every day. I'm still obsessive about order and cleanliness, spending hours tidying things, checking the towels in the bathroom are in the right order, and having more baths and showers than I need.

Not enough records survive to know how many other frightened men had to go through aversion therapy to change their sexuality. Papers were destroyed, and hospitals closed down. Until recently, I never told a soul what had happened. People tend to keep quiet when they've been through that sort of trauma. My uncle Edwin was a prisoner of war in Japan, and he never spoke about it for the rest of his life.

I stayed that way until 1993, when I read about a court case when a group of men and women had been sacked from the forces for being gay. One had been sent to a psychiatrist and claimed he was offered aversion therapy. I could not believe it was still happening, and I went public with what had happened to me. People thought I had made the story up, it was so unbelievable. But when journalists started investigating it all came out.

Once the story was out, I got letters from people all over the world who had been through the same thing, thanking me for bringing it into the open. Many of us had thought we were the only ones being experimented on.

Now I still get asked to talk about it every few months, on TV and radio. Someone recently approached me about turning it into a play. But it has only recently got easier. Only in the last five years have I been able to drive past that building in Chester near the zoo. I used to start shaking and take the long route round so I wouldn't have to see it.

> And at the time it marked a turning point.
>
> I decided I was going to live my life as what I was – a homosexual man.

I had tried girls, I'd got engaged, I'd fought it and fought it for six years. If I do it any longer, I thought, I'll have a breakdown. Now I was going to be true to myself. I was working in a nightclub where people accepted me. I wasn't alone, and I wasn't an oddball. And I didn't need any drugs or electric shocks to cure me.

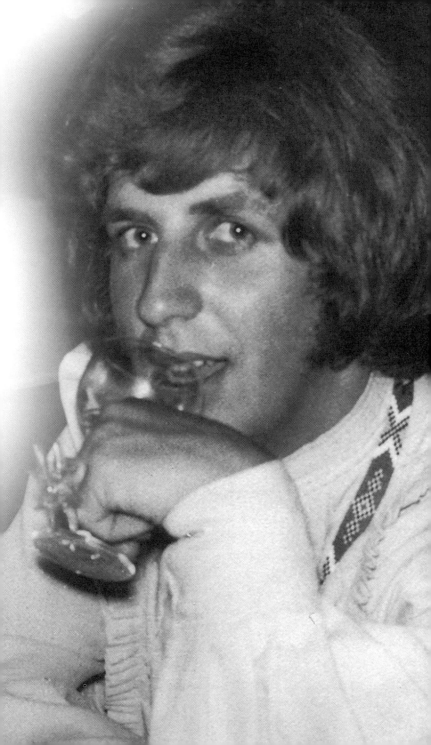

CHAPTER NINE

big Swing Face

"You. Come here."

It was John Stanley – one of the Cabin Club's best customers, and I'd just served the food for a huge party he had brought in.

"What are those on my plate?" he said.

"They're peas," I answered, hovering in my white shirt and black bow tie.

"You've put peas on my plate."

"Yes?"

"I don't like peas," he said.

"Don't make a fuss," his wife hissed at him.

"I will make a fuss!" he said, starting to bellow. "What are you going to do about it?"

"John!" his wife said. "I'm sorry about him."

"Don't say sorry. I don't like peas. What are you going to do about it?"

"Bloody hell!" I said. "You're a nuisance." I picked up the plate and scooped the peas off with my hands. "That better?" Around me his group started clapping, and he had to let it go. We even laughed about it later on.

If there was a Liverpool club where they were having more fun than the Cabin I'd like to have seen it. The atmosphere inside that place was incredible. Liverpool's smart set would wolf down their prawn cocktails, knock back the champagne and brandy Alexanders and dance to jazz on the lit-up dance floor.

And all without a doorman or a sniff of trouble in sight. I don't know where the gangsters were drinking back then, but they left us alone.

And if any stars were in town, they'd be likely to drop by. Frank Ifield had just had a hit with the song I Remember You. He tipped me a pound, which was a fortune in those days. Another singer, Eden Cain, tipped me to serve the soup before the prawn cocktail. When I asked him why, he said it was so he could look down the top of a girl he was with, while she bent over to eat it.

I'd enjoyed myself in the kitchen, coming up with ideas to keep the restaurant ahead of the competition. We were the first place to serve squid in a basket in Liverpool, and the menu was full of fun dishes we'd thought up.

And as well as the cooking I was becoming popular with the punters. I'd come out from behind the hatch more and more, drinking and dancing with them, and staying long after closing, waiting for a lift home from Brian the owner while he played cards into the early morning.

Twice I played with them. I'd got into terrible rows with mum because I never wanted to leave the Cabin. But I knew she wanted a Goblin Teasmade and I thought I'd try and win her the £32 it would cost, to get on her good side. I managed it, and turned up with the box as a suprise. But the next time I lost all my money and decided I'd better not make a habit of it. After all, I was only earning £15 a week.

Once again, mum would start asking me why I was mixing with these smart wealthy people. "Why are you always with people who are better than you," she'd say, over and over again. It was something we'd never agree on.

Characters would come in the club all the time, like one man called Malcolm. He was absolutely gorgeous and I took a shine to him. Later that week his sister Michelle would come down, and I thought she was a stunningly attractive girl. The pair

would keep alternating visits and, with my eyes on stalks and tongue out, I didn't have a clue what was going on. Months later when I asked about it, everyone fell about laughing. Hadn't I realised they were the same person?

Then, for the first time in my life, I was headhunted.

The Swan pub down the road wanted me to be their chef and assistant manager.

Like the Cabin, the Swan is still there in Liverpool, although now it's a bikers' pub. At the time, it was owned by Mervin and Nancy Kieron, one of Liverpool's best-known, eccentric couples. They would drive around in their pink Rolls-Royce, him with a huge handlebar moustache, her dressed all in pink and dripping with diamonds. He was a terrible flirt – he'd turn to you and mutter: "Look at the lovely titties on that woman!" – and Nancy would always find out and batter him.

They wanted the trendy new basket food I'd been cooking in the Cabin to go with the Swan's reputation for the best pint of Bass in Liverpool.

Once Nancy Kieron came in the club, immaculately dressed like Lady Penelope, and sat down to have a drink. She glanced to her left and screamed. A filthy rat, riddled with some disease, was staggering along the table next to her. Everyone watched as it started stumbling, slowed down, rolled onto its back and died.

While at the Swan, I'd still go in the Cabin after work and would still stay there late. There were a few good places to go around there: one of my favorites was the Porthole restaurant, done up like a ship inside. It had vegetarian piranha fish imported from South America, which were supposed to be meat-eaters. People used to go just to see them, although their diet meant they never survived long.

I was still desperate to get into show business, and I had the idea of singing in the Porthole. I pleaded with them and they agreed. But when I got up and belted out The Lady is a Tramp – a song I still sing today from time to time – no one clapped. "Am I doing the right thing?" I thought to myself.

But there was another way into showbiz that I'd been thinking about – being a DJ.

Dancing to records had started to spread around Britain, and I'd read about disc jockeys and seen disc jockeys in clubs in London. They were going down a storm, and I sensed this was the way things were going.

I'm sure someone will phone me up and correct this the minute they read this sentence, but my 61-year-old brain can't remember anyone doing it before me in Liverpool. Apart from Billy Butler, of course. So I decided to give it a go.

"Let me try doing it," I said to Ian.

"But you're a chef."

"I'll do it between my shifts," I said. Just for an hour. Just for half an hour."

He sighed. "The band won't like it. But we'll give it a go."

Sure enough, the musicians weren't too happy – this was a plot to replace a group of workers with one who could do the entertaining on the cheap, they thought. But it got sorted out that they wouldn't be losing any work, and I would DJ for the half hour they were on their break. So, with 10 records, one turntable and my chef's outfit as my costume, I took the plunge.

People turned round from their tables. Some looked curious, some looked shocked. What was happening?

"Everybody dance!" I yelled. "Come on! Clap your hands!" Nothing. But as the loudmouthed chef who had a reputation for yelling at awkward customers, they knew I wasn't giving up that easily.

"Come on, give it a try!" I said, pointing to people. "You, you, go on, get up!"

Slowly I managed to bully them onto the dance floor, and by the time I'd exhausted my 10 records, they were all dancing. I'd got away with it. So each night I'd come over from the Swan and do an hour with my record player while the lads in the band had a rest.

Then one day, Brian called me into his office. "We need to talk," he said. "Sit down."

What had happened, I thought? Was he about to tell me not to come in anymore?

"How do you fancy being a DJ?" he said. "Full time."

I laughed. "Working full time as a DJ?"

"That's right. How much do you want?"

I must have looked like a train had hit me. He was actually going to pay me for doing that? It was money for old rope – I was just putting a few records on and having a laugh. I had a think. What would be the right amount to ask for? I didn't have a clue.

"We'll give you £20 a week," he said.

I couldn't believe it. "What?" I spluttered.

"All right, £25. But that's it. You start tomorrow."

He walked off, and I was left just sitting there in disbelief. I would have to leave the Swan, but I'd done it – I was now in show business. I walked down the street saying "Yes! Yes!" I'd found a route into a new career – and a job where I wouldn't smell of chips anymore.

Mum was in tears, of course. She didn't know a DJ from a hat stand.

"You spent all that time training to be a chef, working day and night, and now you're going to throw it all away," she sobbed. She brightened up a bit when I told her what I would be earning, but she was still worried it was all just a craze, and when people got bored of DJs I would be left on the dole.

The first week doing it flew by. Every night I would get up, put on my records, show off, and have a brilliant time. It was a piece of cake, and that Friday I was embarrassed to ask for my first pay packet. It wasn't a complete jump from one career to another. I was still helping out in the kitchen at the Cabin when they were short, and taking any catering work I could get. Sometimes I'd do the buffet for a big party, then put on a disco for them afterwards.

God I thought I was sexy

Once I'd made an enormous cake, which took hours to bake and then ice, for a birthday party. As I was driving along with it, a kid ran out in front of me and I had to slam the brakes on, sending the cake flying. I ran out of the car and put the boy over my knee.

"What do you think you're doing?" his mum shouted to me from across the road.

"Do you see what he's done to that cake in there?" I yelled. She took a look.

"Little toe-rag – hit him harder! Go on, really whack him! Here, I'll help."

As the weeks and months went on, I got known around Liverpool. More and more people would start coming to the Cabin, until there were queues down the street to get in.

I was making them big money, but I still wasn't taking it seriously. There was the drinking. When you're a new DJ there's nothing worse than being faced with an empty dance floor that isn't filling up. I thought because everyone else was drunk, you had to be drunk too, to get them in the mood. So I made it my mission to get as drunk as I could every night I was on. I shudder to think how many times I drove home wasted. We all did in those days: punters, club owners, even the police.

But for the first time, after a few difficult years, I'd discovered fun, and was having one of the happiest times of my life.

Every Sunday I had to be back home in time for mum's big lunch, or there'd be murder. But after Saturday – the biggest night at the club – the last thing I wanted to do was shovel down roast beef and two enormous Yorkshire puddings. I'd lie in bed at midday thinking of that lunch on the table and dreading it.

"What's wrong?" mum would say.

"Nothing," I'd answer, wishing I was anywhere else.

Around that time I met a couple I've stayed friends with all my life, although sadly they have both passed away now. Austin and June Wilson were some of the richest people in Liverpool, owners of the huge Army and Navy chain of stores. Later, their daughter would marry Liverpool captain and

The gang at Atmosphere, Birkenhead

manager Graeme Souness. Mrs Wilson looked like Elizabeth Taylor in her beautiful gowns and jewellery.

But, like the Wards and the Collinges, they weren't stuck up. They were fun people, regulars on the dance floor at the Cabin, and after I got to know them they invited me to DJ at a house party they were having.

When I got to their enormous house in Woolton, I couldn't believe my eyes. They had what was, I reckon, the only indoor swimming pool in Liverpool at the time. I remember feeling sick with jealously that I had so little and they had so much. Surely Austin could lend me a million for a year, I thought. I could just live off the interest and then give it back to him.

Of course, I didn't realise he was doing that himself – I had no head for business at all.

Their swimming parties became legendary around Liverpool for being wild, exciting nights. At one, everyone was given a blow-up doll on the way in. Mum was mortified one night when I came home with just my tie and underpants on – someone must have pushed me in the pool.

By now I was about to turn 21, and I had a following of fans, a wardrobe that was getting out of control even by my standards, and my own showbiz nickname – Big Swing Face. It came from the name of a big band song by Buddy Rich that had become my signature tune. I had my first set of publicity photos printed with the name and my picture on. I've got long hair, a ruffled shirt and a velvet jacket on, and I look the spit of Austin Powers.

To celebrate my birthday that year, I decided to push the boat out. I had a Champagne and hotpot party, dressed as Barbra Streisand and got up on stage to mime along to Second Hand Rose. Mum came and it was the only time I've seen her tiddly in her life. At the end of the night she was lauging her head off, calling out: "Peter! There's a man giving me a lift home!"

Pete Price
" BIG SWING FACE "
SINGING D.J. — COMPERE
Telephone : 051-525 5281

Sitting there I realised something. I'd gone into DJing thinking it was a bit of a laugh. But this was a business. I needed to get bigger gigs, bigger crowds, more cash. The next few years were crucial if I was to make it in showbiz. I was having the most fantastic time of my life at the Cabin, but it was time to go.

In the early days at Radio Merseyside

CHAPTER TEN

Fog in the South

SO there I was, 21 years old and a DJ. More and more people cottoned on to the fact that you could earn money doing this, and I had to keep ahead of the game. As people in the Cabin started requesting more and more records, I had to keep on buying them.

But then I caught onto the fact that if you're a DJ you can get sent demo discs free. They had big white As on the front, which were great for posing. You'd make sure you left them on the top of your piles, for people to see.

I began to think if I could be a DJ in a club, why not on the radio? I wrote to all the radio stations, sending them demo tapes. I sent one to Radio 1, which had only just started. My friends have heard it, but I haven't dared listen in 40 years. I can hear it now in my head, though. And it's cringe-worthy. I'm completely camping it up, screaming my head off like a lunatic.

One night, I got a seriously lucky break. A man called Ron Castle who worked for a clothes company came in and saw me DJing and, afterwards, asked me if I would be interested in some work. A new boutique called Turnstyle was opening in Bold Street, just down the road from the Cabin, and he was launching it in the unlikely location of Liverpool's Central Station. Guest of honour would be Sandie Shaw, the huge star. Would I like to DJ?

PETE PRICE

I was so excited. Me, working with a name like that, getting seen by everyone who happened to be getting off a train from Wirral and Southport between 4.45pm and 6.15pm.

The big day came and it went all right. I tried not to be put off

You're gorgeous... have you got a brother? Me and Sandie Shaw at Central Station

by Sandie's feet – she never wore shoes and had the biggest bunions I've ever seen. The next time I saw them that big was on Jimmy Ruffin, the Motown singer.

We were slagged off in the papers for holding up all the commuters during rush-hour. One columnist wrote: "While 25,000 Merseysiders are trying to get home, models will prance on the back of a truck under floodlights." But it didn't matter; I must have kept 50 photos of that afternoon.

I didn't sit back and wait for work to come to me after that, though. Every week I was trudging around everywhere looking for gigs, and finding more and more. I did fashion shows at Lewis's department store and people would ask me to judge old-fashioned beauty contests at places like New Brighton Baths. My gay friends found the fact I was doing these hilarious, of course. But I always said: "Why not? At least I'm objective, I appreciate what the contestants are wearing and I won't try to get into their knickers, unlike the other judges."

After a group of us went on holiday to Turkey, I got someone to take a photograph of me in a club over there standing where the DJ stood. When I got back, I told everyone I'd been working in Turkey's top nightclubs, and got my picture taken with a gold-embroidered waistcoat I'd bought from a bazaar.

Seeing how that story about George Harrison had been twisted I thought "If you can't beat them, join them" and was always thinking about publicity stunts to get myself in the news.

I did one show with Simon Dee, a megastar on the TV and radio who would later burn himself out and finish up being a bus driver. For quiet Wirral, this was all seen as a new world at the time – listen to how one of the local papers mum got reported it:

"Mr Pete Price of 5 Bridge Road, West Kirby, who is making a name for himself in the "pop" world as a DJ (disc jockey) is going to work with Simon Dee on Wednesday in a charity discotheque party."

Thanks to the regular crowds I was managing to get at the Cabin, another offer came along from Ron Castle – and this time, it was the big one.

Kaleidoscope was a huge, day-long music festival, lasting from 12pm to 1.30am, on Saturday December 7, 1968. It was being held at the old stadium, where people used to go and watch wrestling (I remember one wrestler, called Jack Pye, had an unfortunate habit of urinating on the audience.) My mate, Merseyside DJ Billy Butler, used to go every week.

Topping the bill at Kaleidoscope was Pink Floyd, with other acts including the Move and Cliff Bennett. I think I was due to compere a section of the show quite early on, because a group of DJs from Radio 1 were coming up from London on the train to do the main bits. But when I turned up on the day with my box of records, Ron came up to me white-faced. There was thick fog in the South of England; the DJs had not set off yet. He looked apologetic: "I'm terribly sorry about this, but would you mind holding the fort while we wait for them?"

I spent the rest of the morning praying for that fog not to lift. And it didn't.

So there I was, for the rest of the afternoon and evening, in front of an audience of thousands and thousands who had all paid 7s 6d to get in. I was introducing pop acts, jazz groups, fashion shows, comedy, the lot. Right at the end of the night, the star DJs arrived, but by then I didn't care. I'd had the most amazing day of my career, and I was done in.

I had managed to impress the BBC by covering at the last minute. And it so happened they were recruiting local people.

The corporation had just launched eight experimental local radio stations across the UK. One, of course, was in Merseyside, transmitting out of Allerton golf course, slightly south of the city.

What were they putting on the air? Well, the sorts of shows they had planned for their schedules had names like Postmark Merseyside, Melodies of Merseyside and Murder, Mayhem and Mystery (some of Merseyside's most dastardly deeds).

As you can probably see, they needed something for the younger listeners, not to mention something without "Merseyside" in the title.

So, for the sum of five guineas, I was to be their first freelancer. My show would go out once a week for half an hour. It would be called *Never Mind the Price* and would review new records, and would earn me five guineas a go. Of course, the format of the show had nothing to do with the fact that we'd be guaranteed a steady stream of fresh music to play – and wouldn't have to pay out royalties.

There was an announcement in the papers, and breathless adverts went up all over Merseyside saying: *"Don't read this – it's priceless!"* giving details of the show. A report said how it was my "first broadcast venture" after DJing for 13 months, and that I'd been approached because of the Kaleidoscope show.

When I met the producer, Jim Black, he terrified me. Jim was BBC through and through, and spoke with a plummy accent, but he talked me through the process kindly as I didn't have a clue what I was doing. My first show was broadcast on February 3 1969. My opening words were: "This is Pete Price – Never Mind the Price. What a cheek!"

We'd recorded the shows in advance, but of course I'd sit in Bridge Road with mum listening intently to the first one when it was on. The next day, someone from the station called me.

"It seems your show went down well, Peter," she said. "We've had quite a few telegrams arrive this morning saying how much people loved it. They're all saying you're the next big star and the show should be on every day. Everyone's very impressed."

I smiled – I'd forgotten about a little plan I'd come up with. You see, I knew a guy in the telegram office, and together we had come up with the idea that he'd get these sent to Radio Merseyside after the show. I owe him a pint, I thought.

The next week after programme two had gone out, I got another call.

"Hello Pete. You had even more telegrams this week – about a dozen or so, saying how much they loved the show. You really must have a lot of fans out there."

But the next week, I'd been rumbled.

"Hello Pete. I've got more telegrams here. One's from Diana Ross saying how she thought you were the world's greatest DJ. The other is from Frank Sinatra asking if you will come and work with him in Las Vegas. Could you ask whoever's sending them to stop please?"

The daft sod, I thought. He'd gone too far and made me look a complete tit.

But Radio Merseyside took off in a big way. Even now, it's the BBC's most listened-to local radio station outside London. Soon they decided to double my show to an hour, calling it *Twice the Price*. As the show was so successful, they allowed me to have guests. I was on a mission and went to London with a tape recorder. I found many stars, but I must tell you about this one.

I asked to borrow a tape recorder so I could go down to London and try to get some interviews. I went to Ronnie Scott's jazz club and spotted Spike Milligan.

"I'm sorry to bother you," I told him. "But I'm a little local radio DJ that gets five guineas a week…" so I went on, pleading with him for an interview. And he gave in.

"Would you like a beer?" he said, holding out a pint for me.

"I'm sorry, I don't drink beer," I said. With that, he threw the pint over his shoulder, drenching a woman behind him, and poured wine into the glass for me. Looking like a drowned rat, the woman laughed nervously.

"Come and see me tomorrow," he said. The next day I got to his office in Notting Hill. Peter Sellers and Harry Secombe had offices in the same building.

I remember the huge canvasses hanging up and the beautiful polished wood floor, and I heard him clumping around upstairs. We recorded the interview – it was bizarre but brilliant.

"What are you doing tomorrow?" I asked him.

"Having dinner with the Lord Mayor of London."

"Why are you doing that?"

"Because I'm hungry."

I went back the next day to thank him for his time, but I was told he was locked in a wardrobe, and couldn't speak to anyone. He suffered bipolar disorder, and must have been in the middle of a depression. Spike was zany and an icon in those days after the Goon Show. He was also very unpredictable.

But so am I. Take for example the time I surprised Shirley Bassey in her dressing room. She was playing at the Empire, and the theatre manager had got front row seats for me, Herbert, mum and Herbert's mum, Queenie. I got to the theatre at 5pm to pick the tickets up, two hours before I was due to meet the others. I'd been trying to interview this woman for years. Backstage at the Empire I found her dressing room, knocked on the door, and when nobody answered I went in.

Then I had an idea. Maybe if I hid there and burst out, she'd let me speak to her. What have I got to lose, I thought. I hid in the shower. I waited for what seemed like forever, then I heard her. She was in a terrible mood, yelling at her PA, screaming and swearing. Now I was scared. Shaking with fear, I pulled the shower curtain back.

She was standing there in a housecoat with her hair scraped back. I froze. "Who the fuck are you?" she shouted.

"I... I... I hate Barbra Streisand!" I squeaked. She burst out laughing. I begged her for an interview, giving her the same sob story about how I only earned five guineas a week and was trying to make a living – and I was a great fan. And she warmed to me. So, as Maynard Ferguson's orchestra played in the first half of the show, I sat in her dressing room in a different world. I asked her what her greatest musical moment had been and she told me it was singing for John F Kennedy. I asked her why and she said: "My strap broke, my tits fell out."

Hanging up was the gown she'd worn on the cover of her album, Something, while walking along the beach. It was such an incredible dress it was impossible to clean, and it was in a right state.

The interview over, I went out to meet the others.

"Where have you been, Peter?" mum said.

"I've been interviewing Shirley Bassey."

"Oh, son. I wish you wouldn't say things like that." They all looked at me with disbelief.

Then she came onstage – the housecoat was off, the gown was on and the magic was back. For generations of gay men, she's been an icon – it's the passion in her voice and the pain she's been through.

After her first number the crowd were ecstatic. "I'm sorry I was late on stage," she said. "But I was being interviewed by a lovely man called Peter Price. Where are you Peter? Stand up."

My legs turned to jelly. She gave me a bouquet to give to mum and a pearl from one of her dresses. There was only one problem – when I took the interview back to Radio Merseyside they said they might not be able to play it because you could hear the orchestra playing in the background, and they might have to pay royalties. I really don't remember how we got round it but it did go out. To this day people still ask me about Shirley.

I said I worked six nights a week, but I meant seven. I'd started working Sundays over the water in Wirral as well. I was doing evenings at the Leighton Court, which we called *Mental Nights* – every time I played *Singing in the Rain*, everyone would start chucking water round.

This got to be a tradition, and the management didn't always approve: when I'd DJ at some places they would confiscate the record and lock it in the safe, just to make sure I didn't play it.

The Wirral group were a completely different set of people, and over the years they've become some of my best friends.

The night moved the Golden Guinea, owned by John Stanley (whose peas I'd scooped up in the Cabin). Then it went to Rupert's, then back and forth from the clubs, but it's stayed the same all those years.

People would asked me how I could work all those nights in a row. But I was a natural night owl – I don't really function early in the morning and I could sleep for England. Plus, I told them, I couldn't remember the last time I had been stuck in a traffic jam on the way to work.

At around that time, I learned another lesson the hard way at the Cabin. I was on the microphone, and I spotted a lady who worked in a boutique nearby.

"Oh, Margot's in," I said, pointing at her. "She works for that crappy clothes shop up the road."

She laughed along with everyone else, but when I got into work a few days later, one of my bosses was waiting for me, red-faced.

They'd had a solicitor's letter. Margot had gone back to the shop and told her boss and he was suing for slander. I didn't even really know what slander was. The management made it clear it was my cock-up, and I'd have to sort it out – all £150 of it. That was six weeks' salary, all for a stupid comment. My wages were docked each week until it was paid off. I crashed my car once, I was so worried about it.

The radio show meant more and more people were coming down to see me, and I knew I had to move on. I knew where, too – in the whole of Liverpool, there was one job I wanted more than anything.

Cabaret clubs, where you went for dinner, saw a few acts then stayed for a disco, were big business in Britain in the 60s and 70s. King of the clubs in Liverpool was the Shakespeare, known as the Shakey.

Since 1888, it sat in Fraser Street, near London Road and Lime Street station. It was one of Britain's most beautiful theatres, and one of the 10 biggest cabaret clubs in Britain, on a par with the Talk of the Town in London and the Golden Garter in Manchester.

It was, if you'll pardon the expression, the dog's bollocks.

It was decorated in over-the-top Victorian style. There were carvings of scenes from Shakespeare plays, real gold leaf on the walls and a jaw-droopingly fancy ceiling. American producer Sam Wannamaker (who was in one of the Godfather films) had taken it over in 1957 to put on plays, calling it a "a place of beauty where beauty could be created."

It had closed down after 13 months and reopened in 1963 as a club and, after a fire, opened again a few years later.

I had heard whispers on the grapevine that they wanted me to be the compere at the club, a chance I'd have jumped at. I kept my ear to the ground, asking people who knew the owner, who ran it for the Robley Group, but didn't hear anything. I decided to ask the area manager, and went into the building to see him.

He wasn't interested. "You're not good enough," he told me in his office, looking down his nose. "In fact, you're not the type of person we're looking for in any way, shape or form."

Well bollocks to you then, I thought, walking out of the building, biting my lip and trying not to notice how stunning the painted walls and plush carpets looked.

I'd had my heart set on being the first host at the Shakey. Everyone who walked past would see my name – "Your host, Pete Price" – on the board underneath whatever act was on that week. Mum would be proud of what I did for a living, instead of asking me why I spent my time putting on records in a nightclub. I decided I'd try some of the smaller clubs and see if I could work my way up.

But then, like the miraculous fog that kept the Radio One DJs off the stage, there was another twist of fate.

The Shakespeare was sold to a man called George Silver. Mr Silver was a multi-millionaire – a huge man with a gleaming bald head and a large, hooked nose. Film buffs will know he appeared in the awful James Bond movie The Man with the Golden Gun as "Fat Beiruit Thug". I'd heard he was looking for somebody to host at the Shakespeare as part of a huge revamp. Was it worth trying again?

I didn't need to. The general manager found me at the Cabin and told me Mr Silver wanted to see me in action, to work out whether I would be suitable at his club. We arranged for him to come and see me one night.

That day I spent hours practising in front of the mirror, sharpening up my one-liners and choosing which records I was going to play. I got the barman to put a bottle of champagne on ice and told the kitchen staff they might have to make their portions a bit bigger. All my friends came along to clap and laugh extra loud and make me look like the most popular man in Liverpool. It was all going to be perfect.

Then Mr Silver didn't turn up.

We waited all night, and as it got towards the end I was furious. How dare he say he was coming and then not show? I was about to be fobbed off for the second time for the job

I wanted more than anything. Well this time I wasn't going to go quietly.

The next morning, I flounced into the Shakespeare.

"Where's Mr Silver?" I barked at the secretary. Before she could tell me he was in a meeting and wasn't to be disturbed I was in there, pushing past the board members.

"Who do you think you are, saying you'll come to see me?" I yelled. "Do you know how hard I worked that night? Have you got any idea what this job means to me?" And on, and on, until I'd shouted myself hoarse and ran out of things to say. The fat, bald man opposite me broke into a smile, watched intently by the rest of the board.

"I like you," he finally said. I stared at him, speechless. "I'm going to call you 'Mr Personality'" He chuckled. "You've got the job."

It was going to be hard work. As the host – as Mr Personality – I'd be doing a bit of everything, earning £30 a week. I'd walk from table to table, greeting the guests as they came in and asking if they needed anything. Then I'd come on, sing a couple of songs, and tell a few jokes. I'd come on in between the acts and introduce them. Then, for an hour after the cabaret had finished, I'd run the disco until it was time to go home. All six nights a week, Monday to Saturday.

Now, though, I had to tell the Cabin that I was leaving. What would my bosses say? They'd given me my first big break that had led to all this by agreeing to let me play records. Plus I was still happy there, and scared of going somewhere else and screwing up. I put off telling them for ages, but when I did they were thrilled for me, and threw me a big leaving party.

So with the farewell ovation ringing in my ears, I went to the Shakespeare. I got my own bright pink mini-van with "Mr Personality" on it, and my own dressing room. It would be my name on the board outside, introducing some of the country's biggest acts. I was 23 and I felt like I'd finally made it. From now on things would never be the same again.

CHAPTER ELEVEN
You've knocked out
the act

ALAN Williams will always be known as the man who gave the Beatles away. He was their manager before Brian Epstein took them over. Now in his old age and full of stories, he can still be seen holding court in pubs all over town.

But he also owned the Blue Angel in Liverpool, and he came to me with an idea for a show.

A singer called Don Partridge had had a big hit record with a song called Rosie. The different thing about him was that he was a busker – he'd been discovered singing on the streets for pennies, so the story went.

So Alan had an idea. Why not book Don for a night, but get other buskers from around the country to support him? He would put the rag-tag bunch on stage at the posh Philharmonic Hall, and I would be the compere.

The acts he found were incredible. One woman he'd discovered had been in a Doris Day film years ago, before her career went wrong. Another man, called the Professor, played the violin beautifully but had started busking after his wife had died. One woman had a good voice, but used to stand on stage trembling because of a health condition. Then there was an escapologist and "Jumping Jack", a man who tap-danced on skis.

Well it was a huge success, selling out the Phil overnight with queues round the streets. But there was one big problem.

A lot of them were on the streets busking for a reason – they were alcoholics.

Alan gave me the job of guarding them for 24 hours before the show. But it was an impossible task trying to get them to walk past a pub and not sneak in. It was like herding sheep. We lost three acts. It was sad to hear the stories they'd been through, then see that some of them were ruining their big chance.

I'd loved working with Alan, but the show was a sideline. The main thing in my life now was the Shakespeare, and I couldn't wait to start.

Because I was now Mr Personality, with the tiny dressing room in the middle of a Pete Price makeover, and the mini van with my name plastered on that was so pink you could see from space. And, of course, all the ambition and passion of a cocky 23-year-old who has just been handed the job of his dreams.

A flyer for the revamped club said: *"Pete Price, the well-known Disc Jockey of Radio Merseyside will be our personality compere to link the acts and provide the extra professional polish."*

The first night's star act was a singer called Julie Rogers, who had got to number one with a song called *The Wedding* (which she's still singing today). Of course, now practically every pop act has had a number one hit, and it doesn't mean they've been all that successful. But back then, when everyone bought records, you were a star overnight if you managed it.

My outfit was waiting on a coat hanger. I was going to wear a black shirt, white velvet bow tie, shocking pink velvet suit and snakeskin boots. They wouldn't be getting a watered-down version in for the first night. But I was worried. Would they like me, or was the old area manager right? Was I completely unsuitable in any way, shape or form?

I found out at 9pm on October 6, 1969. The Shakespeare was full, and everyone was straining their necks to get a look at the new host. I ran onto the stage. I sang *What a Day This Has Been*. Then I told three gags. The audience loved it. Every time I came on in between acts I got a big cheer, and they all got up and danced for my first disco at the end. A star was born, I thought, driving back through the deserted Mersey tunnel and creeping into bed above the shop to find mum, waiting up to hear all about it.

The following night, and for the next month of performances, I was booed, heckled, attacked and yelled at. The novelty had worn off, and the audience at the Shakespeare wanted to put me through my paces. They demanded their pound of flesh.

As every comic will tell you, Liverpool crowds can be some of the toughest in the country if they don't like you. People get terrible nerves before they go out in front of a crowd of Scousers. Sometimes the punters are funnier than the comic onstage. Often they just think they are, but they have a good time trying to put you off.

Dying on stage – the show business term for when nobody laughs – taught me all the little tricks of handling audiences. You bully them. You pick on a heckler. You appeal to the women in the crowd so they'll tell their partners off. If all else fails, you beg, then get on your knees and pray to the gods of comedy to make you funny. You think I'm kidding, don't you?

Kenny Ball, King of the Swingers, at the Shakespeare

I memorised a string of put-downs which got filthier and filthier as the evening went on. "You're sharp. When your head comes to a point, have it lanced," I'd start, before moving on to: "Put your hat on, there's a woodpecker flying round."

Finally, there was: "I wish I was a pigeon and you were a statue," finally, that is, before I started on the really unprintable stuff.

Having this chance to work out what I wanted to do with my act and test it out night after night was the making of me. When I see singers on shows like *X Factor* being thrust into the limelight, sometimes before they've ever sung in front of a paying audience, I feel they're being set up to fail. Working with a difficult crowd is the best way to learn your trade.

At the Shakespeare I was getting to do a bit of everything – stand-up, singing and DJing – trying out new ideas and getting a feel for what would work.

Once people in the crowd got to know me, I had my old Cabin problem of trying to stay sober while I was doing my job. Walking round all the tables to say hello to everyone was in my contract, but it was a four-storey building and the tables never ended.

In cabaret clubs in the 60s you didn't order a couple of Scotches then keep ordering – you asked for a bottle, which you'd keep on the table all night. Everybody insisted on having a drink, and Liverpool people get upset if you don't accept their hospitality.

As my clothes had gone down well on the first night, I got the idea of making them a feature of the act. I decided I'd change into a different outfit while each artist was on stage.

I'd met a lady called Toni Spencer, who was a local clothes designer from Gateacre, and I asked her to make the wildest outfits she could for me. It got to the point where I was spending practically all my money on clothes, going more and more outrageous to keep getting the claps when I walked on.

Whenever famous people asked me about my clothes, I sent them her way to get her extra business.

We'd plan little publicity stunts to keep the Shakespeare in the papers, and as my clothes were one of the things people remembered, we decided to make a big thing of them, and here was a great opportunity.

FAR&NEAR

Job that lost its glitter

PETER PRICE has lost his job as a compere—because he glitters too much.

Each time he appeared in sparkling sequined outfits at the Shakespeare Club, Liverpool, he was greeted by whistles and cat calls. The bosses asked him to wear conservative suits — 'and I refused point blank,' said Peter.

"Job that lost its glitter", the headline in the Daily Mail said. "Peter Price has lost his job as a compere – because he glitters too much. Each time he appeared in sparkling sequined outfits at the Shakespeare Club, Liverpool, he was greeted by whistles and cat calls.

"The bosses asked him to wear conservative suits – 'and I refused point blank,' said Peter."

We said I had been given a month's notice, and meanwhile I managed to get 4,000 signatures and lots of publicity. We then reported my job had been "saved".

4,000 SIGNATURES HELP TO SAVE PETE'S JOB

A PETITION with 4,000 signatures on it was presented to the management of the Shakespeare Club in Liverpool after West Kirby compere Pete Price was given a month's notice in early May because of his appearance on stage.

Although 24-year-old Pete was due to collect his cards this week, he has come to a compromise with the management and will keep his position.

Said Pete: "The petition was started the first day I was given notice because of the way I dressed on stage.

"The management wanted me to wear either a tuxedo or a conservative suit.

"Four thousand signatures were collected in eight days and these included several of the artists who have recently appeared at the club.

"I felt that I wanted to fight the issue rather than leave be cause in this day and age, why should we be told how to dre

"M.

PETE PRICE

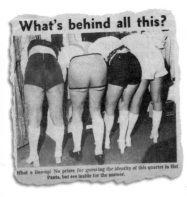

What's behind all this?

What a line-up! No prizes for guessing the identity of this quartet in Hot Pants, but see inside for the answer.

When I really did get banned for my clothes, it made the front page of the Daily Sketch.

I'd taken to wearing hotpants around town to try and start a trend in Liverpool, and one night I put them on for a cocktail party. But it wasn't one of the Wilsons' outrageous pool parties. It was a Conservative Association party at the Floral Hall in Southport. And I'd accessorised the outfit with a heart-shaped apron, bow tie, long white socks, velvet jacket and buckled shoes. I looked a twat. I was thrown out.

"What a liberty,"
I fumed in the paper.
"How stuffy can you get?
It's a most expensive
evening suit. It cost me £55.
Paris has been
forecasting for weeks that
hot pants for men
will be the next
fashion trend."

The Daily Sketch closed soon after that story – nothing to do with me, I hope.

I was becoming a bit of a gob-on-a-stick in the papers. I went to the Liverpool premiere of the Beatles' last movie *Let It Be*, with people like Paul McCartney's brother Mike and poet Roger McGough. Halfway through, I decided to walk out.

"I thought it was terrible," I told reporters. "They have gone far too way out now."

While I was polishing my act, I was getting to meet every star in show business. People would just drop into the Shakespeare when they were in town. Once the impressionist Mike Yarwood came in and challenged Freddie Starr to a drinking contest. Freddie drank him under the table and Mike never showed his face in the club again.

Another time, Tom Jones came in for dinner with Jimmy Tarbuck and Bruce Forsyth. They were all big stars, especially Tom, and we were worried they might get mobbed. So we closed up the whole of the second floor just for them. But that didn't stop the audience. Women were climbing up the pillars, endangering their lives to try and get a look at Tom and have a chance at lobbing a pair of knickers his way.

This wasn't a chance I could miss. I undid my shirt to try and look like Tom, and put his songs on for the rest of the night. After a medley of It's Not Unusual, Delilah and about five others, I got a tap on the shoulder and was told to go up to the second floor.

"Hello boyo, just want to say thank you for playing my music," he said. I don't think I managed to get a sentence out, I was so excited.

I'd offer my services to any of the acts who were at the club. Lots of the touring artists were leading quite lonely lives, constantly on the road, depending on regular bookings and friendly crowds to keep their spirits up. So I would take them out to dinner, or show them where to go in town.

I showed Stevie Wonder the Wookey Hollow night club, and took the Three Degrees for an ice cream at Nicholls of Parkgate.

Sometimes, if they were stuck for something to do in the day, I'd drive them round my old haunts in Wirral, past the shop on Bridge Road and round to West Kirby, pointing out Hilbre Island. I felt proud to be introducing them all to where I came from.

If they were Beatles fans, I'd try to sort out a meeting with the McCartney family: Paul's dad Jim, stepmother Ange and step-sister, Ruth. Jim was a lovely man, who was more than happy to put the kettle on for people like the New Seekers, the Mixtures and Design. After he died I stayed friends with the others, who moved to Hollywood.

I used to say I never knew I had so many friends until I started at the Shakespeare. Week after week, I'd get phonecalls like this.

"Hiya Pete!" the friendly-sounding man on the end of the line would say.

"Hello?"

"How's things, me old mate?"

"Sorry, who is this?"

"It's Derek, Pete, don't your remember me?"

"Derek who?"

"You know, Pete. We used to play football together when we were five. I was just thinking the other day, It's been a long time, hasn't it?"

"Let me guess, you want tickets for Freddie Starr tonight." There was a pause.

"Do you work at the Shakespeare, Pete?"

"Sod off."

Life behind the scenes at the Shakespeare was as fascinating as what was happening onstage. The theatre employed nearly 100 staff, counting the extras who came in at the weekend. It was like a city within a city. There was a market backstage, where you could buy any knock-off stuff you wanted – clothes, booze and tyres were all on sale. There were amazing women who'd worked there for years, who had beehive hairdos with extra hairpieces on top.

It all added up to some of the most memorable nights of my life. The curtain went up, the spotlight came on and you didn't know what was going to happen. I'm still telling stories from the Shakespeare every day, and I could fill this book with them.

There was the stage that had a habit of going wrong. It was electric and could be lifted up and down – the Shakespeare was one of the only clubs that had one – but it just wouldn't work properly.

One week we had sold out for Paul and Barry Ryan, who had just had a number one with a record called Eloise and had brought along an orchestra. What was supposed to happen was this: the stage would be hidden underground. Then there would be a blackout. The musicians would start playing as it lifted them up. Then, with a flourish, the lights would come on to reveal them all, as if they'd appeared from nowhere.

But this time, it didn't happen like that. They had started playing, but that stage wasn't going anywhere. "Oscar!" I hissed to the stage manager. "Oscar, press the button."

The orchestra carried on playing. Oscar shook his head and mouthed to me.

"What do you mean, it's fused?"

The crowd were getting restless as we hissed at each other.

"Why are the fuses in the post, Oscar? Can't you crank it up?" I said, but he shook his head. The audience by now were falling about laughing, as the musicians sat there in the dark, wondering what was happening.

"Right, cut!" one of the directors said. "Meeting upstairs, now."

Five minutes later, I went onstage.

"Ladies and gentlemen, I'd like to make an announcement." The angry crowd stopped bitching to each other, put their knives and forks down, and glared at me. "We have a major problem. The stage has blown up and, erm, we don't have any spare fuses."

They didn't like that. The murmurs were getting louder, and I thought I was about to be mobbed. I took a deep breath.

"Now you've got two choices. We can either give you your money back and send you away, or put them on. But if we put them on, you have to help us. So what do you want?"

"Put them on! Put them on!" every member of the audience yelled.

"Right. Everyone on the ground floor, stand up. Pick up your tables and walk eight paces." The whole audience did it – as if the whole club was moving in one go.

We balanced the orchestra around the hole where the stage should have been (violins on one side, percussion at the back.) And the singers stood on a table that I was holding steady. Picture that – number one hit single in Britain. As I sat there, grabbing a leg every time the table shook, I thought: "I hope there's no encore tonight."

The stage played up again years later, this time when Tommy Cooper was on. I'll be telling more stories about him later, but here's one for now.

Tommy, of course, was the comic who could get away with anything. Often he'd spend the first 20 minutes standing behind the curtain, with just his feet poking out. But this time something was really wrong. The stage was stuck, five feet lower than it should have been.

He told me, and we decided there was only one thing to do: make it part of the act. So we put a set of stairs in the middle of the stage and hoped we'd be able to get away with it.

That night I announced: "Ladies and gentlemen, Tommy Cooper!" All they saw was his red fez bobbing along.

"Thanyouvermuch," he said from down in the hole, and carried on walking around, while the audience fell about laughing. Eventually he's walk up the stairs so everyone could see his face appear. "'Ow are ya? I'm going back down," he'd mutter. Then he'd do the whole thing again. Genius.

Sometimes the stage came to our rescue. Once I was on stage in a slot between acts, singing a ballad called Didn't We. It was supposed to be a nice mellow song to calm everyone down. But there was a problem.

A drunk had been wondering around the tables at the front for a bit, pointing at things and gabbing to himself. As I carried on singing, he took a dislike to me and climbed up on stage. I could see him out of the corner of my eye, lurching around, stinking of booze and muttering curses.

The doorman, Arthur, looked at me, I looked at him and a light bulb clicked on in both our heads.

Arthur was the finest doorman I've ever worked with. He was a gentleman, whose wife worked in the club as well running the cloakroom. He would only fight as a last resort, but this was it.

I signalled for the stage to be lowered down to ground level, and Arthur went down the back stairs. After a while, the drunk realised something was happening, and started muttering: "Whassa stage going...the floor's moving."

All the lights went out apart from a pin spotlight on my face as I went down into the pit. Quick as a flash, Arthur knocked him out.

We raised the stage up, then put the rest of the lights back on. Lying in front of me was the drunk, out cold. I'd carried on singing all along – my face had never gone out of view – and everyone thought I'd put him to sleep. The audience were all on their feet. "See how good I am?" I said, winking at Arthur, who was back at his station by the door.

The final straw for the stage came one Hallowe'en, when Tommy Cooper was on again. It was a huge night in the club – we had a big local company called Tower Shipping in, flashing their money around and ordering huge jeroboams of champagne – exactly the sort of customers Mr Silver wanted. The directors loved Tommy, and were making a big night of it.

I'd decided to mark the night with something different. With the help of two other people, I'd staggered onstage with a tin bath full of water. The Shakespeare was going to have an apple bobbing contest.

"Ladies and Gentlemen," I said. "Tonight is Hallowe'en night, and I'd like six volunteers from the audience."

Six people came up, including one woman with a short dress on. I explained what they had to do, and the curtain was pulled back to reveal the bath. One woman started looking worried. She turned to me.

"Not me. I can't do it."

"Don't worry," I said, "you'll be fine."

"No, I really can't."

"Why? What do you mean?"

"Well, I've got no knickers on."

"What?"

"No knickers!"

"Don't worry," I said. "I'll put a tablecloth on you, you'll be fine."

So we started the competition, the volunteers with their backs to the crowd. And, of course, I couldn't help myself. I took a deep breath, pushed her head down and pulled the tablecloth off, revealing everything to the audience, who started falling about laughing.

But this girl had a temper and she wasn't happy.

"You think it's funny?" she yelled. "You think that's funny?"

She lurched over to a microphone stand and hurled it at me. I ran round the stage, ducking out of the way as she threw a couple of vases of flowers.

Then I heard her effing and blinding again, but realised she'd lost interest in me and was going for the audience, who were all still shrieking with laughter and pointing at her.

"You think that's funny?" she yelled, and grabbed the edge of the tin bath.

It had taken three of us to carry it in, but with superhuman strength she tipped it over, sending a tidal wave of water flying into the audience. It washed all over the directors' table taking their dinners and bottles of champagne with them and soaked most of the first few rows. And it also buckled the stage and blew all the electrics.

The stage may have been awkward, but it had nothing on the stage manager. Oscar was the grumpiest, most miserable, most unhelpful man in Liverpool, and he was proud of it. There was nothing anyone could do about him, either. He'd wired the electrics in the Shakespeare up himself. That meant without him, the show could not go on.

He had a job for life – if we sacked him there wouldn't be any lights that night. When stars were singing and their microphones weren't working, he'd come on and yell at them, shoving another mike in their face and shouting: "Come on, try that one then!" I bet all the acts we were paying thousands and thousands hadn't seen anything like that before.

Even PJ Proby and the Four Tops got the Oscar treatment. It was one of the reasons PJ wouldn't go on stage the following night. We had to get in Freddie Starr from Blackpool at the last minute, which turned out to be better anyway.

Mum would come down to the Shakespeare every now and then, and whenever she did I warned everyone to be on their best behaviour and make a fuss of her. I'd tone my act down, as I was becoming camper and camper. In fact, by then I'd come on, find the prettiest girl in the front row and shout: "You're gorgeous! Got a brother?"

The audience made every night unpredictable in that place. There was a comedy double act called Lester and Smart who were playing one busy Saturday night. They opened their routine with one of them onstage and the other planted in the audience, dressed as a waiter. The gimmick was that the comic would start up and the waiter would start heckling.

So they had started their act – the waiter had started shouting: "Eh, you! You're crap, you!"

But one of the customers, Joey Murray, didn't get the joke and started getting annoyed. "Eh! He's having a go," he said, first to his wife Pat, then to everyone around. "Oo are you, talking to the comic like that?"

The act must have expected the odd person not to get it, so they just carried on. But then Joey decided he'd had enough, and was going to be a hero. He got out of his chair, punched the comic in his waiter's outfit, and knocked him out. I ran into the audience.

"What do you think you're doing? You've knocked out the act."

"Well I didn't know, did I?" he said.

The comic went to hospital, where an X-ray showed he'd narrowly avoided having his jaw broken. We laughed about it years later, although I wasn't happy at the time.

At this point, I should mention someone who came into my life soon after I started at the Shakespeare.

Herbert Howe, known simply as Herbert to everyone in Liverpool, was someone I was vaguely aware of. I'd seen him around the city and noticed his immaculate clothes. At parties I was impressed that he always wore bow ties.

Then one night, the Liverpool Echo was having a party at the Shakespeare, and Herbert was one of the guests. I spotted him from the stage, and thought now was the time to say hello. So I walked off and went down to him.

"Herbert," I said. "I'm Peter Price. We might as well say hello, because we're going to be friends."

And we still are, right up until today. He loved the showbiz world, I loved the world of his glamorous salons. He asked if he could do my hair when he met me – and to this day I still go to his salon for a cut. Nobody else is allowed to touch it. And I know what you're thinking. Everyone who's heard of us in Liverpool seems to think we were in a relationship. Some think we still are. But, hand on heart, we never were – it's just been a great, great friendship.

Over the years our lives have inter-twined in all sorts of ways. We've both been very lucky with the way things have worked out for us.

His mum, Queenie, was like a second mother to me and he was like the brother I never had. Without him in it, my life would have been much emptier.

I look back on those first couple of years as the time I found a career, a great friend, and a big pink van.

The other, less happy memories, would come later.

SETTER

![PETE PRICE]

Above: Peter and the wolf. In those days,
furs were acceptable and I loved this
wolf coat with a passion. Like my
favourite movie stars, I'd nonchalantly
throw it on the floor – high camp.

Left: Now I know where Larry Grayson
got his famous expression. Shut that
door! It was one of my many outfits
made by Toni Spencer. Gold leather
knickerbockers with metallic, lime green,
snakeskin stripes. No wonder no one
ever pinched my washing!

I don't like this red and gold outfit, so I'll tell you about the moustache. I adopted it at the age of 20. It was on and off a few times, like my relationships, but we finally parted company in pantomime when the Alessi twins from Neighbours said it was them or it. I missed it for a while because my top lip would get cold in bed at night.

They don't make them like they used to… This jacket is classic tailoring from the 1930s, which I bought from an elderly man who used to be a male model. I have one in metallic blue, and one in metallic red.

Look mother, I borrowed these curtains and you're not getting them back. Austin Powers eat your heart out!

The hills are alive? Brown suede and gold leather. If you did a twirl, you carried on forever because of the weight of this jacket.

What can you say? It's enough to make Walt Disney thaw out. (Great legs.)

How's this for a flasher? I had to leave the jacket open as everyone used to shout: "You forgot your pants mate." I could've been arrested for indecent exposure. Three of the waiters from the Shakespeare are picking up fashion tips in the background.

Above: This is my famous full length PVC coat. Now you know where binbags came from! Look at it carefully. When it rained, water would just run off it and fill my shoes. The things you do for fashion.

Right: And finally… my birthday suit. The things I do for the Echo!

to
Peter
It was nice talking
with you on your
show.

Affectionately

Shirley Bassey

SHIRLEY BASSEY

CHAPTER TWELVE
I want to come back at the top of the bill

JUNE 3, 1972 and I'm on stage at the Shakespeare, but I'm not my usual self.

Tonight is a special night at the club, and I'm struggling to keep it together. In the middle of a song I break down in front of 1,000 people.

A few weeks before, I had I decided I was going to quit as compere at the club, and this is my last night.

When things were going badly – really, horribly badly – when the usual put-downs and jokes and mock-prayers for the night to be over hadn't worked, I always had one last trick up my sleeve. I'd signal to the band, and belt out *This is My Life*, an ultra-camp Shirley Bassey number. I'd stomp and scream and ham it up, and by then end the crowd would be on my side.

Up until now, it had done the trick. But a few weeks before, it hadn't. They had seen it all before, and they knew what was coming. After two-and-a-half years, it had become the Pete Price show, with anyone else they could get in. It was fantastic when it went well, but when I died on stage, I really died.

In my head I made the decision to leave – half as a two-fingered gesture to the miserable bunch in the audience, but also because I knew I had to move on.

A club in Manchester had head-hunted me. They'd sent a couple of people to watch me at the Shakespeare, then offered me the job.

It was a bigger city and more cash, even if it meant leaving Liverpool for its arch-rival.

After bad nights at the Shakespeare I'd thrown hissy-fits and threatened to walk out before and never had, so no one took it seriously. I think it took everyone by surprise. Just like the Cabin had been, my life was at the Shakespeare. Yet again, I'd go to work and not want to come home.

My final night came, and I did an hour-long set, including nine songs. The management had told me there would only be a handful of people in the audience and given me a fake list, but I walked on to find it was packed to capacity. I spotted mum near the front, in tears as I sang *My Way* then nearly collapsed at the end – what a drama queen.

All the staff came on, and gave me a gold leather jacket they'd asked Toni to make specially.

"I want to come back to the Shakespeare – as the top of the bill," I told reporters. "I've made it big in Liverpool, so now if I try Manchester and then go on to Birmingham, by the time I'm 73 I should be a famous star."

In the time since I had started at the Shakespeare we'd had some huge successes.

There was The Comedians. This was one of the biggest shows on TV at the time and audiences queued round the block to see Ken Goodwin, Charlie Williams, Jos White, Bernard Manning, George Roper and Jim Bowen at the Shakespeare. The thing I remember the most, though, is still the bitching backstage. "He's going to do my gag, the bastard," one comic would say to me standing in the wings watching another perform. "There, he's done it. Wait till he comes off, I'm going to punch him."

When the comic finished and walked off, of course it would be: "Great act, well done," and slaps on the back.

The Shakespeare was still the funniest place you could imagine working. One Christmas, we had a group of executives for a wig company called – honestly – Top Secret. Their TV adverts showed people hanging up by their wigs to prove they'd never come off. But when we brought the men's food out, we couldn't find them. The waiters must have walked past a dozen times before they saw the table of bald men sitting there cracking up. They'd taken their toupees off as a party piece.

Although the audiences were tough on me, they'd been known to give the star acts the same rough ride. In those days every set by an artist was 45 minutes to an hour, period. None of the two-hour programmes you have to put together now if you're a pop star, or the thin, 20-minute sets today's comics get away with.

But the punters still wanted their money's worth, and if you didn't do an encore you were for it.

One singing duo, Georgie Fame and Alan Price, were a sell-out. But when they had finished their act, they walked off and wouldn't walk on again. I had to hide behind the piano because the audience started chucking things at me.

Another group, Herman's Hermits, simply walked off stage

and into their limo, leaving me to take the flak.

There had been the acts I'd loved, like Frankie Vaughan. He would always pop in to say hello, and would send me smoked salmon at Chistmas from him and his wife Stella. Once I thought he was going to lose his famous cool when somebody in the audience kept heckling him. He stopped the music and said: "I want this person removed." But when the lights went up he saw it was Jimmy Tarbuck, one of his best mates, and Jimmy got up on stage to do duets and patter with him – that's how unpredictable the place was.

Mum's health started going about this time, and she was taken to hospital after having a heart attack and was then bedridden in Caldy Hospital, convalescing. She was a huge Frankie fan, and had been supposed to go and see him at the Shakespeare, but she hadn't been able to.

So we decided to surprise her. I went to her bedside, and beckoned for Frankie to come in. What a mistake.

Mum looked shocked, then she fell down back onto the bed. The nurses rushed in with an oxygen mask.

"She's having another heart attack!" said Frankie, turning to me. "Didn't you tell her I was coming?"

I looked sheepish. "I wanted it to be a surprise."

"The woman's got a heart murmur, Peter."

She really did have another heart attack. I'd nearly killed my own mother. Eventually they brought her round, and they posed for the photo that is one of my most treasured possessions.

The day I nearly killed my mother

Before he made it big, Freddie Starr had gone down a storm at the Shakespeare. We had booked him to appear one week, but he had got a call inviting him to play at the Royal Variety Performance. We all loved Freddie, and we realised this was his big chance, so we released him from his contract and I went down with him. Of course, he then became a star overnight.

Then there were the artists who in my experience weren't so nice. With his sharp observations on Northern life, Al Read was the Peter Kay of his time. Except I've always found Peter to be a thoroughly nice person. With Al, nothing you did was ever good enough, even though we'd put ourselves out for him time and time again.

So, after my final night, I left the Shakespeare for good. One week later I decided to come back because I was so homesick for the place and had a nasty shock. I strutted up to the door and saw a bouncer I didn't recognise – and he didn't let me in.

"Can I help you?"

"I'm Pete Price."

"I've never heard of you."

"I've been here for years."

"Five quid."

I went mad, huffing and puffing at him, but I still had to pay that night.

Meanwhile, 40 miles east in Manchester, my new boss was getting ready for my debut. I was to be the compere at Fagins, near the Palace Theatre on Oxford Road.

Fagins was a completely different club to the Shakespeare. It was in a modern office block instead of a Victorian theatre. It was open-plan instead of cosy and intimate. My outrageous clothes were a definite flop here. And, as I told a Manchester Evening News reporter, the audiences were like chalk and cheese.

"If an audience in Liverpool don't like you they tell you where to get off," I said. "Over here they just ignore you." What I wanted to add but didn't, was: "Except when they're giving you abuse because you're a Scouser."

But, much as they may have wanted to ignore me, the public weren't going to get the chance. Fagins spent a fortune on promoting me as the face of the club, dubbing me "Britain's number one compere", and plastering pictures of me all over the adverts for the club.

They even made a life-size cutout of me to stand near the entrance. He was robbed, and later found in a gents' toilet, in a very bad state indeed.

I was driving between Wirral and Manchester each day, but I loved bits of the new city – particularly the gay bars. And while I was there I became friends with my bosses. The Partakis family were self-made millionaires. George had

come to Britain from Cyprus, met a girl from Wirral and built up a multi-million pound business. I had huge respect for how hard they worked, and still keep in touch with their daughter Georgina, who I'd happily have married.

There were five times as many clubs in Manchester as there were in Liverpool, so the competition was fierce to sign up the best cabaret acts. But we managed to get some big names.

When we announced Scott Walker of the Walker Brothers was playing Fagins, people went mad. He was an idol, worshipped by his fans. But he would get terrible nerves before his performances, and his manager kept him hidden away where no one was allowed to meet him, including me.

But I was probably more impressed when one of my heroes came in. The last time I'd seen Danny La Rue had been as a wide-eyed teenager discovering gay London for the first time. Then one night, he walked into Fagins.

I spent the rest of the evening with him, and had a painting by one of my favourite artists commissioned to send him as he collected anything to do with clowns.

It had always been one of my ambitions to bring a record out, and I got the chance at Fagin's. I approached the management with the idea of putting on a night at the club and recording it. Naturally I would top the bill, but we got three regular acts from the club in as well. Live at Fagins made us all proud of what we'd done with the club, even if the LP didn't do amazingly well.

I still looked after the stars when they came to play at Fagins. Doris Troy was a huge woman, known as Mama Soul for her brilliant performances. And the woman could eat. I'd seen her tucking into buckets of Kentucky Fried Chicken, and I decided to take her out to an all-you-can-eat buffet. Eight plates she had, that night.

In return, she took me to meet James Brown when he was playing in Manchester. We were told to call him Mr Brown, and I remember him throwing his arms round Doris as I stood there, starstruck.

Meanwhile, I was still working in Wirral every Sunday night and still doing my Radio Merseyside show. Never Mind the Price was now Twice the Price, and I was getting to do more celebrity interviews and chat instead of simply reviewing new records, and I'd been using my nightclub connections to get anyone who was in town at the time.

The show's finest moment had come one day when we didn't have anyone on. A phone call came through to the producer. She went white and signalled to me to drop everything.

"Paul McCartney's on the line," she mouthed, starting to shake.

"Get off, it's a wind-up," I said, queuing up the next record.

But it was him, on the Red Rose tour with Linda. It was the interview all the national radio stations had been trying to get, and Macca had just called Radio Merseyside for a nice, relaxed chat. That got me some serious brownie points. Afterwards he sent me a bouquet of red roses that I passed on to mum.

Another show I was proud of was an interview with Tony Bennett. He was playing the Empire, and I was due to record it after he walked offstage. But the crowd wouldn't let him leave. They kept on clapping and cheering, and he kept going back on. I looked at my watch and saw they'd given him a 20-minute standing ovation.

"That must have been an **incredible experience,"** I said to him breathlessly afterwards. "I felt they weren't quite with me tonight," he shrugged.

After the interview, he'd asked if I wanted to go for dinner with him, and we'd decided to eat in his dressing room. I was seriously star-struck, even by my standards. I made special notepaper to tell people everyone I'd interviewed on the show – the names included Spike Milligan, Barbara Windsor, the Bee Gees, Shirley Bassey, Mark Bolan and Sacha Distel.

A year passed at Fagins, and I decided I wanted to be back in Merseyside. The Shakespeare had offered me my old job back with more money, and there was talk of being made a director. It was a difficult decision, but I said goodbye in June 1973. The entertainments manager, Roland Ankers, wrote me a reference I've still kept. It said:

"Pete Price is in my opinion the country's number one compere. It is with great regret that I had to allow him to leave Fagins. In his 12 months as resident host he created and atmosphere the like of which I have never experienced.

"An excellent vocalist, a brilliant compere, but most of all a complete professional – all in all a truly great person. A man who deserves to reach the peak of his profession, a man who one day soon must surely be classed with the all-time greats: my friend Pete Price."

At the time, it was the nicest thing I'd ever read about myself.

But the fact remained that this star of the future still lived with his mother in Bridge Road, West Kirby. Mum had given me a section of the house to myself, but it wasn't enough. Now I was back in Merseyside, I decided it was time to move out.

"I need some privacy, mum,"
I told her. "I won't rub it in your face,
but I need to bring people
I've met back with me."

When I saw she was upset, I added, half-truthfully: "I'm just buying it as an investment really, I'll still be home all the time."

There was another reason I didn't tell her about. I knew she was getting older – she had already been in hospital after her heart attack – and I didn't want to live there when she died. It would be too much to bear.

So I went flat hunting, with an absolute maximum budget of £10,000. It was just before the property boom.

I remember the first time I walked into the flat I've lived in ever since. Herbert and I had driven across Wirral, looking everywhere. Then I fell in love. I had chosen it because there was one thing I wanted more than anything – a view of Liverpool. I ran up the stairs and there it was.

"Let me do the talking," Herbert said quietly to me, seeing the excitement on my face. He had come with me because he had a head for business. But as soon as the woman selling it started talking about terms and conditions, I couldn't help myself.

"I don't care, I want it!" I said, as she started talking about other offers. I was terrified of being gazumped. "Great business that was," Herbert said as we left.

Decorating it, I was in my element. Although I loved living with mum, part of me had always wanted my own home. At just 17 years old I had bought an electric fire. I've still got it, and it's now a valuable antique.

Mum had always advised me to put money away in a building society regularly, saying it would help me get a mortgage. In those days it was near-impossible to get a mortgage on a flat in the North of England, as no one thought they'd take off. But mum's plan worked.

Through the bad times in my career, it wasn't always easy to find the money each month. But I finally paid it off when I was 50 – and burst into tears.

PRICE'S LANE

Beatles for Liverpool?

Sculptor Arthur Dooley [...] joined the campaign to immortalise the Beatles.

Mr. Dooley has volunteered [...] build a statue of the g[...] [...] Friends of Mersey[...]

Monument to the Beatles?

THE SUGGESTION that there should be a monument in Liverpool to the Beatles has engendered a fair amount of comment. As many Echo readers have pointed out the most lasting monument surely will [...]

Why no monument to Beatles?

Pete Price.

Monument to Beatles?—It's monstrous

Sir.—Can anyone in their right mind think of such a monstrous suggestion as a monument to the Beatles?

They brain-washed impressionable teenagers and others into hysteria. Any type of monument to them would be a travesty to decent and law-abiding citizenship.—Semi-Quaver, Bootle.

Sir.—In answer to Pete Price's suggestion that a monument should [...] built to the [...]

British Empire. Just for the record, Mr. Price, these four untrained youths also made themselves millionaires.—George Ridgeway, Smithdown Road, Liverpool.

Sir.—In reply to Pete [...]

Dear Sir...
READERS WRITE TO THE ECHO

Beatles 'statue' backed

Support came in Liverpool to-day for a public monument to the Beatles, in recognition of the group's work in putting the city on the map ten [...]

PETE AND THE[...] BEATLES

The final words on The Beatles memorial fro[...] the Merseyside D.J. who started the controvers[...]

Sir. — My mother has just sent me the cuttings from the Echo on the monument to the Beatles idea.

To those people com-[...]

I have every intenti[...] of doing so. You s[...] Mr. Ridgeway a lot [...] people want to help [...] this project.

Lastly in reply [...] Belly Laugh's na[...]

CHAPTER THIRTEEN

you could
'ave me

IT'S April 15, 1984 and I'm round at a friend's watching TV. It's his 21st birthday, but we all still want to watch Live From Her Majesty's because Tommy Cooper is on.

He's going down well tonight, but the tricks seem to be more of an effort for him.

Then suddenly, he collapses. The audience roars with laughter, but something doesn't seem quite right to me. I've seen this act countless times: Tommy came back to the Shakespeare every year I was there, always selling out, and always bringing the house down. I know each gag inside out.

"Something's happened to him," I say. The audience carry on laughing, the curtain comes down and they go into a commercial break.

Les Dennis and Dustin Gee have to come on to do their act but they can't move Tommy's body, and his feet are still sticking out of the curtain. Jimmy Tarbuck's manager Peter Pritchard is trying to giving him the kiss of life, but he's already dead.

At the party, I'm thinking: "What a way to go. I've died on stage a few times, but never like that."

Over the years I'd got to know Tommy quite well at the club. There was the time the stage broke, but there are so many other memories from that time in my life.

He warmed to me as a young entertainer starting out. He was such a huge talent yet, like all comics, he needed to be loved.

So even though the audience were bent double in their seats laughing and on their feet at the end, it was never enough. For him, the old saying about applause being better than any drug couldn't be more true. I've seen so many old performers come out of retirement for the same reason.

In fact, Tommy insisted on me being in the audience every night because of my loud, infectious laugh. When I started up, he'd look into the crowd and say: "Wossall this about? Whos'at?"

Watching him on those nights, I saw how much detail went into his act. His outfit was cleverly made, with shoes that were always too big, and a suit that hung awkwardly on him.

He'd come on with his hands up and his baggy sleeves flopping about. Then he'd say: "I'm stayin' in a lovely hotel," and drop one hand to the floor. A canteen of cutlery would pour out onto the stage. He had memorised every line, every gesture. He was an amazing magician – you have to be to do the tricks so badly, just like Les Dawson had to be good at the piano to play it out of tune like that.

There was a gag I had to do with him during his act. What I did was walk all the way across the back of the Shakespeare's huge stage with an empty glass.

"Hey, woss goin' on?" he'd say, watching me. Then, at a quiet point in the show, I'd walk back with the glass full, spilling it. I was supposed to do it every five or 10 minutes for 45 minutes: no water, water; no water, water.

"C'm 'ere," he'd eventually say, and call me over. "What are you doin'?"

"It's all right for you," I'd answer. "But my dressing room's on fire."

It's the worst gag in the world, but only Tommy could get away with it. When it worked, it worked. But if I got the timing or the slightest detail wrong, I'd get a bollocking.

One night, we had to bring on a double bed, fully made up.

Tommy would then announce: "Ladies and gentlemen, I'd like to do an impression of a man getting up in the morning." Then he'd lie down for five minutes and not move, before slowly lifting himself up. Then he fell back down. That was it.

Other gags only he could get away with? He'd pick up a horn and blow into it, pause, then say: "That doesn' mean much to you. But in 10 minutes, this whole room'll be full of Vikings." There was also a gate we'd put on stage, so he could walk through it and say: "I feel better for that."

When he was playing the Wookey Hollow once he did a routine where he'd have three bowling balls, one made out of hollow plastic. The joke was that he'd throw the light one into the audience. But when he dropped the heavy ones, it went through the glass floor. After a week's run, they ran out of glass for the floor and nobody could dance.

I once remember seeing him with just his shorts on while he was getting changed after a performance. He was very overweight, had huge varicose veins and was standing there sweating buckets. He looked at me. "See you," he joked. "You could 'ave me. Thanyouverymuch."

It's well-known that Tommy could drink, but sometimes it's a miracle we got him on the stage. He'd have 10 or 12-hour drinking sessions – pints with brandies in them, glasses of scotch, the lot.

Once he'd been invited to lunch at the ultra-posh Oriel restaurant by Tower Shipping who were huge fans. He was in a bit of a state after the previous night, but I managed to get him there... just the three hours late. In the limo on the way, he was puffing on a huge £20 cigar. "Can you take me to the bank please?" he asked the chauffeur. He was writing a cheque and when we got to the bank the chauffeur opened the door and Tommy fell out onto the street as a joke, still writing.

Inside the restaurant, everyone packed around him. After he'd ordered his steak and chips, he started doing tricks. The food came and everyone was still waiting for him to do his punch line. And they kept waiting, in tears of laughter. By the time he'd finished, his food had gone cold.

"Excuse me," he said to the waiter. "Could you heat this up?"

Well, they weren't going to do that for Tommy Cooper – they had to cook him a whole new dinner. But by the time it came back, he was in the middle of another joke, and they had to do it all over again. Eleven steaks, he had.

When the wine waiter asked him to try the wine, he pretended to choke, then fall out of his chair, and writhe in agony on the floor. The poor man thought he'd killed Tommy Cooper.

Then he got up as if nothing had happened. "Than' you, that's lovely."

So now I was back at the Shakespeare. Well, almost. First I had one of the best jobs of my life, so I'd better tell you about that.

Two of my best childhood friends, Andie Stabback and Richard Petty, had just got married. Richard used to bully me in the Scouts, and I had a huge crush on Andie but she wasn't interested – I always joke that's the reason I'm gay.

They had decided to move to the Seychelles, in the Indian Ocean on the east coast of Africa, and build a hotel there. They were taking a gamble – you could only just fly there, and it was still about to take off as a holiday destination.

Andie and Richard invited me out to do six weeks running a cabaret and disco. There was hardly anything to work with on the island – if the needle on your record player broke, it would take about six weeks to get a new one. I remember going to

see the Poseidon Adventure at the only cinema and the film catching fire in the projector halfway through. Everyone went mad. At one point we ran out of potatoes and had to serve chips made of breadfruit – get the picture?

But the place was paradise. In the day time we'd go swimming in the sea, lie on the beach or go for long walks. I'd drink tea fresh from a plantation, and visit the sanctuary for some of the world's oldest living tortoises. That year it had become the biggest destination, and stars like Peter Sellers, Princess Margaret, Paul McCartney, crown heads of Europe and, er, the Beverley Sisters, were turning up.

Later on they'd film one of those terrible Emmanuelle movies there, and Andie would have a walk-on part as a prostitute.

The Sicilian mafia were there, with their wives all in black in the sun. I had a crush on one of their sons (could I have been a gangster's moll?). We went tuna fishing with them and they made sure they had a load of fish caught and brought onto the boat so they wouldn't lose face if they didn't catch anything.

There was once a shark on the boat, and I was sunbathing next to it. Suddenly it moved, and I legged it overboard.

I introduced bands, ran discos and hosted the Miss Seychelles beauty contest. I was also on the radio, and I was nearly thrown off the island for insulting the Prime Minister.

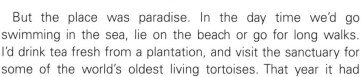

The Governor sent for me to give me a warning. "Will you please not refer to the Prime Minister as 'pissed in a restaurant' on air?"

It wasn't all perfect. Once I was snorkelling with Andie in the coral reefs and she spotted a beautiful piece of red coral. I went to pick it up and she started shaking her head frantically. I ignored her and put it in my shorts. It was fire coral and it lacerated my bum, laying me up in hospital with painful swellings for a good few days. Another time a shark swam past me and hit me with its fin. Of course, the Liverpool papers wrote it up as "Pete's shark attack nightmare" when I got back and I played along.

I had a holiday romance out there and, on my last night, they brought a cake in with the man inside to jump out in a bathing costume. Then there was the gay German prince. I was in the hotel when a valet came up to me, and said, in a strong accent: "My master would like you to go for a drink with him."

"What?" I said.

"My master would like you to go for a drink with him."

"Tell him I'm not interested."

A few minutes later a revolting looking man with a duelling scar down his face and a monocle came up to me, clicked his heels and shouted:

"I am a German prince!"

"And I'm an English queen," I said. "Now piss off."

The first time I came back, I bought eight bottles of Southern Comfort and tried to get them through customs. Typical me, I fell over walking past the officer and they all smashed.

"What have you got in there?" he asked me.

"Erm, a bottle of Southern Comfort?"

"Is that one bottle with eight necks?"

I went out again the next year, but this time I got really unwell. I was itchy all over and was drawing blood scratching and scratching. When I got back to Liverpool, none of the doctors could find out what was wrong with me. A tropical diseases centre eventually found out a sand fly had laid its eggs under one of my fingernails.

There's one more story I need to tell about my time in the Seychelles – because it was while I was there that one of the things I am proudest of in the world started.

I'd written a letter to the Echo just before leaving about a little idea I'd had:

Sir,

Can you please tell me why no one has built a monument to the Beatles? Four lads who put Liverpool on the world map, that gave the world a new dimension in music.

There is nothing in this town to show how we feel about them. No doubt Arthur Dooley would do something.

It could stand outside Lewis's, on the island for the world to see how much we feel about these fantastic lads. What do you think?

Pete Price
Bridge Road
West Kirby

I posted it, got on the plane, and didn't give it a second thought.

About a fortnight later, a package arrived from mum. I couldn't believe what I saw. The Echo had been publishing letter after letter from people about the idea.

Even out here, everyone had been asking me about the Beatles when I told them I worked in Liverpool. Had I met them? What about the rumours they were getting back together? Every time I stuck one of their records on, the crowd had gone crazy. And whenever someone asked me how Liverpool celebrated them, I had to answer: "Well, it doesn't really." They may have been the greatest pop group ever, but half the time, a tourist walking around wouldn't know the Beatles had ever been here.

PETE
PRICE

There's something in the character of certain people in Liverpool that doesn't like rewarding success. Even now you can see it when people like Coleen McLoughlin and Wayne Rooney get slagged off just for achieving something. So it wasn't any surprise I got letters like this:

"Can anyone in their right mind think of such a monstrous suggestion as a monument to the Beatles?

"They brainwashed impressionable teenagers and others into hysteria. Any type of monument to them would be a travesty to decent and law-abiding citizenship."

It's amazing to look at these letters in 2007, isn't it? Today, Liverpool's Beatles Story museum is one of our biggest attractions. We have an annual festival dedicated to the Beatles, shops sell Beatles memorabilia and dozens of people in the city make their livings off them. Yet people were against putting up a statue.

With so many moaners, the council weren't about to give me the money to put up the statue. I had to raise it myself.

I had a new show on Radio Merseyside – now just called the Pete Price Show – and I plugged it to death on that. Back at the Shakespeare, we planned an evening to raise money for the statue. It featured the Black Abbots and Tom O'Connor, and was called a Tribute to the Beatles. After the flyers had been printed, Frankie Vaughan agreed to come along as well.

Tickets sold out and the night was incredible. Frankie and I auctioned off Beatles memorabilia including a giant photo of the band donated by the Echo and a bill poster advertising an appearance in New Brighton in 1962. We'd said we would give Frankie whatever money we raised in excess of the £500 the statue would cost, and in the end we handed him a cheque for £650. It was like Beatlemania all over again, everybody said.

We agreed the statue would go up across the road from the Cavern Club in Mathew Street. I had a scroll made by a calligrapher, saying I had donated it to the city.

I think Arthur Dooley was one of the greatest sculptors Liverpool has ever produced, and I've got several of his works at home. When I got it and handed him the cash, his son set fire to it and he didn't bat an eyelid. I could have swung for him.

By March 1974, Arthur had finished. He hadn't done a conventional sculpture of four men holding guitars and grinning. He'd produced a gold woman, representing Mother Liverpool, holding three babies in her arms. Another one, holding a trumpet, is flying away. The caption underneath reads: "Four lads who shook the world."

It split fans. Some who saw the statue weren't impressed, saying it looked like a cobweb, and Tom O' Connor said he hated it. But I didn't care. Years later, I was amazed when the council lost the scroll saying the statue belonged to the city. The Echo's Joe Riley found it, and it now sits in the Beatles Museum (but still belongs to me).

Meanwhile, the statue is still in Mathew Street today, surrounded by the booming Beatles tourism industry. The latest addition is a Beatles hotel, but there'll be more and more. And I like to think my statue played a small part in all that by getting Liverpool to wake up and start celebrating what was on its own doorstep.

The Best Price is ...

Pete Price Back at the Shakespeare SHOWBAR

Hello There!

Pete Price and I am writing to tell
I am looking forward to seeing
back at the Shakespeare in a
season of fabulous shows. As a
you'll know that the top line club
not only the friendliest and
also the top line club
forward to not only
swing of things but
new friends, so just
acts we are
you'll be able
the
IVE in

	Week commencing		
"	"	16th September	Labi Siffre
"	"	23rd September	George Roper
"	"	1st October	Vince Hill
"	"	8th October	Paul Melba
"	"	15th October	Detroit Emerald
"	"	22nd October	Peters and Lee
"	"	29th October	Freddie Starr

The place is right, the acts are great, the
food is fabulous and certainly not
expensive. It all adds up to the sort of
night you deserve at least once a week.
every week at the Shakespeare. And
don't forget it's a great place for great
occasions, birthdays, anniversaries or
simply for people who like parties. Take
care, see you soon at the Shakespeare.

Pete Price

CHAPTER FOURTEEN
just don't wear it
on telly

THE Shakespeare had special adverts printed: "The best Price is… Pete Price – back at the Shakespeare showbar!"

I loved the attention of being welcomed back to Liverpool as a big star – at least, a bigger one. I was topping the bill in their adverts and my name was the biggest on the wall. But I wasn't kidding myself. I may have lived up to my promise to come back as the star attraction, but it wouldn't last long.

Basically, I was still just the compere – the one who gets the grief when the acts are crap, the one who warms the audience up at the beginning of the night. Part of me was angry with myself for taking the job back at the Shakey. What I really needed was to strike out on my own. I should have been working on my act and taking it out on the road. There were rich pickings out there, bigger money to be made.

But I was terrified of failure. Working in clubs, I'd seen some miserable people pass through the dressing rooms. There were the comics who died onstage, tried and failed to get a shag then drank themselves to sleep. There were the singers who couldn't really sing anymore but kept on going, trying to ignore the audiences laughing or talking over them. They all had mortgages to pay, and for many of them it had stopped being fun long ago.

I was becoming an institution at the Shakespeare – I loved the place and was surrounded by friends. I'd give it a couple of years then see, I thought.

Plus, I was meeting more and more incredible people. There was Larry Grayson, just on the verge of becoming the biggest comic in Britain and turning the Generation Game into the most popular show on TV. I remembered how he'd been a young support act when I visited Danny la Rue's club all those years ago.

When we announced he was coming it was like the Comedians all over again: I'd never seen queues like it. He'd walk onstage and just shrug his shoulders and the place would erupt. As a camp comic, his act was a huge inspiration to me.

Offstage he was a lovely man. He'd worked with the most famous people in the world and told stories about stars like Mae West.

I remember seeing Uri Geller for the first time, flanked by bodyguards because of the Middle East situation, and trying to figure out how he bent those spoons. There was the singer Roger Whittaker. When he arrived, looking like an accountant in his glasses and beard I thought there was no way he was going to entertain our lot. But he ripped the place apart with his singing and incredible whistling. Now he's sold something like 55 million records. Talking of spoons, he also had one of the world's largest collections – I didn't even know anyone collected spoons. He has to keep them in the bank as they're worth a fortune.

Then there was the best of all. One day I was up on the ladder at the front of the building, putting the names of who was going to be on that night onto the wall. There was someone coming that I'd been looking forward to seeing for years.

I'd just got to the M in Monkhouse when he shouted up to me.

I turned round and saw the face that had been on TV every week as long as I could remember.

"Don't say anything!" I shouted. "Wait until I've got down this ladder!"

My feet went, and I tumbled to the floor. I couldn't wait to talk to him. It didn't help my nerves that he looked exactly how he looked on telly: perfectly turned out, ridiculously tanned and beaming. The guv'nor of comedy. The Bob Hope of Britain (except quite a lot nicer and funnier).

After I'd met him a few times, I couldn't believe it when he gave me his number.

How did I feel about him? I was in love with him, in every way except physically. I'd set up interviews with him so I could listen to him talk about movies, comedy and all the other things he was an expert on. With him at all times was his wife Jackie, who guarded him and got him the peace he needed to work. They were the love of each others' lives.

Then came a PR nightmare for the Shakespeare. A while back, we'd featured the first club appearance of a young pop group called the New Seekers. They had been phenomenal, and I'd loved them all.
(I'd even pulled one of the female members, but we won't go into that).

Anyway, since that first gig they had become huge stars with fans around the world, but had decided they were breaking up. We had agreed to pay them the huge sum of £25,000 for their last week as a band. They agreed to do it because we got on so well, and it was a huge coup for the club. We had people coming from all over the world to see their last shows.

For the Friday night show, they were picking up an award in the Hilton London, so a plane had been laid on to fly them up to Liverpool straight afterwards, in time to go on around 10pm.

We waited and waited, but the plane didn't arrive. At 10.30pm, I got a call saying one of the singers, Eve Graham, was ill and they wouldn't be coming. Then I had to tell the crowd. They went mad. Some of them had travelled to Britain to see the

NEW SEEKERS' LAST DATE A MISS

THE New Seekers pop group may face legal action after they failed to turn up last night for their final public appearance before disbanding.

They were due to appear at the Shakespeare Cabaret Club in Liverpool.

But for the second night running, fans went home disappointed after the group claimed they could not play because singer Eve Graham was ill.

"I am absolutely shocked to think they are letting the fans down in this

way," said club compere Pete Price. "They could have turned up without Eve."

And the club management confirmed that they had put the matter in the hands of solicitors.

The row erupted after the management were told of Eve's illness 11.30 pm on Friday.

Complained

of temper and argument and it was far too late to get hold of another group to stand in.

"We had to pay back £3,000 in ticket money, and some fans complained about having to pay for their meals. They say they were there under false pretences.

"I rang each of the New Seekers in turn today, all they would say was I'm

group. We had to give everyone their money back – £3,000 in all – but even then some people weren't happy because they said they'd bought meals under false pretences.

I rang the group the next day, but they wouldn't change their minds – they said they weren't playing without Eve. The managers called a crisis meeting and we decided we'd have to find another group. In the end we flew Blue Mink in from all around the country, and thankfully they were spectacular.

Meanwhile, amid all the excitement and the big names, things were changing at the Shakespeare. Different types of people were coming in and the nights had a different atmosphere.

When I'm thinking about my time at the club, I split it into two halves: before the gangsters started coming and afterwards.

Liverpool's organised criminals had always stayed away from the Shakespeare. I think they were a bit overwhelmed by it, preferring the rougher clubs and pubs. What got them in was the boxing. We'd never done it before, and I'd been nervous about the idea. You see, boxing attracts its own crowd and nothing winds people up like sitting watching it.

We'd put Dave Allen on after the fighting – it was the biggest mistake we ever made in my opinion. Dave, another great who's just sadly died, was one of the best comics we ever had. He was religious, but liked to take the mickey out the Catholic faith. I saw a couple of men in the audience start looking at each other and shaking their heads as his act went on. Later on, there was a fight. It was the first time I remember that happening at the Shakespeare, and it scared all of us. Dave said he'd never work for us again but we stayed great friends. After that, the gangsters got a taste for the place, and kept coming back. As a compere, I felt like I was on a knife edge. They were great audiences, but you had to watch what you said. "I think you're very funny lad, but I'm not bent," one man said to me after a show one night. He handed me a vile sovereign ring. "Take that, he said. "Just don't wear it on telly for a few years."

Of course, as far as the company was concerned, these new customers were good for trade. They booked out their own row of tables, always had expensive bottles of brandy and champagne on the table and flashed their money around. But the money being spent in the Shakespeare wasn't being spent on it, and the place was going downhill.

After the boxing night, fights got more and more common. I remember one couple had started having a row in front of everyone. The people around them were murmuring how she would dance with everyone and he would get jealous. When the doorman stepped in to stop it, she turned on him and we had to call the police.

When they arrived, they took one look at the man and carted him off straight away. It turned out he was one of

Britain's most wanted. He'd been on the run for six months. He'd got drunk, got jealous and got arrested.

Another night I was singing and a fight broke out on the balcony. One man fell all the way down onto a table.

"That's most inconsiderate," I told the audience. "I hadn't finished the song yet." I shouldn't really have made the joke – we later found out he'd broken his back.

Matt Monro, who I thought was a lovely man, parked his beautiful, pristine Rolls-Royce outside the theatre. When he got into it at the end of the night it had been scratched. It was the first time I could remember that happening.

When the Scaffold came to play, hot on the heels of their hit Lily the Pink, they asked if they could bring a documentary crew with them. We all got excited thinking we were going to be on TV, but it turned out they were making a film about the seedy side of Liverpool. It was awful to think the Shakespeare was losing its reputation in front of our eyes.

Then there was one very famous band – I'd better not say any more than that, because they're still around – whose lead singer couldn't keep it in his pants. In the middle of their set one Saturday night, a man got up onstage, shook the singer's hand and walked off.

He opened his hand and looked **terrified.** The man had put a bullet there – that was a sign you were a dead man walking.

With the club going downhill, we had a change at the top. Another company bought out George Silver. I was made an executive director of the club, on the agreement that I'd still be resident host and compere. It didn't mean much more money – we weren't doing well enough for that – but I started getting lots of little perks. And it all went straight to my head.

I now had the biggest dressing room and got the decorators in straight away to give it a lavish makeover and new carpet. I had my own table, number five, that I coulduse for entertaining, and I made sure cheap booze was smuggled in for my guests. And, best of all, I had a say in which acts would be on. The theatre would close for a week in January 1975 for a £10,000 refurbishment to bring it up to standard. The restaurant now boasted "a wide selection of French and German wines" which cost between £1.55 and £6.50 a bottle.

"Let me say that we have no illusions about the Shakespeare," I wrote in a newsletter. "We know that it had a poor reputation for food, service and general appearance, but, believe me, if the people who have criticised the club in the past will give the new owners a chance, they won't regret it." We all prayed they would come back. Just before this happened, we'd decided we had to do something to change the club's reputation. But what would attract the old audiences? Then the management had a brainwave – the Shakespeare's first ever Christmas family show.

Back in 1974, before he had a string of successful theatre productions under his belt, Bill Kenwright was producing a stage version of the Wombles. It would be shown at nine theatres around Britain. The characters had already had a children's TV show, huge hit records and spin-off toys. It was a national phenomenon and was a perfect way for us to get all the local kids in.

It turned out not to be. As far as I can remember, the licensing agreement only stretched so far – the characters on stage were not allowed to sing any of the famous songs and their costumes weren't up to scratch – they looked anorexic, not like Wombles.

Cast members were learning their lines backstage, the papers reported, and the 21-year-old woman playing Uncle Bulgaria admitted to journalists there was no time for a dress rehearsal and it was the first time they had done the show. About half the audience walked out and there was a riot in the foyer.

The other directors put me forward as the public face of the club to announce we were cancelling the show. That meant I had to slag the show off publicly to every reporter that rang me. It was a huge story in the papers: "Mumbles earn grumbles for Wombles", "Wombles panto rumpus", "'Tatty' Wombles have kids in tears" and "What a shombles".

Bill Kenwright travelled up to Liverpool and arranged for 50 underprivileged children to go and see another of the productions. He had lost a fortune. We handed the audience their money back. It was a disappointing show, and I was only the front man, but I still regret going too far in what I said. Bill hadn't meant to put on a second rate show. He'd been let down and he was hurt by the whole thing. I apologised a few years later and he was very gracious to accept.

All this negative publicity had also affected the original Wombles songwriter Mike Batt. We were due to throw a party at the club for orphans, so I decided to ring him and see if we could get the original Wombles up.

He agreed, but we kept it as a surprise for the kids. In the middle of watching stilt walkers and jugglers, all of a sudden the Shakespeare went quiet as they walked on, singing Remember You're a Womble. The children's faces lit up – we'd made their Christmas.

Later on, someone in the club caught one of the Wombles having sex upstairs in his outfit – apparently he had some sort of fetish for the costume. But thankfully none of the kids saw, and they all went home happy.

It meant, though, that we started 1975 firmly in the red. We had a load of acts booked and we weren't sure how we were going to pay them. Even then, fees were phenomenal. We could easily pay a big comic £25,000 for six shows. I looked at the acts we'd booked for the next few months: Lulu, Sacha Distel, Tony Christie. Could we afford to pay them? I hadn't even been given a contract for my new job yet.

I wanted to try something different, and persuaded the other directors to put on a musical.

Hair! had been a smash-hit across the world, running on Broadway and in the West End, but as far as I know it had never been tried in a club.

The punters didn't know what to make of it. It starts with the cast at the back of the theatre walking through in slow motion. They climbed over the tables, picking their way through the people having their dinner, who were a bit baffled by it all.

"Eh! Do you wanna bevvy?" one man shouted.

"You're walking on my dinner," another piped up.

Later on, there was a scene where the cast came out naked. "Look at the cock on him!" I heard someone shout. "Her fanny's fallen!" I thought that this probably hadn't happened in the West End.

But Hair! went down a storm, and I made plans to book Oh Calcutta!, the X-rated show that had caused a national scandal. But at the end of the run, we found the weight of the cast and the scenery had buckled the stage. It was broken again.

One day Les Cox and his team came in to hold auditions for a talent show called New Faces. I was sitting in my office, probably barking out orders, when someone came in and asked me if I wanted to have a go.

I wasn't keen – I'd tried once before at the Shakespeare and got nowhere. Before going on I'd worked myself up into a state about it and had come across a bag of nerves.

"Go on Pete, you only need to walk downstairs, put your outfit on and do it," he said. So I went for the easiest option – the newspaper suit routine.

I'd bought the suit from a boutique in Carnaby Street a few years ago for 15s 6d. Everyone thinks it's a Liverpool Echo suit, but it's actually just printed with pages from some other papers. But it helped me no end. I've got a terrible memory – it takes me ages to learn any lines – so I had the idea to cheat.

I'd go on wearing the suit with a copy of the Echo. Then I would tell topical jokes which I would have cut out and stuck on the inside pages of the paper.

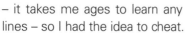

So I went out, completely relaxed, and did a few gags and a song. Then I thanked them and went back to the office, not giving it a second thought. After all, they hadn't wanted me on last year and I hadn't put any effort in this year.

The whole thing was a split-second decision. But it would lead to one of the biggest triumphs – and most catastrophic disasters – of my life.

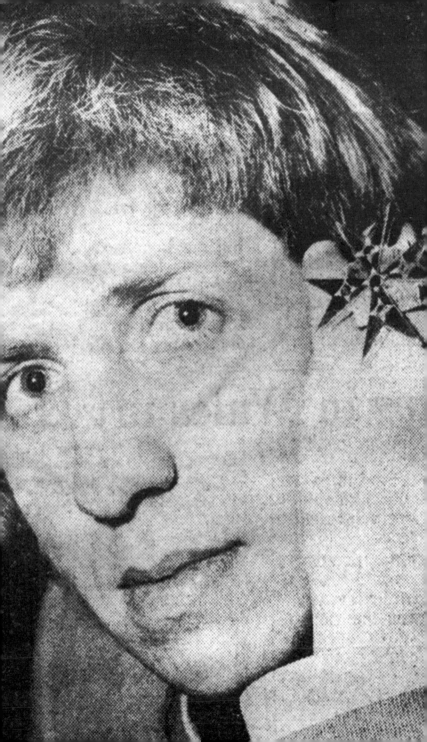

CHAPTER FIFTEEN

some queer things
in the
newspapers

"GOOD evening. My name is Pete Price," I'd say. Then I'd stop and fiddle with the trousers on my newspaper suit, heart probably pounding with nerves. "I'm sorry about this. I've just had chips in it and the vinegar's running down my leg."

I'd pause, hope that got a laugh, then take a deep breath and point to my snakeskin boots.

"Like the shoes? Poof adder."

While they laughed at that one, I'd open my Liverpool Echo and start looking for the gags I'd pinned inside. I'd look up, and say: "I must admit, you do see some queer things in the newspapers."

That was the opening for my act – that was what I'd be spending hours in front of the mirror polishing, ready for 15 million viewers.

A week after doing the audition, I'd got a letter saying I was on the show. I was on New Faces! For the benefit of anyone under 35, New Faces was the X Factor of the 70s, except more people watched it. The other difference was that any sort of act could go on – comics, ventriloquists, magicians, singers and groups.

The opening sequence featured a cartoon busker in a cloth cap who was swept away in a limousine and made into a star overnight, and that was basically what happened to the people who went on the show and did well. Tough panellists would give you marks and if you won, well, it made the careers of people like Michael Barrymore, Victoria Wood, Les Dennis and the Chuckle Brothers.

But comics on the ATV show had to work fast – your slot was only four minutes – and one wrong move could cost you everything.

Not much pressure, in other words.

The thing that was worrying me the most was my comedy persona. I'd been used to effing and blinding at the Shakespeare, and this was out of the question at 5.20pm on Saturday night. A lot of my gags relied on gay innuendo as well, so I had to watch how far I went. Comics like Larry Grayson may have camped it up on TV, mincing around and saying "Shut that door!" but they also made jokes about fictional mothers-in-law and their material was carefully vetted.

Help was at hand though. Bob Monkhouse was thrilled I was on the show and immediately offered his services. He sent me a tape of 40 gags and we went through my material together. It was typical of him to be so generous and put himself out.

The Echo also helped me out by printing a special mock edition of the paper for me to take onstage. It had the big headline "Liverpool comic will appear on New Faces – big chance for Pete Price".

While that was all shaping up nicely, my day job wasn't going as well. Things were going from bad to worse at the Shakespeare. As we slid further and further into the red, I felt like I had been put up as the scapegoat to take the blame for how bad things were. It had got so bad that each week could make or break us. We had booked Sacha Distel and he'd gone down well, but the managers weren't even sure we would be able to pay him (and they didn't). The big refurbishment had been a gamble and it didn't seem to be working.

To escape it all, I'd throw myself into decorating my flat, importing silk from Thailand for the walls and getting a gold-plated bed. I did a feature in the Daily Post about it, where I let slip that I still took all my washing round to mum's. I also used to cook anything smelly, like fish stew, round at her's, so I didn't stink the flat out!

When the day came, I went down to Birmingham to film the show. I'd been on TV before, on the drama series Crown Court. But it hadn't worked out. I was only an extra, and I'd kept trying to build up my part. I'd sat on a cushion to try and get myself in the shot, and the director asked why I was above everyone else. Then I'd started smiling at one of the characters out of the blue to try and get noticed on screen. So this was the biggest thing I'd ever done.

I went into make-up and was fussed over by everyone. Then I put the freshly dry-cleaned newspaper suit on. Years ago, the great ventriloquist Ray Allen (his doll was called Lord Charles) had shown me a trick for putting the trousers on so they didn't get dirty. You fold them up and pull your legs through, then let them drop down – a bit of old-fashioned advice. It's funny what comes back to you when you're nervous.

Is that for real?

The show would be recorded "as live" meaning it wouldn't be edited. If you forgot your jokes or fell on your arse, that's what 15 million people would see. After waiting in the wings and watching the other contestants being picked apart by the panel, I was on.

The band piped up and I sang What a Day This Has Been, my signature song, with special lyrics referring to the show. I was waggling my bottom lip in a funny way when I was singing, I noticed watching the video the other day. Maybe I'd seen a singer do it at the Shakespeare but I looked mental.

"No, no, don't clap, there isn't time," I said as the audience started applauding, before launching into the act I knew inside out.

Looking at the footage now, it's funny how confident I seem. I suppose compared to a bad night at the Shakespeare, a TV audience bussed in from Nuneaton on their best behaviour aren't much to worry about. But you can still see my nerves – I keep saying "he's mental" or "she's mental" after each joke to fill the gaps in case the audience doesn't laugh. And I keep muttering "I can't cope," one of my catchphrases at the time, whenever I'm thinking of what to do next.

But all the practice seemed to be paying off, I thought as I got near the end and sang my final song – the audience seemed to like it, and that meant the TV audience at home would be voting for me.

The way the show worked was that the panel would choose a winner from the seven acts, who would go into the final. The viewers also voted for their favourite by posting a coupon in TV Times, and if they picked differently from the panel that winner would go into another round.

I was up against a couple of singers, a few groups and a Bavarian band from Essex. The panel gave me mixed reviews, and I was delighted when comic Arthur Askey praised my act.

But it wasn't enough. I came second – devastatingly close to the top prize and the place in the final.

The show went out on Saturday April 12 and I started getting more offers of work, making me think I should go out on the road now and not hang around at the Shakespeare. And no sooner had I thought that, than the decision was made for me.

It all started on the Friday. Whispers were getting round that our time was up – the Shakespeare was about to close. One by one, the chairs started to disappear. By the evening it was all anyone was talking about. I had a key to the safe, so I decided to take out the wages I was owed – plus holiday pay – just in case there was a problem. I got the bunches of notes out, counted them, and stashed them away.

The next day – Saturday April 19, 1975 – was a turning point in my life. I went into the club in the afternoon, and started getting things together for that night's show.

But then I got a phonecall from ATV. I'd been voted the viewers' favourite.

Apparently record numbers watching the show had said they wanted me back. It knocked me for six. Ever since it had gone out, people had been stopping me in the street asking me about the newspaper suit. I knew I'd made an impression, but I had no idea I'd gone down that well.

I rushed out of my dressing room to tell people. I wanted to invite people along tonight, smuggle in some booze to Table Five and have a proper celebration. After all, the rest of the directors were nowhere to be seen, and I was in charge that night. But then I saw a group of staff looking worried.

"What's up?" I asked impatiently. I wanted to tell them my good news, not hear about some support act who'd pulled out or a fridge that had stopped working.

They told me the game was up – we were definitely closing. Sacha Distel wouldn't get paid. Tony Christie and Lulu wouldn't be coming to Liverpool now.

The Shakespeare was finished. I was on the verge of becoming a major TV star, and I'd lost my job.

The Shakespeare had been through worse, of course. In 1963 it had nearly been destroyed by a fire, weeks after reopening. It had closed after 13 months when Sam Wannamaker tried to revamp it. This was the Old Shakey, part of Liverpool's history. It couldn't be finished, I thought. But the future didn't look like it was going to involve me.

What did we do now? Did we tell the staff? The punters?

We decided we'd let the other workers know, but keep it from the audience. There was a simple reason for that. It was Saturday – gangster night. Once that lot found out we were closing, they'd take no prisoners. They'd drink the place dry then not pay their bills. So we'd keep quiet, pool the money at the end of the night, then split it between the staff so we all got our wages.

It was all going well, then I spotted one of the waiters. He knew he had lost his job, he was a drunken wreck, and he'd broken down, sobbing. Sat at the bar, he'd told a couple of mates in the audience. And now everyone was finding out.

As I stewed about it in the wings, I got angrier and angrier. How could they have let it get to this stage? Seventy staff would be out on the streets. What would it mean for me – would I be declared bankrupt too? What would having that hanging over me do for my career? Despite the fact that I'd really only been the frontman for the Shakespeare, and hadn't dealt with the accounts, I'd never be trusted again. And I'd worked my arse off for that place over six years.

Well, I decided, if we were shutting tonight, we were going to do it my way. I walked on calmly as the curtain came up.

"Ladies and gentlemen," I said, with tears in my eyes. "I've got a special announcement.

"Tonight is a special night at the Shakespeare because it's our last night. We're broke, we're all out of a job, and the receivers are coming on Monday morning. So let's make it a night to remember."

I thought they'd all rush to the bar, leaving us with a bonus at the end of the night. They had the same idea – except they weren't planning on paying.

It took about five seconds before everyone rushed to order drinks. I'd already moved the champagne and brandy into a safe room – that was my perk. It took another five seconds for people to start pocketing the cutlery.

Then the chairs went, then the fridges, everything in the kitchen, the lights, the sound system, the tables, the tablecloths, the soap in the toilets, the paper in the toilets, and the seats on the toilets. I saw someone trying to get the chaise longue out of back window. One woman calmly measured out 12 by 20 feet of carpet then cut it up to furnish a room in her house. There's a flat in Old Swan where so much stuff was taken it's as if a miniature Shakespeare has been recreated. The till's at the front door.

When the receivers arrived on Monday morning they were able to recover something like three pint glasses and 3s 6d.

And there was a small miracle. We hadn't had any money to pay the act, Wayne Fontana and the Mindbenders. But one customer – probably a gangster – had handed them a cheque for £800. It was their fee for the whole week. And, would you believe, it didn't bounce.

"A nightclub audience got a shock announcement from the compere," the next day's Sunday Mirror reported. "He told them: 'We're closing at the end of the evening.'"

"And the final curtain came down on one of the North's most famous nightspots with an air of mystery. Regular visitors to the Shakespeare Cabaret Club in Fraser Street, Liverpool, heard the blunt closure announcement from Pete Price, compere for six years.

"Afterwards the general manager Mr Bernard Roberts said: 'I don't know what is happening. The staff have had no official notification that the club is closing.'"

As for me, I'd booked a holiday in Miami, so I was off for a fantastic break in the sun. How had I escaped? Simple. Although I'd asked for a contract time and again, the owners had never given me one. There was nothing on paper saying I was a director. Anyway, I had a new act to think up for New Faces.

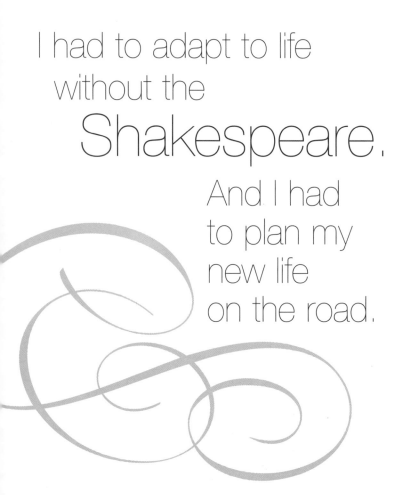

I had to adapt to life without the Shakespeare. And I had to plan my new life on the road.

This time next year I'd be 30,
and it was time to get

serious.

CHAPTER SIXTEEN
the curse
of the statue

"PETER! Is that you?" the giant oyster said to me. "Could you go and get help?"

I did a double take. The oyster thought about it, then piped up again.

"Actually Peter, could you pass some of that whiskey in here, and then go and get help? We're stuck." A hand with several diamond rings on it came out of the shell.

A knees-up in a giant oyster? It could only be the Wilsons. The oyster was actually a bed – a typically fabulous, over-the-top bed – which they'd bought for their new villa in Majorca. I was staying with them there, and loving every second of it. They had left Britain to avoid paying over-the-top tax, and had built a huge complex of flats behind the villa to pay for their plush, eye-popping new home.

Anyway, the bed had broken and trapped Austin and June inside, and when the staff managed to fix it they emerged a little the worse for drink.

Each time I went out to visit the Wilsons I had the same problem. What on earth do you buy a pair of loaded tax exiles as a gift? Each time I visited, I'd cater for enormous dinner parties to give the staff the night off. I'd drink Dom Perignon in the kitchen while cooking for 27, slightly the worse for wear. Then the food would be served on an electric table that revolved at two speeds. It seemed to go faster as the night went on.

But what they liked the most were the simplest things. They loved a certain type of oatcakes from Staffordshire that you couldn't get over there. So once, I ordered six boxes of them from Sainsbury's to take over and keep them well stocked. Except the staff took six boxes to mean six boxes of 24 boxes, and when I turned up to collect them they were piled up. I screamed and walked out. How was I going to get them on the plane?

What an amazing time I had out there. Except the horseriding, that is. Their daughter Danielle, later married to Graeme Souness, told me she was planning to take me riding, and I was dreading it. I begged to stay at home, but I wasn't given the option.

"We don't want to bother with any interpreters or instructions, so just pretend you understand what he's saying. If he looks like he's asking whether you've ridden a horse before, just point to the horse, nod and say 'si'."

"Are you sure this is a good idea? I'm happy to stay at home and make us all a nice dinner, you know."

She smiled. "There's no getting out of this. We're driving you to the stables or we're driving you to the airport."

We got to the stables, and I did what I was told – I should point out at this stage that I'd never ridden a horse in my life and they terrified me. I was dressed in a pristine white shirt, black trousers and shiny cowboy boots.

The stable-hand said something in Spanish to me, and I nodded enthusiastically. He looked surprised, smiled and slapped me on the back. What on earth had I just agreed to? Then he led out a horse which was a veteran from some bull ring, complete with marks from several bullfights. It looked like it could run for miles then rip a few grown men to shreds to finish off. And in my opinion, it didn't like poofs.

I nervously got on, he laughed again, and gave the horse a pat on the bum. It started to trot as I clung to it for dear life. Then it broke into a gallop. I wouldn't have known how to stop it in English, let alone Spanish. It sped up and carried on

going, charging over fields, jumping fences and down pathways. I closed my eyes and started praying.

Then I opened my eyes. We were on the motorway.

Cars were blaring past, beeping their horns. The drivers wound down their windows and yelled abuse at me. After about ten minutes, it got bored and decided to stop, and the others caught up with me.

I was destroyed. My legs were locked and I was covered in bites, I waddled back to the car, and they took me to hospital then put me to bed. They all thought it was hysterical. I've never been near a horse since.

Back in England, I was feeling the pressure. I had my appearance on the New Faces Winners' Show coming up. My picture was all over the TV pages – well, they were always going to use a publicity shot of a guy with a moustache dressed in a newspaper suit.

Here's the news—and this is Pete Price wearing it

DISC jockey Pete Price as no excuse for not eeping up with the news. For the latest addition to wardrobe is trousers, and tie — all in

"When I originally designed the outfit I thought it would be a good idea for city news vendors to wear them to create a new

"I did go into town in the other night," he say "and caused a bit of a sti when a man in a cinem queue got a bit stropp when I walked away befo

"They've just found out that Adolf Hitler didn't start the Second World War," I say, looking in my Liverpool Echo. "It was Vera Lynn's agent." As I see one of the crew doing the hand signal for "wind it up," I just point and say: "There's a funny chap waving at me here. Hello!" And I end on the line I still use today: "Ladies and gentlemen, you've been a challenge …and you've won. Good night."

I didn't win. The audience seemed to like my act, but I got the impression the panel had made up their minds the first time. Lenny Henry was the overall winner that year, and if there's one comic you couldn't begrudge it was him. "You may have seen some of these impressions before, but not in colour," he says on the show before launching into a stream of brilliant impersonations. It was a sign that TV comedy was moving on.

And for me, all wasn't lost. ATV wanted me to come back to New Faces, this time as the compere. I was thrilled. This might give me a route into TV presenting, other shows, anything. Meanwhile, Bob had done me a huge favour as well, by getting me on his show Celebrity Squares. I'd be on with stars like Peter Sellers and Thora Hird – I was one of the first relative unknowns they'd used, only because Bob believed in me.

One thing was annoying me, though. The agent I'd signed up a while ago should have been at the New Faces shows in Birmingham with me, finding me work and promoting me while I had so much exposure, seizing the moment to book me up in advance. But he hadn't even turned up. I got the impression he'd taken me on in case I got big, but wasn't interested in trying to find me anything. It happened a lot in the business with big offices – and it still does. This was scaring me. I'd been grateful the agency wanted me, but now I'd left the Shakespeare I was out of my comfort zone. I started worrying about my mortgage – if I lost my flat I'd be penniless.

A letter I wrote in a magazine to my regular Wirral Sunday night audience, now at Rupert's in Birkenhead, sums up how I felt about the situation.

"I don't think any of my regulars realise just what I think of them as people. You see, working as many clubs as I do you meet so many con merchants and phoneys.

"If you haven't already heard 1976 could be the break I've waited for. The television side of my career is hopefully going in the right direction, but I've still got a long way to go."

When I turned up to compere New Faces I got a shock. I was expecting to have a set script, and be told where to stand at all times. Going off-script or telling too many gags would get me the boot, I'd thought. But the director just let me do whatever I wanted, without any editing, on national television.

And watching my performance now, I wish they'd been tougher on me. From the moment I'm introduced as "one of the most outrageous comics you could possibly meet," I look like a man out of control.

PETE PRICE

Between acts, I change into some of my favourite outfits, like my white cape with the Disney characters on it, and my matching silver jacket and shorts. I suddenly stop in the middle of talking to the panel about one of the contestants and decide I'm going to do some gags instead. Then I just stand up and start telling them. It must have been the panel's worst nightmare – here's someone they thought they'd got rid of months ago, in charge of when they can and can't say something.

When I'm in the audience, supposed to be asking members of the public who they think deserves to win, I'm doing nothing of the sort. I've found a man from Aintree and we're doing Scouser jokes together and slagging off the set ("It'll be nice when it's finished, won't it?") Introducing acts like Roger De Courcey and Nookie Bear and the brilliant club comic Pat Mills (another character gone to that social club in the sky), I start rambling about how I've met them before and what I think about them. And I keep going on about how I love the programme and always watch it at home.

It was the Pete Price show with any bits of New Faces they could squeeze in. In other words, I was signing my own death warrant live on air. Or "as live", anyway.

A few weeks later, I got a phonecall from Club Mirror, the trade magazine for nightclubs. For the first time, they had run a national award ceremony for club acts and I had won in the compere of the year category. It was a brilliant honour – my publicity had described me as "Britain's best compere" for years, and now it was actually true! Other winners included Paul Daniels (novelty act of the year) and Cannon and Ball

(comedy act of the year).

The prize was a slot as compere on TV show Wheeltappers and Shunters, and a bronze statuette.

Now, I don't believe in the supernatural. For one thing, I've been to mediums to try and get any message from mum since she died and none of them has ever told me anything convincing. But this statue, the size of an Oscar, representing a jester holding a happy and sad mask, was different. The bloody thing was cursed.

From the moment I touched it, things started going wrong for me. On the night of the award ceremony, at the Golden Garter club in Wythenshawe, Manchester, I found out I had to do a 30-minute spot. But I was still a compere. I had a few gags and a few songs, but I didn't have a fully fledged act yet. Bernard Manning was compering, which was bad news for two reasons. First of all, if I was such a good compere, why wasn't I doing it? But worse still, it meant Manning had the power to make or break me with his opening comments.

PETER PRICE
Compere of the year
NATIONAL CLUB ACTS AWARDS 1975/76

"I'm really nervous, Bernard," I pleaded, just before the curtain went up. "Do me a favour mate, don't set me up." That was the biggest mistake I made. I waited in the wings to go on, fingers crossed.

"Right, ladies and gentlemen, here he is now, compere of the year. And if he's funny, I'll show my arse in the Vatican."

Everyone laughed. "Funny? He's about as funny as woodworm in a cripple's crutch. Pete Price!"

The bastard, I thought as I took the cursed statue and started my act. It was a disaster. But it wasn't the biggest disaster that night.

In the second half, I had to introduce another act, the Dooleys. Suddenly there was a blackout. I'm trying to get past them and fall off the stage, into the dance floor, in front of everyone.

I was taken to hospital and treated for water on the knee, and decided I would come back onstage, crutches and all, for the big finale at the end.

A man who called himself the Royal Astrologer came on with a donkey. It was holding something in its mouth.

"For a surprise, this is your astrology chart for the year," he said.

"You should have come here half an hour ago," growled Manning. "He wouldn't have fallen off the fucking stage."

Worse was still to come. After seeing my act then hearing about my accident, everyone at the club had decided something: I must have been drunk.

Actually, although I'd drink and work while I was compering at the Shakespeare, I'd never do it as a stand-up in a million years. Any quick-witted responses I'd be able to come up with would be out of the window once I'd had a couple of pints. I was always amazed by comics who could booze all day then go down a storm with a crowd.

But the rumour was out. There was nothing I could do, and I started losing work.

Thankfully I still had a guest appearance on Celebrity Squares to look forward to. Bob talked me through the best way to do it and made sure I got asked a question. In the commercial break I'd spot him chatting to the contestants, pointing me out and saying: "Why don't you give Pete a try?"

What I wanted more than anything, of course, was a regular slot on TV. But word got to me that the head of programmes on ATV, a man called Francis Essex, didn't like me. He wouldn't even see me to talk about ideas. Later on, Bob wrote me a finely crafted letter that I could sign and give to him. "The tone of this might make you puke," he said, "But if anything will get you into FE's office, this should."

It did the trick. Mr Essex looked at me and said: "You realise the only reason you're standing in this office is because of this letter?" But once I was in, I couldn't get any further. I later found out there was another camp comic, Duncan Norvell, who they were grooming for stardom. Another rejection.

Meanwhile, the Shakespeare had passed through the hands of the liquidators and was now under new management – sold to a company called Challor Entertainments for just £8,000. They planned to take it downmarket, forgetting about the big stars, getting cheaper, local acts in and trying to break even.

I doubted they would be able to turn it round now. The bankruptcy had resulted in too much negative publicity. But I was still curious about how it was getting on – you can't just walk away from a place after six years. Now and then I'd pop in to see everyone and gossip with the staff about how business had been.

It was one of those nights on March 20, 1976. It was 10 days after the awards ceremony nightmare and, feeling lonely, I'd wandered in for the first time in a few months.

Mal Craig, who fronted the house band, called me up on stage. We had worked together a lot over the years.

In fact, I sang the last song that night. Hearing the applause at the end took me back to that first night I was in there. All those years, I thought, and I was still in awe of the place.

I hung around for a couple of drinks and then went outside in the rain and drove back across the water.

At about 9.30am I was woken up by the phone. It was a policeman who I knew, and when he'd finished speaking I hung up and sat there staring into space. Then, zombie-like, I got my coat and shoes on and peeped out of the window across the water.

Not again, I thought.
It's as if the place has a jinx.

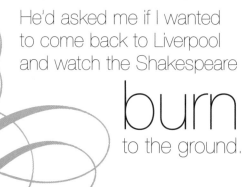

He'd asked me if I wanted to come back to Liverpool and watch the Shakespeare

burn
to the ground.

CHAPTER SEVENTEEN

fire

FROM my window in Wirral I could see the thick cloud of black smoke through the drizzle. And when I parked on London Road, it was clear whoever had started this fire was determined it wasn't going to be put out.

From the front entrance the flames had lit up the street. This wasn't a fire, it was a disaster movie. The bust of William Shakespeare hung over three Victorian windows, saying "comedy" "tragedy" and "music", all now with flames licking out of them.

Around 100 firefighters were desperately trying to get it under control after getting the call at 9am. One was seriously injured. Flames that were 100ft high were belching soot and glass up into the air, where it rained down on the local streets, packed with people staring, unable to take it in.

When the fire brigade had first arrived there, they had heard screams and seen four people in an upstairs window, shouting for help. They were a woman, a chef, a waiter, and David Meakin, the manager.

"On Saturday I was telling friends how pleased I was with the way things were working out for the club," he told the Echo's reporter, adding the same thing everyone was saying – that this was another example of the Shakespeare's rotten luck. Terry Phillips, who owned the Wookey Hollow, said he had been trying to buy the club before the fire. Damage was estimated at £1m, but how could you put a price on it?

After the fire had been put out, it was clear this was not the same as the fire in 1963. "The idea of saving the shell of the building just doesn't exist," a surveyor said to put the idea out of all our heads. It would be made safe, then demolished – even though it was a listed building, the fire had been so bad the usual rules didn't apply.

For days, I had performers from all around the world ringing me up in disbelief. So many people loved it. I repeated all my favourite stories in print and on the air. I hated hearing it slagged off – it was the most beautiful building I'd ever set foot in, the building I'd loved more than any other.

One of my proudest moments was when I'd glanced at a brochure advertising Liverpool to businesses and seen it there, next to the cathedrals, the Mersey ferry and the Liver Building. The artist had even included the billboard with my name on it in the picture.

I wish the person or persons responsible for burning down the Shakespeare would come clean about what they did. They know who they are...

What if it had never burned down? Would it have closed, lain derelict for the 80s and 90s with so many of the city's other old gems, then found a new use? Would it be a comedy club, or luxury flats, or bingo hall, or a chain pub? Or would someone with a bit of passion have put up the money and reopened it as a place where people could go out, have a drink and watch some of the best acts going?

Now Liverpool is a Capital of Culture, wouldn't it be great to see the Shakespeare rise like a phoenix from the ashes?

Well, there was certainly no going back to the Shakespeare for me now. And it was starting to look like a metaphor for my career.

I worked hard on my appearance on Wheeltappers and Shunters and was well-received by the crowd in the studio. But everything apart from the bare bones was cut out.

When it was shown I made the best of it, saying: "The compere's material is always the first to go," but I knew the producers just didn't like my act.

My only glimmer of hope was a pilot show Bob was working on that was my big shot at getting on telly. It was called Comedy Connections, and even for Bob it was a class act. It relied on quick scenes, knowing gags and a big cast of comics – a sort of British version of the American show Rowan and Martin's Laugh-in. It was Bob's baby at the time – he always had a project on the go that he was passionate about.

It was filmed in front of blue screens with amazing backgrounds superimposed behind us. Don McLean was the star, with other comics I knew and liked, like Pat Mills, Bobby Nutall, Dave Ismay and Bobby Patterson. I came on, dressed up to the nines, and delivered camp one-liners.

After we made the pilot, it looked like it was going to get picked up. There was a buzz in the industry about it. It was a huge chance for all of us. The makers had discussed booking the entire cast for a summer season and there was talk of a national tour on the back of the show.

Then, on Christmas Eve, we heard the bad news. An American company had bought the whole series. It would be made, but for a US audience, with comics from over there. The money was just too good for the production company to refuse. We were thanked for our involvement, but told our services were no longer required. Bob felt terrible, and didn't know what to say to us all as he'd hand-picked the cast.

As bad Christmases go, that was one of the worst. Mum's health wasn't getting better, and I was scrabbling around for work.

Imagine going from the comfort zone of the Shakespeare and Fagins to being out on your own – then not getting any work.

For one, six-month period around that time I sank to the lowest point in my life.

The work just stopped. How had it got like this? I asked myself.

Not so long ago everyone in Britain was talking about me on New Faces. I was a Liverpool institution at the Shakespeare. Now I was a failing comic no one seemed to want to hire.

I was broke, into the bargain. I should have been signing on so I had a bit more money coming in, but I was too proud. Someone would see me at the DSS, and word would get round. People already thought I was a drunk but that would really finish me off.

Sitting in the flat, worrying about whether I'd still be there in a month, I'm not proud to say I considered suicide again. I remember being round at a friend's house, crying my eyes out. Now people phone me all the time on my shows saying similar things, and every time I'm back there. But mum never stopped supporting me.

And then, a few months later, something really weird happened.

I saw dad.

It was in some rough working men's club in Bolton where I was about to do my act. I'd heard he had moved there, and asked around for David Lloyd Price, as I wanted to see him again out of curiosity. They pointed him out to me, sitting at the bar. The same pug nose and round, bald face. I remembered the last two times I'd seen him. "I'm just going on holiday for the weekend," as he left when I was 12. The matchbox with a fiver in it: "Give this to your mother."

I walked up to him, in full costume. "Aren't you going to buy me a drink then?"

"I'm sorry," he said looking nervous. "Do I know you?"

I introduced myself. We had a short, awkward conversation about nothing in particular. Then I was on, and I couldn't help myself.

"Ladies and gentleman," I said,

"I'd like to make an announcement.

There's someone in the audience tonight I haven't seen for nearly 20 years.

He's my dad."

There were gasps. Everyone who knew him turned to stare.

"And dad," I carried on, "I've got some bad news for you." I did a twirl. "I'm a homosexual!"

I never saw dad again, so I might as well finish the story off now. In 1981, he went on holiday, to Benidorm for a month. Aged 68, it was the first time he'd been abroad in his life. He'd actually made a will and given it to a neighbour, in an envelope, marked: "To be opened in the event of my death." The note said he wanted his funeral to be in Merthyr.

He was going away to try and improve his health. It's funny to think of him sitting on an aeroplane for the first time in his old suit and raincoat, wondering what was going abroad would be like.

After a week at the Tropicana Gardens, his health hadn't improved. He'd been taken into hospital ill. His brother had gone out to get him and, after treating him, doctors in Benidorm decided to fly him back to Manchester on a hospital plane. But he died in the air. The Manchester coroner gave the cause of death as Legionnaires' Disease – he was one of the first people in the country to die of the rare form of pneumonia, and one of three victims from the same resort.

The papers said he must have had a premonition to write the letter before he set off.

The story went everywhere.

"Pricey's distraught," one mate joked when he saw all the coverage of the case. "There's his dad on the Six O'Clock News, News at Ten, and Granada Reports – and Pete's been trying to get on telly for years."

It was just a very strange ending to the life of the man who'd helped bring me up then vanished from our lives. It sounds cold, but I wasn't that upset. He wasn't much of a father and I had very few memories of him. I was sorry he had to die like that, away from everyone he loved, but I could never have forgiven him for beating Mum then leaving her with all his debts. Months later I got a bill for £28,000 for flying the body back, which there was no way I was paying. I hardly knew the man.

Mum had never had another relationship after him. Once, when I was still a boy, I persuaded her to go on a date, but she'd got cold feet. She brought him back for a coffee and insisted I get up and sit with them, eating their fish and chips. "He loves his fish and chips," she said, putting me in the middle so he couldn't try anything. I was like a zombie in my red pyjamas, and it was clear I was the only man she needed in her life.

CHAPTER EIGHTEEN

you're sharing with the bingo* machine

"LOOK what you bastards did to me!" I said. I held up my hands, covered in smudged fingerprint ink and waved them at the table of police officers sitting in the club.

It got a decent laugh – but they thought it was part of the act. None of them would believe the real story. And no one since has had the chance to believe it – I've never told it before now.

It began on a Friday night. I'd been doing a gig at the Willows in Salford with the Three Degrees. Afterwards I'd gone over to the Valley Lodge Hotel for a friend's wedding and had started celebrating. The hotel was owned by the Partakis family, of Fagins in Manchester (I told you they were wealthy).

It had been a good day. In fact, I'd taken someone from Liverpool with me who I'd been after for a while, and I thought tonight could be the night.

Then Georgina Partakis rang me up. She said they'd had a last-minute booking at the hotel and they needed the room. Would I mind spending the night at their house instead? I got into my car and drove there, about a mile up the road. I'd stayed there before, and this wasn't just any house. I'd been drinking and I knew I shouldn't really, but it wasn't far.

It turned out a police car was tailing me all the way. As I went past the Ferrari garage in Knutsford, they pulled me over.

The policeman came up to the car holding something I'd never seen before – a breathalyser. I was just over the limit, and he took me back to the police station to give them a blood sample. I waved to the guy I'd been after, who was stuck in my car in the middle of nowhere. He didn't drive. Maybe I wouldn't be getting lucky tonight after all.

Sitting in the station, I couldn't believe my bad luck. Police were only just starting a real crackdown on drink driving – trust me to be one of the first people they made an example of. Of course, drinking and driving was a really stupid thing to do and I'd never do it now. But everyone still did it. At the Cabin we'd thought nothing of it, and for someone who worked late and relied on his car, it was the easy option. From where I was sitting, I spotted my blood sample sitting in a safe, ready to incriminate me.

Then I had an idea. No one was around but me. The safe door was open. Surely if the sample vanished, that would be it – they wouldn't have a case? I sat there thinking it over. I sat there some more. Then I grabbed the little bottle of blood and legged it.

All hell broke loose. There were about 15 cars after me that night. I had stolen evidence from a police station, I suppose.

I had ran into the road and got a taxi back to the Partakis's house, but they found me there, cuffed me and led me back to the station where I got the old good cop, bad cop routine: "You know, you could be talking five years in prison for perverting the course of justice." I've since spoken to hardened criminals who've told me I was right. If I'd just held out against them they'd have had to give the case up through lack of evidence. But I cracked. So I led them to where I'd hidden the sample: a bush next to the dog pound for the police Alsatians.

I was charged with drink driving, fined £100 and banned for a year. At the next day's lunchtime gig – would you believe there were police in the audience? – I still hadn't managed to get my fingers clean. I said to them: "Look what you bastards did to me," which got a huge laugh.

The driving ban was another big blow to my career – but self-inflicted this time. I couldn't really afford a driver on the money I was on – by the time I'd paid him some of the gigs wouldn't be worth doing. People I knew would see me waiting at bus stops all over the place.

Later, they'd say:

"Oh, we thought we saw you at the bus stop."

"Yes, that was me," I'd say.

"Oh, if we'd known it was you, we'd have given you a lift."

"That's why I was sodding waving at you!"

So I had to get a driver. It had to be someone who I'd be able to talk to, and who wouldn't show me up when I was turning up to jobs. I found a group of five lads who I could use at different times, as a bit of work on the side. "One week we could be in some shithole club," I told them, "the next week we could be in a TV studio, or even abroad." But I was worried about whether they'd be able to cope. Seriously – in my busiest years on the road I was doing 70,000 miles a year, and after a day's driving you're knackered.

In the first month of my ban I was appearing on the Les Dennis and Dustin Gee show in London. It happened to be on the same day they were filming Top of the Pops in the next studio.

"If you behave," I said to the driver, Eugene, "I'll take you next door to watch Top of the Pops. But you've got to be cool. You can't get starstruck or anything."

"I'm cool, I'm cool," he said.

Once he spotted Billy Ocean and Gary Glitter, he completely lost it and I had to drag him out of there.

That night I had a gig in a horrible London club. Afterwards, we walked past Stringfellow's and Julian Russell the manager and a close friend, shouted: "Pricey, get in here now."

"Behave yourself," I murmured to him as we went in.

"There isn't much room," Julian said, "so we're going to have to put you on Barry Manilow's table."

Well, Eugene started hyperventilating with excitement. The doorman wasn't happy – he though he was drunk. It got worse – he collapsed – and I had to get him to hospital then stick him on a train back to Liverpool.

The next driver was even worse. We were travelling from London to Amsterdam to do a couple of shows for the Army. He came down on the train, picked up the car, and we drove over to Harwich to get the ferry.

But once the ferry set off he started getting seasick. By the time we got to Amsterdam, he'd been throwing up for hours. I had to drive again – still banned – because he was ill.

There isn't much to say about driver number three except he tried to nick my car. Oh, and he finished up in Paris, earning a fortune as a male escort (honestly).

That was just two months' worth, with another 10 to go. I started trying to figure out the trains, and once spent eight hours stuck at Crewe station. What a Godforsaken hole.

I've mentioned it before, but I think now would be a good time to talk about dying onstage. It's every comedian's worst nightmare, and no one in this business knows more about it than me.

If you think standing in front of a miserable, heckling crowd is bad, try doing it in gold knickerbockers and a matching waistcoat. You have to believe in what you're doing.

As a comic, if you sense the audience don't like you, you have to have a high-risk strategy. Even though you've heard them 100 times, you'll have a good idea how strong a joke is. You might remember how hard you laughed the first time you came up with the gag, or heard it. You'll remember what different audiences thought of it – whether a rougher crowd or a posher crowd will like it. And in your head there'll be the A-list, the B-list and the C-list.

Normally, you'll ration you're A-list, your Angelina Jolie and Brad Pitt-level jokes. You'll sprinkle them among the lesser, Charlotte Church and Gav Henson gags, and pad the whole thing out with your real time fillers – Peter Andre and Jordan, let's say. You'll take an audience up, then bring them down; up, then down.

But if you're going down badly, you have to get them laughing at any cost. So the A-listers all come out – bang, bang, bang – Mick Jagger, Barbra Streisand, Prince William, the Beckhams.

If it works, the audience are back on side and you can relax. But if it doesn't, you're stuck with an unimpressed crowd and nothing left but the Cheeky Girls.

And then there really is nowhere to turn. If you were a band, you'd say screw 'em let's play loud. If you were a singer you'd start belting the songs out. As a comic, you just stand there, take the flack, look and the clock on the wall and wish you were anywhere else. And remember: two spots a night was the gig, lasting 30 or 45 minutes each. Then you're off, and no one will speak to you if you've died. If you're lucky, you'll get paid. Les Dennis was famous for never leaving a club without his money – and I wish I had his bottle. But in a pair of hot pants it was harder to stand your ground.

Here's something none of the old comics will admit to you. The Comedians TV show had us all crapping ourselves. That show took every joke there was going round the 70s club circuit and stuck it on telly. Every one of us watching it cursed it. Sometimes you had a feeling the club itself just didn't like you. If you wanted musical backing you couldn't just bring along a tape – you had to supply expensive sheet music (called "dots") to the house band. At one club I was waiting for the pianist and he walked in with his guide dog. "Don't worry, he'll be fine," the manager said. "You just worry about the singing."

In social clubs it was always clear that once you were working for them, they owned you – especially at the sorts of places where everyone had their own seats. Ordinary working men turned into little Hitlers once they became concert secretaries. And some of them would have their own private key to the fruit machines, which helped pay for their holidays. Pity they couldn't have spent it on the wallpaper.

They made it clear you were sharing your dressing room with a bingo machine that was topping the bill that night.

Doing one gig underneath an enormous crucifix, I knew there would be no blaspheming that night – even though that was all I was itching to do. It was a good Catholic club, with the priest sitting at one of the top tables. I could get away with one of my favourite gags: "I saw the priest yesterday. He said: 'I prayed for you.' I said: 'You should have rang – I was in.'"

But I couldn't get away with this one: "Mary Magdalene was lying in the gutter and she was going to get stoned. Jesus came up and said: 'Let any woman without sin cast the first stone.' Just then, a big brick hit her on the head. He turned round and said: 'Mother, you piss me off sometimes.'"

And how's this for an introduction? At one establishment – the Boothtown British Legion (that was pure Phoenix Nights) a member of staff makes an announcement: "As you know, Harry the club secretary has passed away." Everyone bows their head. "I'd like to pay tribute to this great man with two minutes' silence."

Flowers and wreaths were placed on the stage. I'm waiting in the wings, wishing Harry were here so I could kill him all over again.

The man looks up. "Thank you, ladies and gentlemen. Now here he is, Pete Price!"

Sometimes I wouldn't even get a chance to do my act, the crowd would be so bad. Once I'd had a publicity photo taken next to Herbert's Rolls-Royce in a fur coat. Big mistake. The men at Gateshead WMC or wherever it was had decided I wasn't going to be getting any laughs out of them. I could have been Eric Morecambe himself and I'd have died.

The Liberace look didn't work in social clubs as I found out – it irritated people.

When you're on the road and you're not on star money, you stay in pro's digs.

These strange places were all over the country, and acts have got stories to tell about all of them. One, outside Taunton, Somerset, was run by a woman called Winnie Small.

Her and her husband had divorced and they'd divided their bungalow up into two, with a partition. She had Parkinson's disease and was in a wheelchair, and knocked holes in the wall when she crashed into it. She'd come in, hands shaking, to serve you your mug of tea and bowl of soup – but by the time she'd put it down there was nothing left in it.

Once at Stanley British Legion I went on and before I said a word they were shouting: "Get off, you're crap!"

"But I haven't done any gags yet," I shouted back.

"Off! Get out!"

I went out of the door and they'd thrown all my clothes in a heap. I wasn't having this – I wanted my money. So I went to the police station. But when I'd told them my story, the constable looked at me and shrugged. "Well, you must have been crap."

Around this time I went round to see mum one afternoon and she got something out to show me with my cup of tea. It was an interview she'd done with a local paper. She hadn't told me anything about it, they must have just rung her up and she'd decided to say yes. She'd never been interviewed in the paper all her life – she was so shy, after all.

I've still got the picture they took of her, holding a framed photo of me and saying: "He isn't too old for a slap." It's hanging in my lounge, and we've used the frame round it on the cover for this book.

She says she can't get used to seeing me on TV: "I sit at the table and find it difficult to stop my teeth from chattering." Then she says her dream is to see me happily married with a family.

"I'd love to have grandchildren, but as Peter says, with his work being so demanding now it wouldn't be fair to expect any wife to put up with such a life."

Then, in May 1977, I got the phonecall I'd been dreading, ever since I was a child.

It was early in the morning, and my Auntie Mac (who wasn't a real auntie, but better) rang me. The night before, mum had been very poorly while I had been out working. She'd said: "I don't want to disturb Peter, because he'll have had a late night." The next morning she had had a heart attack. An ambulance had arrived to take her to Clatterbridge hospital.

I got in the car – I wasn't banned at this point – and got to hospital before her ambulance did. Standing in A&E, I saw her being rushed in, on a stretcher with an oxygen mask. Mum asked for her teeth, because she didn't want to be seen without them. She had about five pairs of false teeth that were dotted around the house.

All I remember about the waiting room is feeling numb and empty. After a while a nurse came out and told me mum was dead. The heart attack had killed her, but she was also in the late stages of cancer, we found out later, so it was probably a kinder way to go.

I did a double take and looked at the nurse. She was Pat Maley – the first girl I'd ever snogged. I hadn't seen her since we were teenagers. You couldn't make this up.

After that, I drove to Auntie Mac's in West Kirby and cried and cried. She said she would take care of the funeral arrangements. But I wanted to do it, and out of nowhere I found the strength.

I walked to the shop, threw myself on her bed and lay there for a couple of hours smelling her bedclothes.

Then I started on the work. I put a notice in the shop window saying she'd passed away. I went to see the vicar at the church at the bottom of the road, spoke to the undertaker and started ringing round her friends. Then, at the end of the long day, I went for a walk to Hilbre Island. After that, it becomes a blur.

It's time to thank my mum

It's time for me to thank my mum. I wasn't her biological child but that didn't matter because she "got to pick me", and that has always meant so much more to me.

You see, I was given away. Discarded by my birth mother. But if there is a god up there – and I sometimes question it – he gave me to a wonderful, compassionate, loving woman, Hilda May Price.

I sometimes wondered while I was growing up where I'd have finished up if mum hadn't found me. Maybe I'd have been stuffed in an orphanage without any love. Maybe I'd have been fostered from home to home, put into care with many thousands of sad, lonely children or even given to someone who wouldn't have accepted what I was. Thank God I finished up with Hilda my mum... my life... my reason for getting up each day.

She was my best friend, the sister I never had, my provider, my guidance while growing up. The day she died my heart broke and never mended. The biggest part of my life was wiped away. All I have left are memories.

The day the lingering smell of you disappeared from our house, I panicked. I was so angry. It was all I had left. And it was like losing you all over again. So I have always clung to the memories of you – and mum, thank you, because you left me with so many. Every night I would kiss you goodnight while you slept. I would hug you whenever I got the chance. When I used the house phone, you'd always shake the box for the money. Money didn't grow on trees in our house – it grew in that moneybox from where, somehow, you conjured that **£19.53** when I really needed it.

You were always full of little miracles like that. You'd moan about my pile of washing but somehow it would be done, ironed and back within the hour. You'd always give me the biggest dinner. You would always manage to spoil me even when we had nothing. You always supported me even though you didn't always understand what I was about.

If every child had a mum like you, the world would be a better place. Thank you for being you, for that smile and for the way you dedicated your life to me. I still talk to you every day and I still tell you everything.
I know you are somewhere around me, that you are watching over me.
You are my hero, your strength is with me, your support is with me.
You came along, you looked inside my heart.
I hope one day I will be with you again. Watch over me until then.

Peter Lloyd Price

CHAPTER TWENTY

Stalking
George Michael

FUNERALS bring out the worst, as well as the best, in people. One member of mum's family came round, what seemed like hours after she'd died, and started looking round her house.

"I'm so sorry about your mother," she said. "If you're selling that wardrobe, I'd love it."

I didn't feel some members of mum's family had treated her very well, and it was time to wipe the slate clean. It probably wasn't the right time at the funeral, but I decided to tell a few people what I thought of them.

Some family members were even complaining that my Auntie Mac shouldn't be in the first car to the church. I told her she was more family than they would ever be.

The Presbyterian Church in West Kirby was packed – everyone in the area knew her. Herbert had offered to fly back from America, but I'd said no. I've still kept all the cards I was sent from people. Hazel Collinge wrote: "She was very proud of you Peter, and that is the greatest gift a son can give to his mother." Tommy Ward said it was better I had not seen mum the night before as I would have felt helpless. "People only die when there is no one who cares to remember them. That will not be the case with your mother." I'd been questioning my religion after mum died – and I couldn't understand why she'd been allowed to have such a hard life – and so I was in desperate need of comforting words like these.

And Angie McCartney wrote that she would be happy to be a "deputy mum" if I needed one.

In fact, Angie did something I'll never forget at the funeral. I was standing on my own by the coffin, and everything suddenly came back to me. She saw how upset I was and ran down the aisle. "Do you want me to stay with you?" she said. I told her I was all right, but I'll never forget her for doing that. It had been the loneliest day of my life.

A few weeks later, I was on tour with Shack. One night, incidentally, I went to a sauna in Watford. I saw this guy and thought: "I know you from somewhere." I started talking, and fancied him, but he wasn't interested.

We got changed together, and he put baby oil on from top to bottom. Then he put on the espadrilles that Wham wore. "It's George Michael," I thought. He said goodbye, but I started following him. He lost me in WH Smiths. I told all my friends I thought he was gay, and they all laughed at me.

I was staying with Marty Christian from the New Seekers and his wife Carol, in the beautiful village of Heronsgate, near Watford.

Driving home on the M1, words just came into my mind. "Hilda, Hilda my mum. In all the worlds, you're number one." I spoke to Marty about it, and he told me if I wrote the words down, he'd set them to music. I was knocked for six – I'd never written a song in my life. It had just popped into my head.

Then we got a deal with Pye records who recorded artists like David Bowie and Status Quo. We met Eric Hall, the agent known for his over-the-top wardrobe and catchphrase "Monster, monster!" It was amazing going to the offices in Berkley Square for meeting about it.

It sold but it wasn't a huge success. On the B-side, there was a country song. Marty had tried to get me to sound like John Wayne – can you think of anyone less like John Wayne?

But soon afterwards I was walking around Soho and a gay

man, out of nowhere, ran up to me and said: "Oh God, you must have really loved her!" and ran off. Then, further down the street, another one shouted out: "It's so sad about your mum!"

What was going on? Why was this happening? I asked at the record company and they'd taken out a full-page advert in a gay magazine for the single.

I don't know

what mum would have thought
if I could have told her
she'd become a gay icon.
But I was popular in all the clubs that week.

Meanwhile, work wasn't going badly. Through Angie McCartney – well, it wouldn't have been though my agent – I had been booked to appear on a big tour. The artist I was supporting was Gary Glitter.

Of course, when I tell people now, one question follows without fail. And no, I didn't have a clue. When, in 1999, he was convicted on charges of downloading 4,000 pornographic images of children and was listed as a sex offender, I was as shocked as many of the other people who knew him. We were all shocked a few years later when he was convicted of child abuse in Vietnam. I'd just thought he was a cracking bloke. We loved him, and didn't have a clue.

They'd booked me for this – something like his seventh farewell tour – because he wanted to change his style, and move into the big theatre clubs. It was an audience I knew like the back of my hand, and the gigs were a huge thrill. I was working well by now – I'd finally learnt my craft.

At the Apollo in Manchester, he had a new group supporting him – the Bay City Rollers. Of course, in the time since he'd booked them, they had gone huge all over the country. On the night, Glitter arrived in his turquoise Rolls-Royce. The Bay City Rollers fans decided they'd take the mickey and they all started singing "Grandad, grandad, we love you." He went mad – he wasn't even 35 then. He was a big star, and he believed all his own hype. The eyebrow would go up and he'd throw his hands in the air, wherever he was – there was no on-stage and off-stage with him.

Everyone, of course, knew he wore a wig, even in those days. One of the tabloids had put up a reward for a picture of him without it on to try to make a bit of mischief. But he never took it off.

Once after the show we were sitting in a sauna having a few drinks, and he was in there with the bloody great toupee still there. "What's it like sitting in here with that hat on?" I said to him. Big mistake. He didn't speak to me for a week.

People would try and pull the wig off when he leaned into the crowds, but there was a system in place so no one could get any pictures to flog. Two heavies were standing at the side of the stage with towels and if it came off, there'd be a blackout, they'd frantically cover him over and bundle him off.

One hotel we were staying in had a full-size stuffed rhino in the hall. Glitter was up in his room having a spliff and his group decided they'd play a trick on him. They hoisted the rhino up to the second floor and pushed it into his room. He looked up and screamed as he saw this thing charging at him, being shoved from behind by the band. He got in such a state, we thought he was going to jump out of his hotel window. A week later I was belting out My Way at Batley Variety Club, and everyone started laughing. I wasn't happy at all but I didn't realise the rhino was being wheeled along behind me. It became the tour mascot. At the end of the tour I was owed a bit of money and asked Angie for it. You can write a cheque out on anything, so she wrote it out on a giant, solid hardboard cutout of me, and handed it to me. And I hope you know me well enough to know what I did with it. I got funny looks at the bank that day.

Later Glitter went bankrupt, and I remember meeting him for lunch at the Bowler Hat in Oxton, where he was staying, and sitting down to order. "Two dozen oysters and a bottle of champagne," he shouted.

"Gary, you've gone bankrupt," I said. "You even owe this place money."

"Fuck it."

It was around this time while I was away on a summer season in Guernsey that another thing happened that knocked me for six. One of my closest friends, Paul Pollard, rang me up.

I'll just tell you about how I met Paul. I'd been at the Shakespeare and he'd came up to me and said: "Hello, you're great. I got the tickets for tonight from your mum."

"You what?"

"Yeah, she let me into your room and I just found them."

"My mum let a complete stranger into my room? Is she mad?"

Anyway, over the years Paul and I have had some ups and downs in our friendship, but he had always been there for me. He loved my mum and I loved his. So anyway, Paul had rung me up to tell me he'd found my birth mother. When I'd gone away he'd offered to help me find her and I'd said fine, only half thinking he was serious. But he'd done it. Only he could do that.

"I've been to see her," he told me calmly.

"You've what?"

"I've been to see her." He told me where she lived.

"That's crazy. You've really been to see her?" I kept asking.

You hear stories about people who are adopted and go their whole lives without finding their parents.

When I got back from Liverpool I was still in shock – the reason why's all in the next chapter. I was excited about seeing her, but the guilt was terrible. The way I saw it, Hilda May Price was my mum, no one else. She'd only just died and I knew how she'd have felt about what I was doing were she alive. But I was looking for love.

Paul arranged for us to meet, somewhere in Liverpool where she wouldn't be seen. She had to be careful, she said, because of her husband. He didn't know, and nor did their stepchildren.

I still remember sitting in the car for 10 minutes panicking then going along with Paul. I got the shock of my life – it was Pete Price in a bloody frock. She was the spit of me.

The rest of that first meeting is a blur. Except for one statement she made. I was mortified when she said: "I'm sorry I brought you into the world with your problems."

I remember question after question I had wanted to ask her but couldn't yet – we were complete strangers. And afterwards I was guilt-ridden for a month. I felt like I'd cheated on mum with this new woman. The whole thing didn't feel right.

Later she told me Paul had just knocked on door and said: "I'm a friend of your son's." She said her stomach had turned over, but she had always expected that knock at the door.

After that first meeting I went round to her house, when her husband was out, and we spoke every so often. Then we broke it off. Her husband passed away, and I rang to say I was sorry he had died. It meant a lot to her – she had no other children of her own.

After that we started seeing each other more and having longer conversations. Then one day, she showed me a photo of my father. It was a formal-looking portrait which showed off his strong face and dark colouring.

The first thing that flashed into my mind was: "Thank goodness for that – he's got a good head of hair." Our eyes were the same, and I could see some of my features in him.

She told me he was a Polish-American GI, and she had met him at the end of World War II, but she didn't give many more details than that. It had just been a fling, she said, but she had kept the photo all these years.

They were only a few details, but they sent my mind racing. All my life I hadn't dared ask about these things because I didn't want to upset mum. Now I'd lost one mother and gained another. And the whole thing had left me as mixed up as you could imagine.

So I did what
I always did
– threw myself
into work,
this time like
never before.

CHAPTER TWENTY ONE

by the seaside

FROM the day I started out on the road there was one thing I knew I had to do – get booked for a summer season.

It's struck me I should explain what a summer season is for younger readers, as they don't really exist any more – not like they did, anyway. Summer seasons were variety shows playing at the big seaside towns up and down Britain. They were strictly family entertainment, with comics, groups, children's characters, magicians and a big headline act.

Why did I want one? Imagine this: you're a comic on the road who's a bit short of work. Then you get a season. Suddenly your diary's full up for weeks. For the biggest gigs, that can mean all summer and most of the spring and autumn too – 30 weeks from April to October.

You're playing two shows a night, packing in the crowds with a bunch of other entertainers, getting to know each other and going out on the lash at the end of each night.

Then, if the show's a hit, you go and do it all again the following year in another town. The same production moves from Eastbourne to Scarborough, Margate to Lowestoft, and plays in front of a whole new audience. And there was no shortage of bums on seats. Back then, hundreds of thousands of people from across the north would go for their two weeks in Blackpool. There was Scottish Fortnight, where everyone north of Carlisle would swarm to the place.

My first summer season wasn't 30 weeks, and it wasn't Blackpool. But it was a start. I'd be compering Showtime '78 in Guernsey, topping the bill alongside dancers, another comic and the singer Holly Day.

Holly and I got along from the start. She had the same habit of going off and changing clothes between her appearances – she was the epitome of an over-the-top club singer, with a huge talent. She should have been a star.

It was a happy couple of months. Guernsey was one of the most beautiful islands I'd ever seen. Plus not much goes on there, so there wasn't anything to compete with our show. The papers seemed to like me: "Affecting a slightly camp style," one wrote; "he soon won over the audience with a number of quick jokes, some of them a little earthy."

No, Guernsey was fine. The problems started on my last day.

At the time I was driving a Mercedes sports car, which I couldn't really afford. It needed repairs and I took it to a garage. The bill was going to be £1,800, so I decided to get rid of it, and bought a new Rover for £10,000 cash. Looking at it now, it was a revolting car, but I must have liked it at the time.

I planned to drive the Rover back to Britain, not declare it, and not pay any VAT. It sounds like a bit of a dodgy scam, but quite a few people I knew seemed to be getting away with it.

The morning came for me to leave. I was going to get to Southampton and drive straight off the ferry to Rupert's, where they were throwing me a welcome home party – I had been away too long.

I drove up to customs, with all my stuff in the boot.

"Have you got anything to declare, sir?" the man said to me. I said no. It can't have been very convincing. I said: "Is there a problem with the car?"

He looked right at me. "I'm going to ask you again, sir. Have you got anything to declare?"

"No."

To this day, I think someone tipped them off. They swooped into action. "We are confiscating this car, sir," he said, and asked me to get out.

I fell on my knees and begged them,
in front of everybody,
"Please don't do it, please."
I made a right show of myself,
pleading with him to let me off.
He didn't.

I was stuck at Southampton with two suitcases. I went to court and three months later they gave me the horrible car back, once I paid a fine of £3,000. The whole thing was so stressful, I lost a stone in weight worrying about what they'd do to me. For years afterwards, I never got through customs without their being some sort of search. I've had everything except a telescope up my bum.

While I'm talking about that summer in Guernsey, I should mention Holly Day and Tony's wedding. Holly had had an on-off relationship and eventually they decided to get married. But the wedding was not going to be traditional.

At the end of the ceremony – top-hat-and-tails plus Lancashire clogs – we were all given hankies. We were told to wave them and sing the couple off to Goodby-ee – the Gracie Fields song. She'd brought her dress from a second hand shop. It began to dawn on us that the whole thing was a send up.

The coach pulled away to the hotel for the reception. "Stay on the coach," they said. The couple went in and came out after a few minutes, having a row. They told us the hotel didn't have anywhere for us to go. They'd double booked. Holly suggested we went and looked for a fish and chip shop instead. So we all went along, tension building, and pulled up outside several chippies. The last place we went to was closed, with the shutters down. By this stage, we were all starving and about to murder one another. Then the shutters flew up, and the place was done up to the nines.

The whole thing was a trick, and we all start tucking into a choice of fish chips and peas or pie, chips and peas. What a cracking wedding.

With Guernsey over, I focused on getting into the big seaside towns, where I'd be guaranteed months of work. The next year I didn't manage to get in. But then I got a new agent.

I don't want to mention my other agents, but I felt they'd fobbed me off too many times. One would actually talk down the phone so it sounded like there was a bad line, then take his phone off the hook – like something a 10-year-old would do. He'd do it to me all the time. Once, I was working a club near his house and I had a problem ringing him. I went straight round, barged through the front door and caught him red-handed. The phone was hanging there on its cord. "Don't ever do that to me again," I yelled at him. This man had my livelihood in his hands.

Then I realised what a good agent was like. I met Mike Hughes: the star-maker.

Mike wasn't a particularly cuddly man. He'd never be a shoulder to cry on. But he knew how to keep his acts working and I found myself wishing I'd been with him all my career.

To him, every minute was an opportunity. "What're you sitting there for moaning?" he'd snarl in his whiny voice when I came into his office, after making me wait 40 minutes. "I could be making money." He was making big money, too – his clients included Les Dennis and Dustin Gee, Russ Abbot, and Roy Walker. I was terrified of Mike and so were all the acts – I didn't meet him face to face for two years – but he changed my life.

You'd get a monthly printed-out sheet showing your bookings, and then you'd be on standby for anything else that came in. He didn't like you taking holiday, as he wanted you to be available for whatever came up, 52 weeks a year. One thing I do regret is that I was never able to talk him into getting me panto work – he said I was too openly gay for that audience. Seems funny now doesn't it, when you think of Julian Clary, Paul O'Grady, John Inman and Danny la Rue who all packed audiences in.

Anyway, straight away he started getting me better money and better gigs. Better and, occasionally, downright bizarre. "I know you don't want to work away from home at New Year," he told me in 1979. "But I've found you a job and it's only five inches from where you live."

The last two New Years without mum had been unbearable, so I agreed. Then I found out it was five inches on the world map. The United Arab Emirates, to be precise.

I was doing New Year's Eve in the Ramada hotel, Abu Dhabi, in a show aimed at ex-pat Brits out there. With me would be Elaine Delmar, a fabulously beautiful jazz singer, who brought along a pianist who'd worked with Frank Sinatra.

We turned up at the airport, expecting to be flying out on Concorde. I wasn't too bothered – it was just a laugh to be getting away. Then we found out we'd been moved planes and Elaine started to look annoyed.

"I've got a bad feeling about this," she said to me in the check-in queue. "I'm not sure if I really feel like going – I think there are going to be problems."

"What have we got to lose?" I said. "The money's in the bank. Let's just go and enjoy ourselves."

At the other end, a Rolls-Royce picked us up and drove us to the hotel, which had been shipped over from America and rebuilt in the desert.

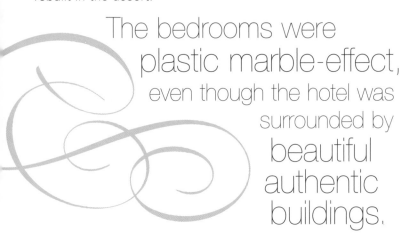

The bedrooms were plastic marble-effect, even though the hotel was surrounded by beautiful authentic buildings.

In the morning we were having breakfast by the pool. The manager came to greet us, and Elaine said: "I would like to get the piano sorted straight away." He went white. "Piano?" They hadn't got one. Pretty basic, you'd have thought.

"I'm going to have a fit," she muttered to me.

The poor manager was saved at the last minute by one of the local princes who agreed to bring a piano along from his palace. But then, I asked where the turntables were for my records. He turned white again, vanished, and came back looking embarrassed. No turntables. Elaine began laughing uncontrollably.

"The assistant manager says you can come to his house," he said sheepishly. "If you play the records you want, he'll record them onto a tape for you."

I started going mad – this was New Year's Eve, not some spotty teenager's birthday party. We wanted to get back on the plane. But they took us to the desert and gave us the most wonderful party, which cheered us up.

The evening came and, as the audience took their seats, we realised it wasn't going to be full of the ex-pat Brits we had been told would be there. The tickets had been so expensive, only the richest locals could afford it. We spotted some of their bodyguards with rifles, ready to fire at midnight. Bugger me, I thought. These people wouldn't understand my English New Year. "Elaine," I said; "I'm a DJ working clubs in England. I can't do this. There's no way this lot are doing the hokey-cokey, the birdie song, the twist and the locomotion."

I came on, sang a song and started telling gags, and everyone looked at me like I was a lunatic. I'd have to work harder with this crowd than I'd worked in my life.

After half an hour of the full act, things started going well (maybe because of the amount of business the bar was doing). Soon, I'd even got a few of them up dancing.

The fireworks came at midnight, and I ran under the table to hide from the gunshots. By this stage I could spot a lot more people secretly sipping drinks. Elaine came on and she couldn't get through one song – everyone wanted a picture with her.

There was supposed to be a beauty competition with a diamond watch as a prize, but they were all too drunk to listen

– it was bedlam. I stormed off. "You do it," I said. "I can't be bothered. Oh bollocks." The contest went on without me while I quietly got drunk. The 1980s had begun. A few hours later still, all the princes demanded we have breakfast with them. We had to go around every table having a fresh meal, feeling rough. We missed the plane, but neither of us minded. We stayed on an extra week and had a ball.

Then, back in England, I can still remember how thrilled I was when Mike rang me to tell me he'd got me the prize – a summer season in the Princess Theatre, Torquay. Cushier still, Mike's sister Margaret ran a hotel in Torquay and had sorted me out a great deal on a suite. I loved the resort, with its palm trees and cream teas, and enjoyed pottering around the villages nearby.

I'd be on the bill with two big names. The Batchelors were a group of classic old-school crooners who were getting on a bit. The Wurzels were West Country farmers who'd just hit the big-time with a series of novelty records. One group's fans included nuns, priests and squeaky-clean old ladies. The other's were hard-drinking and foul mouthed, and liked their cider.

Each band hated the other, and both insisted they were topping the bill. Their agents went to the papers to bitch about each other.

"Things are turning nasty for the Mr Nice Guys of the Princess Theatre Summer Show," the local paper wrote. "An ugly confrontation is looming between two of Britain's top groups – the Batchelors and the Wurzels – over who has top billing.

"The Bachelors are in the star dressing room, but recently the Wurzels are said to have been voicing their objections to playing second fiddle."

It was such a bizarre falling-out it looks like a publicity stunt now, but they really did hate each other's guts. Each night there was murder backstage. The groups would take swings at each other and I'd just have to get on with it. The stage manager would shout from the wings: "Stretch it, stretch it!"

At the time, Terry Wogan was doing jokes about traffic cones, and I decided to adopt one. I'd lead it onstage as if it were a dog, and every night the crew would surprise me by dressing it up differently.

I was dreading the last night, though. Like pantos, the last night of summer season is an excuse for the cast to play tricks on each other. The pianist will get on and find his keys had been taped up, that sort of thing. But when it came to the Batchelors and the Wurzels, things weren't that subtle. They just lobbed fruit at each other. And we're not talking tangerines: melons were flying across the stage. Meanwhile, they swapped my cone for a real dog, which had been eating something that didn't agree with it.

One final memory from that summer – Lee Evans hit me. I'd gone to see Tom O'Connor with Lee's dad Dave Evans down the road at Paignton. We got into some sort of argument and he took a swing at me. He was only a kid and what a big star he's turned out to be.

Next year, Mike the star-maker came through for me again. A long season – seven months – at the North Pier, Blackpool. I couldn't believe it. This time I was on with the Krankies and the Black Abbots. I thought straight away: an hour's drive from home, with cheap petrol.

The North Pier isn't the best location ever dreamed up for a show. To get to the theatre, you had to walk all the way down to the bottom of the pier and by October the waves were lashing at you and the wind was trying to blow you into the sea. The roof came off once, which put a lot of artists off. It reminds me of the time I walked all the way down Southport Pier to do a gig (before they started running a little train) arrived exhausted, and found 32 bloody people in the audience.

So it wasn't the easiest place to work, but I loved the rest of the cast. Ian and Janette Krankie and I hit it off straight away. There's a postcard she sent me with a rude picture, on which she'd written: "I hope this is the first of many openings to come." While we were there, she got pulled over by the police for being drunk on a bike. She was dressed as Wee Jimmy Krankie, naturally. What a girl.

We were on at 6.10pm and 8.40pm every night. My slot was only 16 minutes, and there was no departing from the script. I did my routine, gag for gag, and there were no dirty jokes. If I said so much as the word "bloody" I would be fired. So naturally, a conversation something like this was going on in my head:

"Do a dirty joke."

"Shut up you, I can't"

"Ooh, he looks nice."

"Don't look at him, he'll put you off."

"Say bollocks."

"Pack it in."

Doing a short set meant I was getting in the odd late gig too, so some nights I would be earning double money. In those days, Blackpool's gay scene was just starting up, so there was plenty of fun to be had after the shows. And the whole cast went out and partied hard in the clubs. Occasionally I worried about my health – I still had a bit of a weight problem and I was drinking a lot – but I tried not to think about it.

Lynn and David

I also made friends with a great guy who was in the fashion industry and has helped style me for more than 20 years. David McCarthy had been into Rupert's and was a real womaniser. I'd never liked him – I thought he was a right cocky git. But I got him and a group of girls tickets to the show and we hit it off. David ended up marrying one of the most important ladies in my life, Lynn Bidd. Their children Ellis and Layla, sister Julie, mum and dad Vera and Ron are very special to me. Not forgetting David's mum, May. I love them all dearly.

The next year, the same show – Black Abbots, Krankies and all – moved to Great Yarmouth. Now, I'm sorry to say this if you live in Great Yarmouth, but it really is the arse-end of the world. So much so, I used to drive home every weekend just to get away.

My digs were in a horrible house that smelled of cats. Getting up one morning, I looked next door and saw a tree which had been covered in milk bottles for decoration. The owner always dressed in full military uniform and lived with his "au pair" who did all the cooking and cleaning and I shudder to think what else for him.

I couldn't keep my mouth shut about how hideous Yarmouth was. I had to make a speech to local dignitaries while I was there, and I think I might have said something like: "Now I've been to Great Yarmouth, I know why there are no motorways there." They nearly ran me out of town for that.

Then there were the snakes. When spring comes, legend has it, all the locals come round and take all the signs down from the beach, because they're bad for business. All very well, but the signs warn people that Great Yarmouth is a breeding ground for adders.

Once, we were out on the beach for a barbeque and one of the dancers shrieked out: "I've been bitten! I've been bitten by a snake!"

"Shut up," we said to her – she was always coming out with stuff like that. But then she started going a greenish colour. It turned out she had gone for a wee in a bush, and had walked into a nest. A snake had bitten her... well, you get the idea.

Janette had to drive her to the hospital, with everyone telling the same joke about a woman who gets bitten in the same place: her husband phones the doctor, who tells her: "The only way to save her is to suck the poison out."

"What did the doctor say?" asks his wife, in agony. The husband thinks for a minute.

"He said you're going to die."

That was Yarmouth.

Then we come the most terrifying summer season of them all. It was Blackpool again, Central Pier this time, with Les Dennis and Dustin Gee. In my opinion, two comedy geniuses, and if Dustin hadn't died tragically young, I think they would have been the next Morecambe and Wise. I could tell Dustin was one of those people who just don't look after themselves. He knew he wasn't well, but he just kept partying.

His death, in panto in Southport, was a tragedy; Jim Bowen said stepping into his shoes was the hardest thing he ever did.

My favourite gag Dustin did was when he'd turn round and his face would be transformed into the spitting image of tough-guy actor Robert Mitchum. Then he'd go back to himself and say, in a camp voice: "I could never do the voice."

Les, meanwhile, was a diamond. I remember ringing him up the other year when he was on Ricky Gervais's Extras. "I've just seen you naked," I said. "You know, I used to fantasise about you. I don't any more." He understood.

Also in the show was Bella Emberg – Blunderwoman from the Russ Abbot show. She was a kind, sweet lady who was very insecure and had no idea how much people loved her.

So that was the cast. It was a top-quality show, and I'd done well to get it. Then the tragedies started.

One night, I was on, in my newspaper suit, Blackpool Gazette in hand, telling the crowd that you see some queer things in the papers these days. I was closing the first act when my eye caught the promoter at the back.

He was leaping up and down mouthing "Cut!" and sliding his hand across his throat. I carried on, wondering what's up. Had I said something I shouldn't have?

He started jumping up and down, pointing to me and mouthing: "Died. Died. Died."

I didn't understand. I wasn't dying, they were finding me quite funny.

"Third row. Third row."

And then I saw her.

A woman had suffered a fatal asthma attack. Her last memories of this world had been my act. She had a smile frozen onto her face, which set me wondering which gag had killed her. They had to have an interval while the ambulance came to take her away. I nervously opened the second act with the only gag I could think of. I looked at the death notices in the paper and said: "Isn't it amazing how people die in alphabetical order?" People laughed, nervously.

I felt terrible for the woman, and who'd would have thought I'd be seriously ill soon after? I started to feel really poorly, like the weakness you get from flu which makes even lifting a teacup a terrible effort. I'm not a person that gets ill, and it began to worry me. I was rushed to hospital, and it was worse than I could have expected. I had the liver disease hepatitis.

Two weeks later I'd lost a stone, I was bright yellow and I was terrified. I can't remember what kind it was now, but the health inspectors were called in to try and find out where I'd caught it.

I asked them the question that had been bothering me since I started feeling ill: was I still able to work? They looked horrified that I'd want to, but I explained how important this season was to me. We worked out that I could just about do it. The health inspectors asked the cast and they said no problem.

So I'd rest up all day, then get a taxi to the theatre and do my 20-minute spot in the first half. I was staying at a gay hotel, where they all made a fuss and looked after me. The make-up would disguise the fact that I looked like a character from The Simpsons. Then I'd go straight backstage and lie down until my bit in the second half.

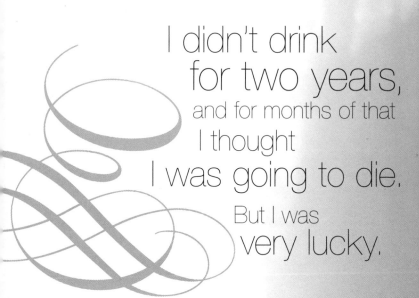

I didn't drink for two years, and for months of that I thought I was going to die. But I was very lucky.

CHAPTER TWENTY TWO

who put that
hole
in the ship?

BELIZE, in Central America. If, sitting in a rainy greasy spoon in Great Yarmouth I'd made a bet with myself that nowhere in the world could be as miserable as this, I'd just have owed myself a fiver.

A terrifying country, full of creatures whose only purpose is to attack you. In Belize City, the nightlife consisted of sitting outside counting the turds floating down the river. A dreadful, dreadful place.

What had brought me here? The army. I was on a tour with Combined Services Entertainment, who organise entertainment for the forces. In the 1940s they had Bob Hope. Nowadays they get Nell McAndrew. In the 80s, it was me.

I soon adapted to the sort of thing the soldiers liked to hear. You'd think they'd want to bluest comedy going, but actually they don't at all. I suppose they can get that sort of humour anytime. They want you to be cheeky but not take it too far.

So I'd taken my act to Salamanca, a dense, terrifying jungle on the border of Guatemala, best known for the movie Dogs of War – and a notorious drug trafficking route.

And did I mention I don't like insects? I can hardly imagine that's too much of a surprise to you. Even flies set me going and moths scare the hell out of me.

I was with an odd collection of acts. There was a ventriloquist who had a monkey, which terrified the locals. To them it was like a voodoo doll. We checked into our hotel, which had no sanitation, and then the medics came out with needles. They gave us every shot in the world. We're also handed a pair of flip-flops for when we shower because, we were told, there is a certain type of worm that burrows into your heel, keeps going until it's reached your heart, and finishes you off.

We would be entertaining the Scots Guards and the Gurkhas, and our first gig was in the middle of the jungle. We flew in on a helicopter, into a clearing. They'd tie the soldiers to each other on night patrol when they went on expeditions because it was so easy to get lost in the dense, pitch black jungle. On the way, they'd told us about the spiders that can paralyse you then gorge themselves on your face... so I was really looking forward to it, honest.

The organisers had put up a stage lit up by the headlights from two tanks. The dancing girls and the organist came on, then it was me.

But as I started doing my act, I saw something flying towards me. It was a bat, and it went straight into my hair. I was off, screaming like a banshee, and the soldiers thought it was the funniest thing they've ever seen.

An officer came up to me and slapped me in the face. "Don't you realise the bat's trying to help you?" he shouted.

"What do you mean, help me? It's attacking me."

He pointed to the speaker by the organ. At waist height, two feet away was a tarantula, merrily walking towards me.

The organist was frozen, the drummer didn't know what to do and I had completely lost it. They took me to a missen hut to calm me down. But soon I heard a slapping sound on the tin roof.

"Is that the rain?" I asked one of the soldiers.

"No, that's the rats," he said calmly. Later I spotted one of these things. They weren't rats. They were more like dogs.

"If you think I'm sleeping in the tent tonight..." I said. "I'm going in the Jeep." I climbed in with my blanket and

spent the whole night listening to things banging against the car saying: "We'll have you, you bastard." By now there was only one place I wanted to be, and that was Wirral.

Somehow I got through the run of shows, and they asked me back to civilization for a couple of days to relax. But the terror didn't stop. While I was shaving an enormous beetle trotted along the floor. If I'd tried to stamp on it, it would have survived, and carried me along the floor like a roller skate.

That day, we went waterskiing, and suddenly my boat started speeding up.

"Too fast! Too fast!" I shouted.
Then they pointed – there was a shoal of barracudas behind us.
"Faster! Faster!" I shouted.
I start trying to run on skis and nearly overtook the boat.

My act had gone down well with the Gurkhas, and they asked me to join them for breakfast – I was thrilled. I woke up at 4am, got dressed up and travelled down the dusty road. I found their customs fascinating – they can't take their daggers out without drawing blood, so they give themselves a little cut each time. I was handed a chicken leg 2ft long and started tucking in.

"This is very nice," I said, relieved.

"It's iguana."

I spotted another iguana – probably the mother of the one I was eating – sitting by our table with her tongue out. I tried another dish, a sort of curry, and the chilli in it melted my jaw. It felt like my face was paralysed on one side.

And then a scorpion walked across the table. Bang – one of the soldiers spotted it and chopped it in half with his machete. I couldn't leave the place fast enough.

When I say Belize was the worst place I ever visited, I don't mean it was the worst tour. CSE treated their artists like royalty, even in places like that. A few years earlier, I'd done three tours for NAAFI entertainments, which wasn't nearly as good.

The first was in 1978, and I was with a group, who I won't mention because the lead singer, who has since become a comedian, was an arsehole. "Are we going away with you, you queer?" he sneered when he saw me. He was one of the most homophobic people I ever met. I got in the van and they hadn't even put any petrol in. We were driving to Europe. What had I done? Had I made a mistake? Then they nicked things from every hotel we visited and kept everything in a filthy state, which drove me crazy as I'm so tidy. Touring with them was a nightmare.

When we got to Gutersloh in Germany, I was doing my act and the singer started trying to get me off stage. He was stood at the sides, mouthing curses at me. I still had five minutes of my slot left, so I wasn't going anywhere. But then he came on, probably drunk, and shouted: "They want to see me as well you know, you twat." Then he started fighting me. One of the soldiers pulled him away, and he was sent home. The audience thought we'd scripted it.

The tour reached Ghent in Belgium where it was traditional to put human manure on all the fields – it was like driving through a fart for four hours (mind you, you should have seen the size of the carrots). The next show was miserable, and my most vivid memory is starting my act, feeling something on my head, and looking up to see four soldiers urinating onto the stage. Believe me, show business doesn't get much worse than that.

As well as keeping it clean in front of the soldiers, I knew never to do any gay jokes. In those days they would have gone down very badly. So I butched up, and didn't mention my sexuality.

But I went into town after one show, and this soldier started coming on to me. He told me he wanted to stay over. "You're taking a chance, aren't you?" I said. In the middle of the night he got up, without me knowing, and stole my brand new car.

I reported him and I got the car back in one piece. It was kept quiet, but I understand he got a good hiding.

Worse was yet to come: Berlin, more than 10 years before the wall came down. First of all, one of the acts drove us all the wrong way along the motorway. Then, miraculously still alive, we had to drive down the long corridor between east and west, through endless checkpoints. The whole thing took about two hours. It was winter, and there was thick snow. It was so cold, when you breathed it hurt, and my moustache had frozen.

At one of the checkpoints, I looked out and fell in love. I saw the most beautiful soldier standing there silently in the snow with a sad look in his eyes. One of the people I was with had explained how they all wanted things like jeans and chewing gum, but weren't allowed them. So I opened the car door took out a can of Coke, and rolled it over to him. I glimpsed him moving it into the snow with his foot. He smiled at us, and I wished we could have got him in the car.

Then it went wrong. We'd been distracted talking about the beautiful soldier, and we took a wrong turning. It took five minutes for them to send a helicopter and armoured cars to surround us. We were arrested (and I'd had the 1812 Overture on in the background for a laugh, but it wasn't). They got us out and interrogated us. They kept asking us the same questions – why had we been going that way? What were we trying to do? Eventually they let us go, but the whole thing terrified me. None of us were smiling at the time – we were just feeling bloody lucky to have got out alive.

I did three tours entertaining troops in Northern Ireland – four days, four shows. I wasn't mad about going after my last experience there. That was during my early days on the road, and I'd been booked at the Abercorn club Belfast, which I later found out was a notorious meeting place for terrorists. The people loved you coming over – the welcome was fantastic. They loved to see anyone from England as they were getting such a bad press. I'd done my set, walked offstage and gone back to the Royal Avenue Hotel, where I was staying. I opened my room door. Sitting on the bed was a man in a mask with one hand in his inside coat pocket as if he had a gun.

"I believe you've been talking to soldiers," he said. I lost bladder control with fear, and passed out.

He was leaning over me when I woke up, trying to revive me. "It was a wind up, don't worry," he was saying. I got up, yelled: "Is that your idea of a joke?" and legged it to the airport. Soon after, the hotel was blown up.

But there was one trip with the forces that stood out. November 1 to 11, 1983 – my tour of the Falklands.

I was on a variety bill, which also included a couple of dancing girls and a strongman, Tony Brutus, who'd do things like picking up two people in chairs hanging from a bar across his back. He wore a traditional medieval-looking strongman outfit, complete with enormous boots, like something out of panto. We'd had him at the Shakespeare and he always went down well. He was so drunk one night when we'd been on a bender entertaining the troops that he climbed into bed with me.

"Tony, what are you doing?" I asked.

He jumped. "I… oh, I'm lost. Wrong bed."

"Too right you're lost."

He also, by the way, peed in my suitcase.

When Tony came back to Britain, he wanted a cup of tea more than anything, so we stopped off at a layby and went over to the caravan. "One cup of tea please," he growled.

"Sorry, we're closed now," the man behind the counter said, closing the shutters.

"No, you don't understand. I really want a cup of tea."

"Well you can't have one. We're closed." He walked out and started locking the door.

So Tony turned into the Incredible Hulk. He put his hands under the caravan, roared and turned the whole thing on its side.

"Right," Tony said. "Give me a cup of tea and I'll put it back."

Meanwhile, on the ship, the dancing girls had gone down well with the soldiers. Every officer we met tried to pull one particular girl, who was gorgeous but seriously thick.

"My dad bought me a motorbike," she said in a Lancashire drawl. "But he got angry with me because I kept burning my face."

"How did you do that?" I asked.

"Well I was trying to smoke a cigarette riding it."

She almost blew my cover on the ship. "Ooh, is he your type," she'd say loudly, pointing out a soldier after she'd had a few drinks.

"They don't know!" I hissed. "Shut up, will you."

One high-ranking soldier came and sat with her – the fourth that night who'd tried it on.

"Are you enjoying it here?" he asked in his posh accent.

"Well," she said, wearing the same blank expression she always wore, "I don't really understand what we're on here."

"It's a supply ship," he said.

"A what?"

He explained it to her. He told her how it was carrying bullets, gun parts and other essential military kit. "Oh!" she cried out. "It's a supermarket!" She looked thoughtful. "You haven't got any hair lacquer, have you?"

Well the man, who was determined to get into her knickers, got in a helicopter, flew it to the mainland, found a shop and got some for her. The whole trip must have cost about £5,000 of taxpayers' money. She looked at what he'd bought. "Oh, I can't use that. It's not the right type."

All in all, we visited Mount Kent, Coastel III, Oreford House, Fox Bay East, Ballion Stream Camp, Goose Green and Kelly's Garden, as well as Ascension Island.

We got there in an enormous Hercules plane which was completely dark inside. And Tony Brutus may have been able to tip caravans over, but he was a nervous flyer. He freaked out so many times they had to strap him to the wall of the plane in the end. But watching the plane fuel in mid-air was an incredible experience.

On the flight from Ascension Island to the Falklands, going into land with thick fog, we had to pull up very suddenly. We had nearly hit the mast of a ship. There was no way we could land, so we headed off for Rio de Janeiro. But then there was another problem. An electric storm was all over Brazil. What next?

We had been in the air for 20 hours so far with terrible rations and a flimsy toilet surrounded by a sheet of tarpaulin. There was an international incident brewing.

We did three detours according to the pilot's map that 47 Squadron gave me, and finished up landing in Buenos Aires. Yes, Argentina, with whom we had just been to war.

We were arrested and had our cameras and passports confiscated. An armed guard put us in a very nice hotel, and the senior officer ordered drinks all round. It was hysterical, we were under arrest for two days, and we got bladdered.

I don't know what went on behind the scenes, but eventually we were allowed back on to the plane and continued back to the Falklands.

The sights we saw on that trip were incredible. Ascension Island has the strangest rocky surface I'd ever seen, used by Americans to practice landing on the moon. It featured the worst golf course in the world – the balls just bounced off the rocks and you couldn't get past the first hole.

We were based on the supply ship Fort Austin, but we travelled all over the islands, sometimes doing shows for 20 men, sometimes 1,000. One night we were doing a show on board and someone had crashed another ship into the side. But a rear admiral had done it, so no one was allowed to say anything.

"Well, I'll say something you all wanted to say," I announced as my opening gag that night. "Who put the hole in the bastard ship?"

The admiral raised his hand sheepishly. Afterwards I was hero.

One of the joys onboard ship, was using a proper toilet. And I'll tell you why. In the barracks the toilets had no walls. There was a line of 20 people all together, passing the paper along while passing the time of day. I decided to wait until 3am before sneaking in. Sadly everyone else had the same idea.

We traveled to one of the most remote parts of the islands to speak to the soldiers, and I passed a group of lads who saw me and muttered: "I just dreamed I saw Pete Price!" Then he looked again and screamed. "What are you doing here?"

The soldiers had a nickname for the locals who were living on the islands. They said they were all inter-bred and some of the ugliest people in the world – I suppose there isn't much to do on the island except breed. They were nicknamed

"Bennys" after the woolly-hatted thicko in the soap Crossroads. But it got into the paper and the soldiers were told to stop. So they called them "Justs" – just Bennys – and they never worked it out.

It was a fantastic time, and CSE made sure we were treated like royalty. But even so, I thought one sergeant was being particularly nice to me. He'd always be asking me if I wanted anything else, and telling me how well my act had gone down.

Then I twigged. It was the soldier who'd robbed my car all those years ago. He'd been promoted, and was terrified I'd say something.

What a fortnight. I've still got a map of everywhere we visited and it's hanging in my hallway. The tour had been two of the greatest weeks of my life.

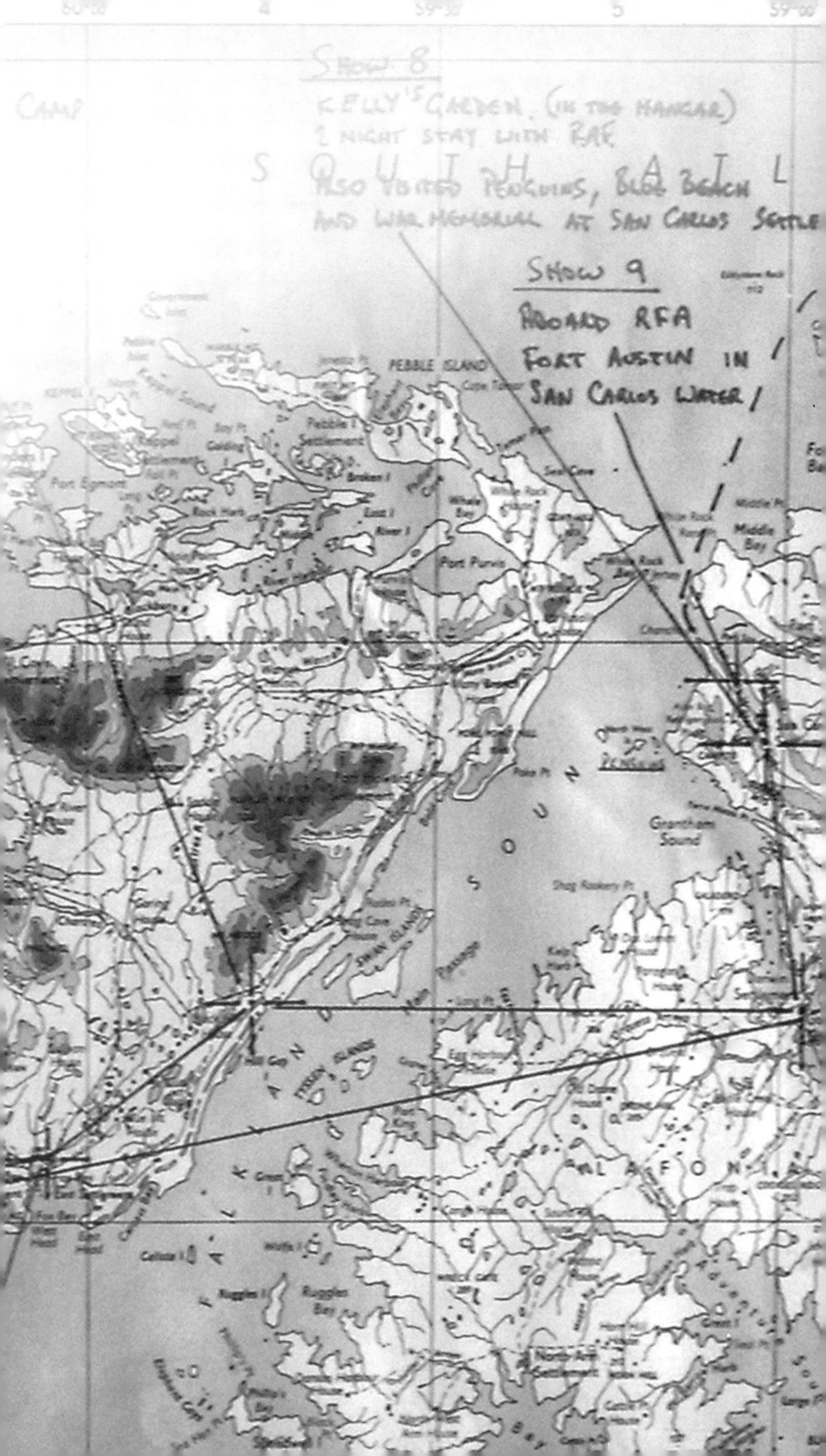

60°00'
4
59°30'
5
59°00'
CAMP
SHOW 8
KELLY'S GARDEN (IN THE HANGAR)
2 NIGHT STAY WITH RAF
ALSO VISITED PENGUINS, BLUE BEACH
AND WAR MEMORIAL AT SAN CARLOS SETTLE
SHOW 9
ABOARD RFA
FORT AUSTIN IN
SAN CARLOS WATER
PEBBLE ISLAND
Pebble I Settlement
Port Egmont
Port Purvis
Grantham Sound
S O U T H
A T L

CHAPTER TWENTY THREE

Brookside's biggest fan

"We'd like you to come along to talk to us about a role in a film," the man from Alan Bleasdale's company told me. I couldn't believe it. I'd never done any acting before, unless you count that appearance in Crown Court as an extra.

"Who am I playing?" I asked.

"Well," he said, "You're a has-been gay comic who dies on his arse."

I laughed nervously. "Do you think I'm being typecast at all?"

The film was No Surrender, the first movie from Bleasdale, the incredible Scouse writer who'd taken the country by storm with Boys from the Blackstuff. He'd written the role for me.

Then it got even stranger. Peter Wilson, Austin and June's son, rang me and said: "Are you sitting down?"

He told me he was in the film too. "I'm playing your boyfriend," he said. I was absolutely gobsmacked.

The first day's filming came, and I'd got a picture in my mind of how movie stars turn up to sets. I wore a fur coat, and I was dripping with jewellery. Everyone else was standing around in jeans and T-shirts. After experiencing a day's filming for myself, I understood why they dressed like that. It was knackering, and the next day I came in wearing a jumper and a woolly hat, too.

Alan wanted me to stand up in front of the club audience and die. They'd set the club up with lots of people I knew there watching, and told them to chuck beer mats and turn against me while I was doing my act.

Weeks later, I was driving along and listening to him doing an interview about the film on Andy Peabold's Radio One show. "Why Pete Price?" asked Andy who was an old mate of mine, after talking about the other stars.

Bleasdale said something like: "Pricey's a legend in Liverpool. When he was the compere at the Shakespeare, people used to go just to watch him die on stage." He went on to say I had begged him for a part, and it was great how I was openly gay. I had to pull over at a layby. I didn't think I'd died that much at the Shakespeare. I certainly hadn't begged him for the part. And, worst of all, I hadn't come out on radio yet. Andy phoned me straight away to apologise.

But the cast of No Surrender was incredible. Michael Angelis, James Ellis, Bernard Hill, Ray McAnally, Joanne Whalley – even Elvis Costello playing a magician. The plot was that a dodgy manager had set up a night at a club and invited along a bus full of Protestants, a bus full of Catholics, a terrorist hiding from the IRA and a group of people with learning difficulties.

I watched it again the other day and even though it's now 22 years old, it's a hilarious black comedy which has become a cult classic.

"I hate poofs," Bernard Hill, playing the doorman, says as I walk into the club. "Uphill gardener. Dinner-masher."

"Never judge a book by its cover," I say to Bernard after coming off stage.

"It's all right," he replies, in my favourite line of the film. "I don't read."

The premiere in Liverpool was a fantastic night, with us all arriving in limos, although a lot of my stuff had been cut out, along with a lot of Elvis's material. In fact, blink and you'd miss us.

The film had a second premiere, too, round at the Wilsons' mansion in Majorca. We all got dressed up in black tie for a special screening. "See?" June said to me as it got to our bit.

"I always knew you were trying to sleep with my son.

Recently, one of the production team on the Ricky Tomlinson drama series Nice Guy Eddie asked me to do a cameo as a compere because he'd seen me on No Surrender.

My career on the big and small screens hasn't been what I hoped it would when I started in this business. You can see this is quite a short chapter. But counting all my appearances, it's amazing how many I've totted up over the years.

I divide it into two parts: before and after radio. Before was the era when it meant a huge amount to get on TV, and I was trying to get a regular slot to perform. Afterwards, TV started to mean less and less, and I was increasingly in demand as a radio talk show host who could comment on anything and everything.

So in the early days I was grateful for anything I could get to boost my profile and put on my publicity. I'm really proud of Stardust '82, the Les Dennis and Dustin Gee Laughter Show, and the other variety shows I did. I've also done stand-up on one of Michael Barrymore's shows with Joe Longthorne and Danny la Rue in 1988. My best ever appearance was Sky's Stand and Deliver, my one-man show.

More recent TV appearances were Kilroy, Granada Reports, The Time the Place, ITN and Sky News (slagging off Heather Mills). I was even on Newsnight, with Jeremy Paxman.

People also often ask me if I would go on a reality TV show. I just tell them: can you see me working with insects or sharing a shower with 10 other people? I swear like a trooper, and I'd be worried about getting caught picking my nose.

After Comedy Connection there was another show where I nearly made it, but didn't quite. I was on a pilot of the Madhouse, which became Freddie Starr's and later Russ Abbot's Madhouse. It was a huge series, but it didn't happen for me.

One of the sketches went a bit wrong. In those days I wasn't the lightest, and they'd put me in a wedding dress about two sizes too small, and a moustache and beard. I'd come on and Faith Brown was singing. She stopped and asked: "Who are you?"

"I'm Robinson Trousseau," I'd reply. It was a crap gag.

But when it came to filming, the wardrobe man, as camp as a nine-bob note, couldn't do the dress up. I had to climb up some stairs, but I couldn't do it because the flipping thing was too tight. Suddenly, I fell off the stairs, the dress fell off, and I wasn't wearing any underwear. "Cut," the director shouted, as I scrabbled around trying to cover myself up. The audience collapse laughing. I was told the cameraman had zoomed in, and I've been waiting for that to come back to haunt me one day on It'll Be Alright On The Night.

There were shows like Punch Lines, Celebrity Squares and 3-2-1 with Ted Rogers and Dusty Bin, which must be the most complicated game show of all time.

One of the most enjoyable shows was a Through-the-Keyhole-type programme, House Style. They'd been impressed by my flat and asked if I'd be featured. A German lady directing said: "I would like you to get in the bath and make some bubbles." I ran a bath, then came out to get her in my swimming trunks.

"Why are you wearing them?" she said, smiling.

"I hardly know you."

Three of my friends, Claire Sweeney, Bob Monkhouse and Les Dennis, have been on This Is Your Life, and I've been a standby guest each time, even though I've never have been featured. On Claire's, the most recent, someone grovelled to me about it. "You might or might not be on," she said.

"I don't mind," I told her. "Once I'd have been upset, but not any more." I'd rather Wendy Darlington from Claire House Hospice got the publicity.

From 1999, I did weekly and twice-weekly shows for Channel One, the short-lived Merseyside TV station run by Trinity Mirror. It was the same phone-in format as my radio show, with guests. The scary thing is I wasn't in control of the delay. We thought out a system where if I started shaking my papers it alerted the producer that someone was going to swear, so he could bleep it out.

Living legend Lauren Bacall shares Paul's sofa with me and Philip Olivier

And in the last couple of years, I've been thrilled to be invited on Paul O'Grady's show three times. I know he wrote the foreword to this book, but I'm constantly amazed about what he's doing to teatime TV. He gets astronomical viewing figures for the time-slot, and the show's always unexpected and hilariously funny. He has made teatime TV history. It's also

annoying, because that's the time of day I like to have a nap.

Once, I was sat on his sofa with Lauren Bacall, a Hollywood legend. I had brought along a copy of the recording of Applause, a musical based on the movie All About Eve.

She had won a Tony award for best actress, and I went to see the show in London in 1970, and joined in the 15-minute standing ovation. I had waited at the stage door to try and get that signed, but it had never happened.

She was thrilled to see the album after all those years. Lauren signed my album and said to me: "Call me Betty." I nearly died. I also struck up a friendship with Sharon Osbourne through Paul. I was hiding backstage to surprise him, and she was there too because Ozzy Osbourne was a guest on the show. Paul said to Sharon: "Have you met this character yet?" We instantly hit it off, and had exchanged numbers within about five minutes.

Finally, there's one TV appearance I need to talk about and, actually, own up to.

It was a slot on a Gloria Hunniford show where they wanted to pit soap experts against each other to see who was the biggest fan. I was up against two complete anoraks. One knew everything about EastEnders, and I mean everything – he was able to tell them Pauline Fowler's telephone number in the show. The other was a national expert on The Archers.

I was representing Brookside, on which I made three cameo appearances. Once I was playing myself, as a DJ at the opening of Grant's restaurant, alongside Paul as Lily Savage. Another time I was doing a fashion show with Sarah Greene.

Anyway. I won the quiz – even correcting Gloria when she told me I'd got something wrong. How did I manage it? I had the answers in my back pocket. I'd gone to the Brookside press office and said: "Help me – if I'm going on this, I want to win." They'd set the questions, and I'd spent all my spare time since then memorising the answers.

So sorry, EastEnders and The Archers, **I cheated.** But it wasn't a serious quiz, and I always preferred Brookie anyway.

PETE PRICE

RADIO CITY GOLD
The beat goes on . . .

RADIO CITY GOLD 1548 AM

CHAPTER TWENTY FOUR

be friendly
be nice

I TURNED 40 in 1986, and decided not to have a massive party; I had a better idea. Instead I booked a table at one of my favourite restaurants and sent out dinner invitations to eight men I knew, keeping each one in the dark about who else was coming. When they turned up they all knew of each other, but some of them had never met and they were all a bit puzzled as to how I'd chosen the group.

"Well," I said to them after we'd sat down and the starters had arrived. "Do you know why you're all here?"

I looked round at them all and cackled. "You're all the men I've been in love with over the years." A couple of them dropped their forks, and they all started studying each other. Did I have a type, they must have been thinking. How could he fancy me and also him over there? It was a hilarious night – I recommend all of you try it once (Just for the record, I never did have any of them). That birthday was a milestone, and it made me think about my career. As life on the road had continued into the mid-80s, it was starting to get me down.

It wasn't that I was struggling to find work, like in the early days. Mike Hughes was doing me proud with bookings, and I had a good reputation in the business. There were fly-overs, where I'd go somewhere, do a couple of shows, chill out for a day then get on a plane back. My mate, the ex-mayor of Holywell Shaun Boyle who resides in Singapore and manages hotels, flew me over to work on an ex-pats party in his waterfront bar. When the phone goes, you never know where the next job will be. There were tours of holiday camps in summer, the clubs, and the bits and bobs on TV. I'd seen so many acts jack it all in, and I had lasted the course.

How do I rate myself as a comic? Pretty good. I'd be the first to admit I'm not the greatest writer of gags, but it doesn't really matter. Over the years I've learnt to judge a crowd – what sort of jokes they want, how in-your-face they want you to be, and I'm proud of my timing and my delivery. And now, when people phone up the show to tell me I'm a crap comic, I just ask them how I've managed to keep earning money for 35 years. I must be doing something right.

Just the other day a guy came up to me in a club, hugged me, and told me he'd once given me a standing ovation. I'd been working at Walton Prison, and he'd been inside. I'd been scared of going in, but when I finished my act, they were screaming and cheering – it went on for about 20 minutes and it was incredible. I walked off and said to the warden: "Wow, they must have really liked me."

"That always happens," he sighed. "They just don't want to go back to the cells."

So I wasn't struggling. But, unless you're a star, block-booked for months and staying in the best hotels, life on the road is never easy. I worked it out, and at my peak I was travelling 70,000 miles a year – nearly 200 miles a day. Think of the days you've travelled 200 miles, then think of doing that day in, day out. People say it's an easy life, you're only on stage for an hour and a half. But you have to get there on time, set up, rehearse, do your band call, perform, then get home. You're talking 20-hour days sometimes. And, although I was earning decent money, you had to subtract 15% for the agency, 10% management fee, digs, mortgage for the flat and everything else. My car alone was costing me £11,000 a year to run – I might as well have been married. What I'm trying to say is that, as I reached my 40s, I wanted to be at home. I'd come close to making it a couple of times, but it hadn't happened. And the health scare in Blackpool had made me think. I'd cut back on the boozing and now I needed my own bed. But I also needed money.

Julian Russell, who I'm delighted to say is a lifelong friend, introduced me to his best mate Louis Parker. He was a showbiz mogul, managing the Prodigy and lots of other groups. He knew everyone in the business.

Louis asked me to DJ for a few of his parties at the Stables club in the Talardy Hotel North Wales. He'd been to my Wirral gigs, and loved the regular crowd there. He knew if he booked me I'd get coach-loads of them over and it would be a fantastic night. But this man didn't do parties by halves. Once he organised a barn dance - and brought in bales of hay, and about 20 live chickens, clucking around. They got drunker and drunker on our spillages, and we got more and more irritated with them as the night went on.

Another time he threw a beach party, and brought in four tonnes of sand. Then he offered a case of champagne for the best sand castles. Needless to say, no one won as we were all kicking everyone else's over. Then, at midnight, he threw the back doors open to reveal a giant inflatable pool in the garden.

Unfortunately the pool burst, and as I looked out from behind my decks I saw a tidal wave about to burst into the room.

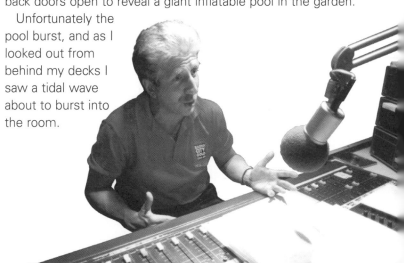

Louis died an incredibly sad death from cancer a few years ago. For his funeral, at St Asaph Cathedral in Denbighshire, they had to close off the village. The head of a chapter of Hells Angels. Boyzone, the Prodigy, and most of the rest of the showbiz world was there, many flying in by helicopter. I was devastated that I couldn't make it because of work.

I try to keep the last memory of him in my mind: coming down moel famau on a scooter wearing a Viking hat with a teddy bear on his back. I still go up and see his grave in Llangollen whenever I have a chance. A cow called Daisy looks after the spot for him. We definitely lost one of life's characters.

Radio had happened in a funny way. I knew a woman called Carmel Brown who produced a show on one of Radio City's stations. She knew I was a complete soap opera addict, making sure I taped them all. I'd taken it very badly when Coronation Street's Hilda Ogden, played by Jean Alexander, left, and Pat Phoenix, who played Elsie Tanner, died in real life. I have so many fond memories of evenings at her house.

Why don't I come on the show, I said, and do a 20-minute section just talking about the soaps? No one thought it would work. Nowadays most papers have a soap column, there are soap magazines, soap websites get thousands of hits, and TV shows are dedicated to discussing them. I like to think I started a national trend.

The boss at Radio City was impressed when it took off. A few years before, I'd also been doing a late-night slot called the Peaceful Hour (which I'm doing again today) where I read out dedications to mellow music. It was all helping get me known again around Liverpool after being away: I had my foot in the door if anything came up. Not that it was a particularly glamorous door. The old City building, on Stanley Street, was infested with rats. There were rent boys hanging around outside the entrance: "Put the light on and I'll give you a freebie," they'd shout as I went in to work.

Then Dave Lincoln offered me a full-time job there. It was a dilemma and a half. The money was crap: a big pay drop from what I was on. Mike Hughes had never thought I should go on radio, saying it damaged my image, and he advised me not to do it. But I decided to take it, and we parted ways with no bad feeling.

Looking back, I know going to radio was the right decision. The work was drying up. Social clubs started putting on weddings instead of club nights because it was an easier way to make money. Then, through the 90s, the old clubs started to close down. The people who ran them hadn't moved with the times, and membership was in decline. Seaside towns were dying, too, as more people went abroad. My job would be presenting the late-night phone-in: I'd tried breakfast with Phil Easton, the legend. I loved it, but it wasn't my time of day.

At 7am on my first programme, I came out with the phrase: "Nipple clamps."

Phil said: "Is this going to be the tone of our new show?" After spending my life working late in clubs, getting up at 5am was a bit too much of a shock. Funnily enough, when I spent three months covering for Kev Seed's breakfast show recently, it went really well, so maybe it is for me.

I started off with music and talk, with music acting as a sort of crutch for when I ran out of things to say, but soon I'd got confident enough to do pure conversation. Strange, isn't it:

If someone had asked me 10 years earlier if I saw myself as a radio talk show host, I'd have said never in a million years.

Very soon, the show got a name for itself. When people call me a shock jock I always deny it. I'm just passionate, I believe in everything I say and never sit on the fence.

I'm not a DJ any more – I'm too old. I'm a broadcaster, thank you very much.

Everyone who works with me knows when I get angry on air, that's the real me. I don't like layabouts and scroungers – now you know how I was brought up, you'll understand why – and I don't like people who moan about other people's success. And no matter how much homophobic abuse I've had over the years, if I'm in the wrong mood it can still set me off.

But overall, in those early years it was a fun show. The Echo would always help me out by putting in little stories about what we were doing. We had extra-large T-shirts printed, saying: "Be friendly, be nice, go to bed with Pete Price." A woman rang me to say she'd got married and gone away on her honeymoon. Her husband was lying on the bed feeling horny, and she came out of the bathroom wearing one of those T-shirts.

They hadn't done anything that night, she told me, because they'd been laughing too much.

I thought of the listeners as my extended family, so we decided to take it a step further. If people wrote to me asking to be adopted, they'd get certificates saying I was now the head of the family and their dad. We sent out 8,500 of the things, and I'm still getting Fathers' Day cards.

I told the listeners I'd be their equivalent of a priest (my producer at the time, Nick McLeod, had actually been one before he went into radio).

They'd ring me anonymously and confess all sorts of things. That's the thing about radio: you're part of people's everyday lives. You could be in the bath with them, in the bedroom, in the car. I'd had lots of lonely times in my life over the years, and

I think that made me sympathise with a lot of the listeners.

One day in 1993, we were talking about the news story that had swept the world. A three-year-old toddler called James Bulger had vanished while out shopping in the Strand Centre in Bootle with his mother. Lots of listeners had been ringing in to say they hoped he would be found. Then we saw the CCTV footage of two young boys taking him away.

I was speaking to someone on the phone, and Nick signalled to me. "Drop that call, take this one."

It was James's grandmother, Helen Bulger. I was stunned – it brought the whole thing home. All I remember is her saying: "I hope that little angel will come through my door again."

As the story unfolded, and the media came to the city, the show became the voice of Liverpool to the world. I had phone calls from people in tears who remembered seeing Jamie being dragged up the street by Robert Thompson and Jon Venables and had not reported it because they did not realise what was going on. The pair had told anyone who asked: "He's our younger brother, and we're taking him home for being naughty" before they murdered Jamie in the most unforgivable way. We found witnesses that helped the police work out what had gone on that afternoon. I had become the voice of Liverpool.

In the end, we had a five-hour phone-in for people to pour out their grief about what had happened. They were weeping uncontrollably down the phones. And it wasn't Liverpool being "self-pity city" as someone branded us. This was a terrible tragedy.

I'm still in touch with James's mother, Denise, and her second husband Stewart, and I went on the march to protest about Thompson and Venables getting parole.

But the whole thing affected me more than I ever thought it would. I needed a week off work because I thought I was having a mental breakdown. Thinking about the murder day in, day out had been too much for me – I can't imagine what it was like for Jamie's relatives.

When I came back, I had a new idea of what my job was. I'd been half-joking about being like a priest, but in a way it was true. Jamie's murder had changed my life by making me realise radio was more powerful than I'd ever thought. I started hearing about loyal listeners who had died – I still do – and each time it affects me.

Over the years I've helped people find their cats, dogs, and in a few cases, their real parents. Later on, in 2000, Radio City moved into St John's Beacon, the ventilation shaft for the shopping centre which used to have a revolving restaurant in the top. I remembered how much of a treat it used to be to go up there to eat, and was blown away all over again by the stunning views.

My dear friends Phil Easton and DJ Darren Proctor, with me on the day we signed for the Radio City tower, which I lovingly call the penis in the sky

In 1998, when Corrie character Deirdre Barlow was in prison despite being innocent, I started a tongue-in-cheek campaign to free her. I even went outside a prison in Manchester to demonstrate. The papers nicked the idea off me, and the whole thing turned into a massive national campaign, with Tony Blair getting involved.

But doing the show was getting me hassle as well. Once, a man came down convinced I had killed John Lennon, and was trying to break in and get me. Another time I had got into my Mercedes in Stanley Street, and a pregnant woman came up to me: "You cut me off before I had made my point," she yelled, and whacked my car with a baseball bat.

One day, I got a letter from a woman called Elizabeth saying she loved me and was a huge fan of the show. Then, next week, another came, then another. Soon two were coming a week. Then five or six – and they were getting a bit saucy. Everyone at City thought it was hilarious. But then they started getting downright rude and suggestive, and I'm no prude. We kept them all in a file.

Six months later, I was coming out of a gym in Birkenhead and a woman was waiting outside. She was about 32, wearing shorts, and actually looked quite presentable.

"Hello," she said, "I'm one of your fans."

"Oh, hello."

"I'm Elizabeth," she said. Then it dawned on me. It was her.

"Not the Elizabeth who writes to me?"

She smiled. "I've just cycled from 20 miles away to be here today."

"That's a long way," I said nervously.

"I only cycle because... I imagine the saddle is your face."

I wasn't sticking around. "I can't talk to you," I muttered, and walked to my car. That did it – she started screaming as I drove away.

A few days later I got a letter apologising for her behaviour. But then she started up again, this time sending me tapes with her singing along to Lionel Richie. A dog was howling in the background as she performed Three Times a Lady and Hello.

It got worse. I opened my post one day and nearly keeled

over. Elizabeth had gone into a photo booth to do a self portrait for me. We think she stood on her head in there from the angle that came out. She had a great beard. How did she balance on that seat? But now I was getting scared, and I brought in the police.

At the same time, we had a man who called himself Major Hewitt. He used to phone in and complain bitterly and with a passion against the police. He was sending me letters where the pen went through the page, accusing me of being in the Gestapo. Then he went too far, writing something I can't repeat. I attacked him on air, and said I'd be passing it on to the police.

The phone rang the following evening. It was someone describing himself as a sergeant. "Because of your persecution, Major Hewitt has committed suicide," he said. "He's drunk a bottle of whisky in his Rolls-Royce with the exhaust pipe on. I think you should give him five minutes silence." At that point I knew it was a wind-up.

"It's you!" I yelled. "You're Major Hewitt. It's you, it's you, it's you!"

Well, the police were investigating both people, and in the end they cracked it. "You'd better sit down," the officer said to me. "Elizabeth and Major Hewitt are actually husband and wife." It turns out he was a known Nazi sympathiser from a posher part of Merseyside, and they'd warned him in the past for executing dolls tied to trees (you couldn't make this up).

Well, Elizabeth's next plan was her worst yet. She'd sent me an expensive ring, and booked a sailing club for our engagement party. Then she'd found out where people I knew lived and sent invitations out.

The police gave them both a warning. She got in touch with me to apologise, and I replied, saying if they got in touch again, they would be prosecuted. Since then it's stopped, thank goodness.

One night on the show, I got a call which threw me into a dilemma. A man rang in saying he was a paedophile, and he wanted to talk about it. I had to make a split-second decision, and decided to bite my tongue and let him have his say.

He confessed to having raped his own child when she was six. He was in therapy, but still had the typical technique of coping with what he had done: he honestly believed this child wanted him to do what he'd done. By the end of the interview, my hands were bleeding as I had dug my nails into them so hard. The angry calls kept coming for two weeks. But I'd done it because I wanted to know what made him tick, and I would do it again.

Another call, which was less serious but still made me shake with anger, was when one man came on telling me he thought it was his God-given right to teach his son how to go out and rob.

And then, there are the final two episodes.

After Jamie Bulger,
I didn't think anything else could distress me.

I was wrong.

CHAPTER TWENTY FIVE

Michael and Terry

Michael had been on the phone to me before. He was 13, although if you heard his voice on the show you'd have thought he was much younger than that. When he rang me, I got the sense that it was a cry for help. He was saying his mother had died, and he had no home. He didn't know what to do, and was talking about committing suicide. He said where he was, and immediately my night-time family leapt into action. At night, every late shift worker and taxi driver has got my show on, so if someone's got a problem, there'll be someone around to sort it out.

Two women listeners saw Michael, picked him up, and brought him to Radio City. I wasn't really involved, I just went down to speak to the police.

Six months later, my current producer Jay Hynd was working with me. I was talking to another caller, and Jay said: "Can you take this call straight away." It was Michael. I asked him how he was.

"I'm still the same, but now it's getting serious, because I wanna take my life," he said.

"Why is it still the same, Michael?"

"Cause I'm more unhappier now than I've ever been in my life. Cause things are getting on top of me now. I want my mum and that. I just can't handle it no more. I just feel like I want to die again."

Something clicked inside me that this was serious.

"I dunno, what do you reckon I should do tonight, Pete? Your advice? Before I start acting... stupid or something like that? Just get my head sorted and just go somewhere."

I told him the first thing he had to do was go to the police.

"But I feel scared to go to the police station on my own. I... I... I can't handle it. If someone will just come with me... I can't really face the police on my own."

"Do you want me to come and get you and take you to a police station?" I said.

"That's up to you. If... if you got the time for it, then..."

"Well, I haven't got the time, but I'll put music on and I'll leave the show, and I'll come and get you. And I'll take you to the police station."

"Yeah, OK." He sounded so relieved. But I was worried. What if it was a set-up? Would people think I was a paedophile for putting a 13-year-old in my car and taking him for a drive? Well, it was something I had to do. I rang the police to tell them what I was doing. Jay got into my seat and started running the music, taking calls from dozens of worried listeners at the same time.

I spoke to the listeners from my car, on the phone. "I've got to go and sort this 13-year-old child out. Otherwise I will never sleep and I'll never forgive myself. So I have got to do this, so I'm actually driving now down Scotland Road.

"I hope I'm doing the right thing," I added. "I really hope I'm doing the right thing."

All the way, taxi drivers were beeping me to wish me luck. When I got there, the police had arrived and a taxi driver had turned up as well. "Erm, you know it's illegal to use your phone while you're driving," Michael said to me.

He looked like he sounded – a lot younger than he actually was. He was quite well dressed and polite – I remember saying: "He's just a nice little lad." We took him to St Anne's Street police station.

The story has a strange ending. A few months ago, we did a programme asking who's told the biggest lie. It was a great show. One security guard said one of his colleagues had got a month's compassionate leave after his mother died. But a year later she'd died again – he'd actually forgotten he'd already used that as an excuse.

Another woman came on whose husband used to say he was going off to look after horses. In fact, he was going back to his second wife – he was a bigamist.

But one of the other callers was Michael. He said he had lied about his mother being dead as he had been at a low point and needed sympathy. It was brave of him to admit it and I was pleased he was getting on better, even though he had been through a bad spell.

Terry was a completely different type of caller. He was one of the regulars. These are the people who ring day-in, day-out. I've got a policy with these people – I won't let them on every time they call, because it would be boring for the listeners to hear the same voices every night. But I'll let them on about once a week. Of course, some of them get around it by disguising their names and putting on different voices to get past Jay.

Anyway, Terry was one of the regulars and loved a good row. He was a grumpy old man – I'm told he used to go into his local tobacconist and just stand there arguing with anyone who came in.

One night I'd decided to put three of the best regulars on a conference call: Nora, Rita and Terry. This row would go all over the place, covering world politics, veering off to talk about Saddam Hussein and George W Bush, that sort of thing. I'd stay in the middle trying to keep everyone calm.

That night, I sensed Terry was breathing heavily, even for someone who smoked as much as he did. He was in full flight arguing with Nora. Then suddenly she was carrying on speaking and he wasn't talking over her anymore. He'd gone quiet. "Terry wouldn't miss a good row," I thought as Nora carried on slagging him off. I sensed there was a problem.

So I went on air, and asked for anyone who knew Terry to go and check him out. Someone rang in straight away: "I live down the same street, I'll go and check."

She rang back to say the light was on, but she couldn't see or hear anything inside. Now I was really worried. I rang the police but the inspector said it wasn't a priority. I begged him to send someone round, saying I wouldn't have asked him if I didn't think it was important. But he wouldn't do it.

So, while Jay and I carried on running the programme, we found out where he lived. I tried the police again, quite cross now. Surely common sense would tell them to send a car round – it would be good PR. But he wouldn't do it. I had to abandon the show again.

A taxi driver took me to his house. The phones were going frantic – Terry had been on so many times, people felt like they knew him. When I got there, a neighbour had broken the door down and people were standing around looking upset. Terry was dead, with a phone in his hand.

It was one of those moments that made me think what a burden the show can sometimes be. I feel like I spend my life counselling people, with nobody there to return the favour. I may yell and scream and come across as quite tough on air, but underneath I'm anything but. Once I went to a therapist to try and get some counselling, but he just told me all his

problems. The session came to an end and he apologised and gave me my money back.

I went on air and told the listeners the news about Terry. Nora said: "I'm sorry he's dead." Then she paused, and added: "But the point he was making was wrong..." and went into another rant. Only on this show, I thought.

Years before Michael and Terry, I'd come out to my listeners. Although I'd always been openly gay – screamingly gay – as a comic, radio had been different. I'd made the documentary on my aversion therapy, and had been nervously counting down to the transmission date. As it got nearer, I thought about how I would handle it. I told the listeners about the documentary, and said: "Afterwards, we're devoting the whole show to the programme. You can ask me anything. And then, after that night, we'll never mention it again."

The people phoning up tearful never stopped that night, and I'll never forget the support the listeners gave me. I knew I had done the right thing.

Over the years on City, this feeling of a family has carried on growing and growing. Lesley Marshall, my PA, has been an incredible friend to me, and everyone who's worked with her loves her dearly. She's another one I'd have married if I were straight. When Lesley's

Lesley and me

mum died, she and her father asked me to speak at the funeral and I was so flattered. But I have to watch my language around her – she's got a swear box and she makes a fortune.

It reminds me of the time I spoke at the funeral of Queenie, Herbert's mum. Frankie Vaughan had given me his trademark straw boater that he'd worn at the London Palladium. I'd hidden it behind the pulpit. I spoke words from my heart and finished up by saying: "I'd like to tip my boater to a true lady on behalf of myself and Frankie Vaughan."

A little field mouse sat in the church staring up at us all. We were amazed. Herbert was thrilled at my words and gave me a picture of his beautiful mother in a glittering frame. Afterwards he said when he saw the boater, he'd thought: "Oh my God, he's not going to sing Green Door is he?"

The stars I've interviewed keep on coming back on the show. I have the three soap queens in my life – Barbara Windsor, June Brown and Sue Nicholls who are all great fun to have on.

And, of course, there was Bob Monkhouse, which brings me to one of the happiest memories in my life. Out of the blue, Bob and Jackie invited me over to their home in Barbados. I went there five times in all, and each time they was the perfect hosts – they sent a driver to pick me up at the airport and arranged all sorts of surprises when I was there. Oh boy, could Jackie Monkhouse cook. I used to say to Bob: "Don't tell me what we're doing tomorrow – I don't want to know because I'll get too excited." Out there, he'd be on the phone to everyone – the controller of BBC1, Margaret Thatcher. Everyone would be asking his advice. Every day, he'd be working on something – and when he wasn't, he'd play on his Gameboy or beat Jackie at Scrabble to keep his mind agile. Jackie and I would go on long walks while he was working.

That's why when, late in his life, his joke books were stolen, it was such a tragedy for him. He played along with the press sending him up over it, but those books weren't just full of lists of gags. They had all his little cartoons in, all his observations and his life thoughts. When he finally got them back he was elated. He was always working on something, making his own tapes of his favourite music and thinking up the next brilliant project.

Once, he casually handed me a section from his autobiography. "Do you want to have a look at a few chapters and tell me what you think?" he said. Was he serious? What on earth would I be able to tell him? I get a quick mention in his first book, but when the second, Over the Limit, came out I couldn't believe what he'd done. I had mentions throughout the book. There's even a picture of us together. "Pete Price – and I hope this paparazzi snap will lead to rumours of a gay romance," he jokes in the caption. "Then we can sue the papers and make a fortune." It will never leave my lounge.

Watching films after dinner with Bob and Jackie was hilarious. He'd stick the movie on, with both of them in their chairs and me in the middle. Then straight away he would be there, leafing through his reference books. "I think the best boy was the same one used in that film we saw the other day, because he would have worked for the studio around that time," he'd mutter as I tried to concentrate on the TV. "Yes!" he'd shout out; "That's him!" Jackie, meanwhile, would start saying: "I'm not going to like this film, Bob," and would ask him what was about to happen all the way through. It was hysterical. After they'd finished and gone to bed, I'd rewind the movie and watch it again on my own, to see it properly. "If you want some ice-cream, make sure you have it in a dish," Jackie would say to me, ruling the house with an iron fist and being a typically generous host – and what a host. I, in turn, tried to be the ideal houseguest, leaving them alone when I knew they needed privacy. When I first arrived at the house, Bob gave me a hilarious job to do. His home on the beach had an incredible view, with flowers festooned everywhere. "Put this hat and these sunglasses on, Peter," he said; "And wave to that boat when it gets nearer."

A sightseeing boat came along and I heard the guide on his megaphone. "Up there is Bob Monkhouse's house and there's Bob, standing at the balcony. Wave to Bob, everyone!" I waved and everyone on the boat was jumping up and down, taking photos, while Bob got on with his work.

One night, someone who works high up in the media – let's leave it at that – and her husband came to Barbados. They were desperate to meet Bob and he'd very kindly taken them out to dinner. The next night they asked if they could return the favour, but he'd made plans to see Jeremy Beadle and Des O'Connor. "You go," Bob and Jackie said.

I went along, and they'd booked the Cliff – one of the world's most exclusive restaurants. Everyone was there: Luciano Pavarotti, the Countess Rossi, Bernard Delfont. Because everyone had seen me with Bob, they were all waving at me as they thought I must have been someone important. Bob had made me feel like a star wherever I went. Once I was there for Christmas and we went to someone's house where the crackers had cost £10,000 for 10.

Anyway, the wine menu arrived, and this lady's husband – a fat man with a loud voice – immediately started getting mouthy. "I'll have the bottle of Dom Perignon I ordered, please." He told me he'd phoned in advance to order it so it would be properly chilled. "But you don't need to worry about that here," I whispered. "I think they know what they're doing."

When it arrived, it was frappe – he must have insisted they put it in the freezer. I couldn't keep a straight face, and decided there was only one way I was getting through this meal. I excused myself, snuck to the bar, and downed a double brandy. It was going to be a long night.

"I want lobster, with two portions of chips," he yelled at the poor waiter as we ordered. I had to sneak off to the bar again as he picked up the soup bowl and licked it clean. Through all this, his wife acted as if nothing was wrong. She must have got used to it over the years and loved him very much.

His lobster arrived and he picked it up and tore into it like a man possessed. But after he'd wolfed it down, he decided he was still hungry and asked for steak and chips. He plunged his knife into the steak and sent the plate flipping over our heads to smash somewhere. Time to go back to the bar again. Finally, the pudding arrived – he'd gone for profiteroles, obviously still not full – and he started flicking them across the table with his spoon, onto his wife's plate. I met up with Bob later and he couldn't believe it.

I remember being in pantomime when I heard Bob had died on Monday December 29, 2003. I knew he had been ill for a while, but had kept it out of the papers: the last couple of times I had spoken to him on the phone we had talked about it. But even so, his death of prostate cancer was a surprise.

I was distraught because I couldn't go to his funeral as I was working. But he would have understood, as the show must go on. Towards the end, Bob had been heartbroken when he wasn't able to write anymore because of his condition.

He was
the kindest,
most interesting,
most generous,
most brilliant man
I ever met.
And I miss him
every day
of my life.

CHAPTER TWENTY SIX

I want to turn myself in

IT'S time to come clean about drugs. On my show I've always been anti-drugs. I've seen them ruin friends' lives. I've listened to too many callers who've had kids taken off them because of addictions, been beaten up and mugged by drug addicts, or lost friends.

But I'm not completely guilt-free myself. When people ask me what I've done, I always tell them I have taken drugs, it was a one-off, and I'm not prepared to discuss it. But I've always tried to be as honest as possible with my listeners, so here's the full story.

My first drug experience was at catering college, which makes it the early 60s. A friend had given me some marijuana to smoke, but I'd tried smoking tobacco and didn't like it. "I can't afford clothes AND cigarettes," I'd said. "So I'm sticking with clothes."

So, using my newly found cooking expertise, I decided I would make a cake, and put the cannabis in that. I baked an absolutely gorgeous fruitcake, sprinkling the weed into the mix just before I put it in the oven. Then out it came, onto the rack to cool down, and I went to the cinema with some mates.

We got back in, ready to get high (with a nice cup of tea to wash the cake down, of course). But it was gone. I went into the living room and saw mum sat with my aunties, playing cards.

"Woooooooo! Hiya Peter!"

Mum said, swaying in her chair.

"What's wrong mum?" I said. Then I saw the cake crumbs on their plates.

"That was very nice of you to bake that cake for us as a surprise, for the card school," she said. Mum was stoned, I never got any cake, and after that I didn't bother trying it again.

Cocaine was different. I was at a huge show business party, with one of the biggest groups of the day and many stars. In fact, I was the only person there I'd never heard of. This party had everything you could ask for: expensive booze, cigarettes... and a mountain of cocaine as big as a wedding cake. Everyone there was on it.

"Why don't you try it Peter?" the host said to me, finding it hilarious I'd never done it before. I was drunk, and didn't really know what I was doing.

"What's it like?"

"It'll make the party go for another eight hours – you'll feel amazing," he said. "Trust me."

So I did it and, yes, I did feel amazing. I understood why so many people were snorting it. It scared the shit out of me.

But then the guilt started. The party had been on Saturday night, and by Sunday I felt terrible. How could I have done something like that, after everything I'd said on radio? I vowed never to do it again: I had an addictive personality, and I knew I'd have got hooked. But the guilt just got worse and worse as I lay in bed hungover. By Sunday night I'd decided what I was going to do – I owed it to my listeners.

I walked into a police station on Monday morning.

"All right Pricey," the constable said. "Great show last night. What can we do for you?"

"I've taken cocaine and I'd like to turn myself in." He did a double take.

"You've what?"

"On Saturday night I snorted cocaine, and now I'd like to turn myself in."

"I think I'd better get the sergeant."

As he went round the back, all the coppers were whispering and staring round. They couldn't believe their eyes.

The sergeant came out, asked me how he could help, and I repeated what I'd said. He looked me in the eyes and shook his head.

"Do you think I'm doing the paperwork for that?" he said. "Now go on, piss off." What a prat I was. I've never done it since.

It's time to go back to 1993 for a Christmas I'll remember forever. Remember how I'd said Mike Hughes wouldn't get me panto work because I was gay, and I was always disappointed? I had been chasing pantos but I had a reputation as a cheeky comic so I had to prove myself. Well, that year I managed it, joining John Inman, Julian Clary and Paul O'Grady in what must be the campest art form out there.

I was thrilled. I've always been passionate about pantomime – a certain type of person sneers at it, but it get so many kids along to the theatre for the first time. I remember how excited I was going to my first panto, at the Liverpool Empire, starring Dickie Valentine. The year after that I saw Morecambe and Wise in a pantomime – and it doesn't get much better than that.

Also, as I've found over the years, being in a pantomime makes Christmas and New Year bearable. With mum gone, I tend to go and visit friends over the period. But there's always that moment after lunch when the family I'm staying with opens their presents, and you know you aren't really part of their Christmas. I always tell them I'm going for a walk and get out of their hair for a bit.

I only had a small part in this panto, but it was a big show – Dick Whittington at the Empire. And it starred the Blakeney sisters, who played the Alessi twins in Neighbours, and were

big names over here but even bigger in Australia, where they had been child stars. This was their first panto, and they were two of the nicest girls you could hope to meet. Recently I met one of the Corrs and did a double take – they look identical.

Straight away I knew panto was for me. I loved the look on the kids' faces when some special effect worked well or the baddie got punished.

On the last night a panto's cast play pranks – just like in summer seasons – except the Blakeney twins didn't understand the sort of tricks you were supposed to do. They'd never seen a pantomime, let alone been in one.

So instead of putting the prince's jockstrap in the treasure chest for a laugh or something like that, Gillian, playing the princess, did this: when the prince asked her to marry him at the big finale, she looked into his eyes, said: "No" and walked off. We all thought it was hilarious, but there were little girls in tears. She never went back – the prince never got the princess.

The following year I was in Rhyl, playing dame for the first time. Doing the press shots the summer before, I was walking down the beach covered with make-up and in a frock. I didn't even recognise myself, but a Scouser walked past and said: "All right Pricey, how are you?" They're everywhere, I thought.

As you'll have noticed, Rhyl is a long way from Liverpool, where my radio show started at 10pm. Stan Boardman, the star who I was appearing with, knew this very well. On stage he may have been the perfect professional, helping me along and never trying to steal scenes off me. In fact he taught me a lot about the craft of panto. But off stage, Stan made it his personal mission to keep me from getting there on time. He was a sod.

Once, he handcuffed me to a caravan that was part of the set. Another time, he dropped me in the wishing well. In the script they had written me three clauses to get out. One night, after I'd escaped some prank, I didn't have time to change, got into my car dressed as Dame Claire Voyant – the ugliest woman you've seen in your life – and sped down the motorway. I got pulled over.

The policeman took one look at me, said "I don't want to know. Just go." That was the closest shave, and I managed to get in on time every night. If anyone thinks show business is easy, try doing two pantos a day and a four-hour phone-in. No wonder I have to take two weeks off in January every year.

My fellow DJ Billy Butler also taught me loads about panto, and also liked winding me up.

I was sitting in the dressing room with nothing on but my tights, high heels and bra. "You're on! You're on!" he shouted.

I panicked, and legged it onto the stage. The audience gasped – I bet a few kids needed counselling – and Billy was at the side of the stage. "In 10 minutes! In 10 minutes!" he said.

Billy, Mickey Finn and Shaun Styles were playing naughty school kids and I

was the schoolmarm in one scene. Every show they'd batter me, so on the last night I took my wig off, shouted: "So you think you're clever?" and got them back. I threw them all off the stage. That'll teach them, messing with a poof. But they had the last laugh. They emptied my dressing room, filled it with smoke and put police tape all around it, as if it was a crime scene. Billy and Stan may have wound me up, but there's one co-star that puts them to shame when it comes to winding me up. He tries to lick you, has bad breath and steals every scene off you. Schnorbitz the dog.

In one scene in Jack and the Beanstalk, I got changed by magic into Schnorbitz. That involved crouching with him in a confined space. Two things stick in my mind from this. One, he had a wind problem. Two, I was allergic to the bloody thing.

Jane Joseph is responsible for bringing panto back to Liverpool – apart from the Everyman Theatre's annual show, no one had been doing it for a while. And through my friendship with her I've got into thinking up ideas for the shows. She's a

generous producer and director, so if you come up with something that works, she'll put it in. I worked my way up the cast list in her pantos, and ended up topping the bill several times.

We brought the slapstick "slosh scene" back to Liverpool, where people pour paste over each other. I was working with Roy Brandon, who's a veteran of panto. We had so much fun, we were like kids playing,

although it was all scripted carefully.

There was a problem though. We could never get the consistency of the slosh right. It was either too thick or thin. One night I saw him holding the bucket – there was steam coming off it. He had to pour it into my hat so it would squirt 10ft into the air through a hole in the top. But when he poured it, the hat started to melt with the heat. "He isn't going to put that on my head," I thought. But he did. Another night they'd put too much red colouring in it, and I was pink for days afterwards. Everyone was standing at the sides of the stage, wetting themselves.

Jane asked me who I'd like to play my other sister in Cinderella and I suggested the comic Mickey Finn. He'd always wanted to be an ugly sister and he was thrilled. Except just the sight of him in drag cracked me up and made it nearly impossible to work. Especially when he walked on as a Christmas pudding and I walked on as a Christmas tree, complete with flashing lights.

One panto I'll never forget was Aladdin, when I played the laughing policeman. I was appearing with my mate Kev Seed, and had been for a few drinks after the show in the Living Room. I walked round the corner of Whitechapel and, from nowhere, someone punched me in the face and knocked me out. All I remember is someone saying: "You do know who you've just hit?"

They never caught who it was. I'd just done an interview about the new CCTV cameras in the centre of Liverpool, but guess what? They weren't working that night.

I had a broken cheekbone, but nothing would stop me going on stage that night. Kev had mentioned the attack on his show, and I had 300 cards waiting for me. A doorman from the area said to me: "Pricey, I'm not gay, but if you find out who did that, a load of us are going to take him up to Snowdon and leave him at the top without his legs to walk back. How does that grab you, Pricey?"

And finally, there's the kid who made my life a misery one year when I was in Snow White. A seven-year-old mini crime wave. We think they'd lifted his asbo so he could come and see us. It started with the boiled sweets. This kid was chucking them at me from the first row and he was an impressive shot.

Then we did the ghost scene, where the kids are supposed to shout "He's behind you."

This kid was running about frantically, shouting: "He's behind you!"

"Where?" I said, teasing them.

"Behind you!"

"Where?"

"Behind you!"

"Where?"

"I've just fuckin' told you!" he shouted, and everyone in the audience cracked up.

Later that night, when the prince was holding Snow White in his arms, he looked in to the audience and said: "What should I do, kids?" They're supposed to shout: "Kiss her," but this kid wouldn't have done anything so tame.

"Shag her!" he bellowed.

Since I started panto, I've also been in a play – the only one I've ever done. It was called Slappers and Slapheads, produced by Kevin Fearon, and it started off in the Royal Court in Liverpool, and transferred to the Palace Theatre in Manchester. I thought it was a hilarious play, full of great writing, and I played the DJ at a club based loosely on a notorious Liverpool nightclub. The plot, showing how a group of characters' relationships intertwine, was brilliantly clever and it got great reviews.

I'd come in 15 minutes before and start playing records, insulting the audience as they came in. Then they play started and I was one of the characters. I kept saying "I've got to go, I've got to go" before leaving in the end of the first act to do my real-life show on radio. I never saw how it ended, and eventually they videoed it for me to watch.

But there's one performance I'm proudest of out of everything. It saw me fulfil the ambition of a lifetime, and I still can't quite believe it happened.

Think about all those nights dying on my arse in the early days and you'll realise how much it meant to me. I got a gig at the London Palladium.

For all my childhood I'd dreamed of being on that stage. I'd heard about performances there by Judy Garland, Ella Fitzgerald, Bing Crosby, Marvin Gaye and Frank Sinatra. Years ago, if you got a spot at the Palladium, you were a star overnight.

I had a 20-minute slot, supporting Joe Longthorne for a charity concert. Backstage it was a dump, but Mickey Finn had told me what would happen when I walked on. "You'll forget where you are, and just stand there, thinking of every person who's walked on before you," he said. My set went better than I could have hoped. I went into the packed audience to watch Joe after I'd finished, and I've never seen him better than he was that night. He's just had the all clear from cancer as I write this, but he's still very frail and I'm thinking about him all the time. I thank him from the bottom of my heart for filling one of my lifelong ambitions.

After the concert I drove back to Wirral, but I don't remember a minute of the drive. I must have been daydreaming all the way, on cloud nine.

The Palladium gig was a charity function, and through the years I've always tried to help out when I can, ever since I started in show business, from mum's lesson that you should always put something back. In that time I've seen a hell of a lot of artists giving their time and cash without making a big thing of it.

But Bob taught me an important lesson. "Adopt one charity, and concentrate on that one," he said. "Put all your energies into it." I knew how many people he secretly helped, so he didn't exactly follow his own rule, but it was good advice.

I chose Claire House in Wirral. Wendy Darlington and her husband John got me into it, and as soon as I saw it I knew this was the place I wanted to help. As a children's hospice, it helps everyone under 18 with a condition that is either life-threatening or life-limiting. And it must raise a staggering £1,440,000 a year to keep going, all by itself.

The first time I was invited to the hospice, I was frightened of going in. A lot of people are, until they've actually seen Claire House. But inside it's the most loving, amazing place you would imagine. Little old ladies see me in the street and give me £10 or £20, which always knocks me for six.

A few years ago I was hosting a charity event called An Audience with Claire Sweeney, which was in aid of the Sparkling Star Appeal for the teenage wing of Claire House – which is now open (and by the way Claire is our wonderful president).

A day at the races with Claire's mum and Tony

There I met Coleen McLoughlin for the first time. Her sister Rosie, who has Rett Syndrome, goes to Claire House for respite, and she's been a phenomenal supporter. Coleen did great work publicising the plight of children's hospices through her documentary with Trevor McDonald that featured Rosie.

I was doing an auction and Wayne and Coleen were both bidding – for the same thing. I let the money go up a bit then shouted out: "You do know you're bidding against one another, you soft sods!" They both roared with laughter.

Claire, meanwhile, was brilliant. I'd known her growing up, and since becoming a big star, she's never changed. And lots of people love her just for being herself.

That night, with just 300 people, we managed to raise £80,000 at auction. Then Peter Johnson came up to us at the end and said he'd been so touched by the night he wanted to match it, making it £160,000 in a night. I was so proud.

PETE
PRICE SHOW

STOPPER

DAVID LEE for PANTO PANTOMIMES in association with METROPOLITAN BOROUGH OF WIRRAL

Fri 22nd Dec 2006 to Sun 14th Jan 2007

SUZANNE COLLINS (Nikki Shadwick from BROOKSIDE) AS

Pete Price ("Don't Pull The Rope!") as Buttons
radiocity967

Cinderella
A Spectacular Family Pantomime

Jo Arnold as Fairy Godmother
Keith French as Dandini
and Full Supporting Cast
Lucken's Miniature
Shetland Ponies & Coach
The Liverpool Theatre School
The Rita Proctor Teensteppers

MR. MEN

Returned by
Public Demand

Roy Brandon

Pauline Daniels
As The Wicked Baroness

GLITTERING
SCENERY AND COS...

Directed by Brian Marshall
Written by David Lee
Musical Director Eric White
Choreography by Rita Proctor

NO INCREASE IN SEAT...
SPECIAL PARTY RA...

Above: People ask me who Buttons is – he's the boy next door that never married and people always wonder why. The sad thing is, Cinders could have had me – her loss! As for Pauline Daniels, I always loved the line she used when somebody shouted: "He's behind you," and she replied "Oh it's only Pete Price, I'm perfectly safe." I'll get you one day, Miss Daniels.

Crowa Productions proudly presents

Snow White
AND THE SEVEN DWARFS

at the Royal Court Theatre, Liverpool
from December 23rd 2003 to January 18th 2004

Liverpool's most lavish and spectacular family pantomim...

Tickets from
£3.50
Family tickets from
£20.00

DARREN MIDDLETON
as the Wicked Queen

PETER PRICE
as Muddles

LEANNE CAMPBELL
as Fairy Liquid

LOUIS HURST
Radio City presenter as Ethelred the Henchman

and
MAX RUBIN
as Prince Regent

SUZANNE COLLINS
(Brookside's Nicki Shadwick)
as Snow White

featuring by popular demand
'The Twelve Days of Christmas'

ROY BRANDON
as Dame Nursie

magic...

Above: The sister
Herbert never had

Right: I told you to
take the label out
of the shoe!

Who is my inspiration for the make-up?
Bette Davis? Joan Crawford? Cruella
de Vil? Bet Lynch? Barbara Cartland?
Trinny and Susannah? Dot Cotton?
Margaret Thatcher? Edwina Currie?
Anne Robinson? Janet Street Porter?
All wrong. It was... Vera Duckworth!

Crown Productions Proudly Presents

magic 1548

Master of Illusion
Richard
De Vere
as FLESHCREEP

Brookside's Ali Gordon
Kris Mochrie
as JACK

Radio City 96.7/
Magic 1548
Pete Price
as SIMPLE SIMON

Tickets from
£3.50
Family tickets
from
£20.00

JACK and the
Beanstalk!

The one and only...
Schnorbitz

At The Royal Court Theatre, Liverpool
From 22 Dec 2004 - 16 Jan 2005

Liverpool's most lavish and
spectacular Pantomime

Liverpool's top comic
Mickey Finn
as OLD KING COLE

From Channel 4's Court Room
Chantelle
Joseph
as PRINCESS JILL

Roy
Brandon
as DAME TROTT

Produced and Directed by Jane Brown
Choreographed by Beverley Norrie-Edmunds
Musical Director Ian Rowlands
Student and Junior Dancers from
Dolphin Dance Studios, Liverpool

Marc Lawlor
as THE SPIRIT OF
THE BEANSTALK

Royal Court Liverpool
1 Roe Street, Liverpool

Would you believe they came on in the middle of the pantomime, live on stage, to ask me to move my car? The stage hands had set me up. The audience was in hysterics.

Why I love pantomime so much. People all year round, young and old, shout to me: "Don't pull the rope, leave the rope alone" which is my catchphrase. Pantomime is so important because it's the first taste of theatre for many children. That experience stays with them for the rest of their lives. The only problem is, how do you explain an ugly man wearing a frock?

Here I am playing Dame Claire Voyant.
Which reminds me of the time I visited a
fortune teller in Blackpool. She looked
deeply into the crystal ball and said:
"Your sex life is going to change."
God was she right. The ball rolled off the
table, hit me in the bollocks and I was
laid up for two days.

Leanne Campbell, who played Cinders, was my bezzie mate and she annoys me. She arrives on the first day of rehearsal for every pantomime, word-perfect. The consummate professional. I based my character on Jade Goody and every misguided woman who gets up in the morning, leaves her pyjamas on, never washes, goes down to the shops, cooks the tea, watches Coronation Street, scratches her bits and then goes back to bed in the same pyjamas

DAVID LEE for PANTONI PANTOMIMES in association with METROPOLITAN BOROUGH OF WIRRAL

Sat 17th Dec 2005 to Sun 8th Jan 2006

Scott Wright
(Coronation Street's Sam Kingston and Celebrity Holiday Reps)
as Aladdin

Pete Price
("Don't Pull The Rope!")
as Wishee Washee

radiocity967 magic

ALADDIN
and His Wonderful Lamp

Roy Brandon
as Widow Twankey

Neil Collet
as Emperor
The Liverpool Theatre School
Rita Procter Teensteppers

Jo Arnold
as Princess
Carina Gillespie
as The Slave of The Ring

Peter Edbrook
as Abanazer

A Magical Family Pantomime

Musical Director Eric White
Written & Directed by David Lee
Choreography by Rita Procter

Floral Pavilion Theatre
NEW BRIGHTON

CHAPTER TWENTY SEVEN

cranks, pranks,
and a night on the radio

I NEVER stop being amazed at what kids think is funny. They seem to be on a mission to send me seething into my grave. I thought I'd give you a taste of what I have to put up with on a daily basis, so what follows is a diary of one night on radio: Thursday May 31, 2007.

In between the entries are a few of the best prank calls. If they give you a taste for hearing me get tortured by the listeners, you can download more at www.radiocity.co.uk – not that I need to tell most of you braindead people that.

9.30am

I wake up and every morning I say: "Good morning world", kiss my mum's photo and think about my lovely boss, Richard Maddock, for giving me this incredible chance on Radio City.

I can't sleep in like I used to be able to, when mum would keep the shop quiet. After a bit I'll phone Jay Hynd to talk about what we both need to do for the show.

Jay's now 25, and has been working on the show for four-and-a-half years now, starting off just answering the phones, but becoming a fully fledged producer.

He tells me he was wary of me when he was on work experience at the station and would see me walking through. "You'd always be dead loud," he says.

PETE PRICE

Caller: I was with my girlfriend, we was having a little party in town, we went out for me girlfriend's sister's do like.

And I'd fancied me girlfriend's mate for a while, like, and what it was, was I snuck off with her to have a bit of, er, nookie, shall we say on the radio. And, er, went back to this car park. I don't think I should say the car park.

Pete: (wary) No, don't say the car park.

Caller: Anyway, we went into this multi-storey car park and I was getting it on in her car, basically. And what happened was I was on CCTV. From the car park. And... and they filmed everything. And what it was was, it was my girlfriend's cousin who works at the car park, and I didn't know.

Pete: (in disbelief) Hang on. Let me get this straight. You fancied your girlfriend's mate. You decided to sneak off, go into a car park, have a bit of nookie, and it was on CCTV?

Caller: Yeah, and that was how I got caught. Because it was my girlfriend's cousin who was working in the car park.

Pete: So your girlfriend's cousin's got a copy of you, having a bit of nookie with your girlfriend's best mate? In the car park?

Caller: Yeah and now all the family know. And, you know, I don't mind a bit of fame, but I don't want my family to know nothing like that.

Pete: Well, are they selling DVDs?

Caller: I don't know, she's passing it round all her mates and all kinds. She's finished with me now, like, but...

Pete: Well dare I ask, I mean, apart from the car rocking, did we see much else.?

Caller: Well, erm, you know we did get out the car and go round, like – I mean you can't just stay in there can you? It gets a bit hot.

Pete: Pardon? You're telling me you had sex outside the car as well as inside the car?

Caller: Well, you've got to, like – you know what I mean? On the bonnet and all that? It's what the ladies like. I thought they wouldn't have been able to see you, because it was on the 11th floor or something like that.

I mean, I'd fancied her for ages. It's not as though it was a one-night stand, like.

Pete: It wasn't a one-night stand, it was a stand on the front of the car, against the bonnet and the back of the car, and inside the car.

Caller: (Laughs) I know mate. And I honestly do regret it, like. But that's my 15 minutes of fame, anyway.

12pm
Jay gets into work and does work on the show – he might be phoning round for guests, doing research, or putting together packages. He might bob downstairs and do a few vox-pops – quick interviews with people on the street – to get listeners talking about a subject.
Meanwhile I'm ringing him every half an hour with ideas. I'm constantly thinking about the show, even carrying a dictaphone with me so I can record ideas.

Caller: (German accent) I was out with a few friends of mine in town. Had a great time, we had a few drinks. And afterwards I couldn't get a taxi so walked ahead. I was walking for about 20 minutes or something and then the street lights around me, they just went out and then I blacked out and woke up, what, 10 minutes later and I'm in a spaceship.

And when I tried to escape, I befriended an alien. He would like to speak to you. (Makes weird noise. Pete hangs up).

9pm
   Jay and I get into the Radio City tower – an hour before, like in the theatre – to work on that night's show. I've had a nap in the afternoon – if I don't get my nap I get grumpy – and then watched Channel 4 News or a bit of Sky News, writing down what's going on that listeners will want to talk about. Tonight, a Thursday, is the last show of the week, so we're doing a light-hearted programme on the Battle of the Sexes. I've lined up comedian and actress Pauline Daniels as a guest, who's bound to come out with lots of funny lines, along with old hands Scott Hughes and Claire Murrow from City who should bicker nicely.

Caller – Mark: About this bird flu, what are the symptoms?

Pete: Well, what they're worried about in this country is that it's going to mutate to be caught from human to human.

Mark: So what are the chances of it coming over here?

Pete: Well, they're worried about it mutating from human to human.

Mark: Well, I had a chicken in my oven tonight and… I think I caught it.

Pete: (realises it's a wind-up) With a bit of luck, you could die. Goodbye.

9.55pm

I sit down in the studio. In front of me are three screens – one showing the calls Jay has cued up, another showing the emails and texts and a third showing that night's running order and also the websites. Then there's all my radio equipment. I'm amazed I can work it all (not all the time though). I've got a load of emails to wade through, and soon they'll start coming thick and fast from listeners. On a busy night, we'll get up to 800 emails and 200 texts. But they can also post messages on my forum, or on Radio City's website, or ring me on my personal mobile. There's no escape.

Jay is in the room next door, and we can see each other through two glass windows. I'm scribbling ideas as we count down to the news. I haven't got nervous before the show for years now – I feel so at home on air, I know I'll be able to get round any little mishaps that happen. Jay calls it my old-fashioned showbiz attitude: I'm always shouting: "The show must go on!" whenever we're up against it.

We can speak to each other in the middle of a call – I just push one button to turn off my microphone so it doesn't go out over the radio, and another to talk to him. With a minute to go, my mind goes blank and I have to ask him Scott's surname.

"Hughes."

"Thanks."

Then I have the idea of cueing up It's Raining Men to fit the programme's theme. I tell Jay and he obviously doesn't like it. We shoot each other evil looks.

"Why It's Raining Men?"

"Because It's the Battle of the Sexes, Jay."
"That doesn't work."
I hear the jingle introducing the show and do it anyway.
And then I'm off, talking at 100mph: "Good evening and welcome to the programme, it's the last one of the week.
 "It's called the battle of the sexes: who works harder? Who is the breadwinner in your house…"

Caller – James: I said to my friend I've got a thing about Peter Price by the way.

Pete: What?

James: I said I've got a thing about Peter Price. I said, he's a verbal bully.

Pete: Can I ask you something? Why do you listen to my show, James? Why do you not just, after tonight, switch off and never listen to me again?

James: 'Cause I've got to listen..

Pete: No, but you'd do us both a favour James.

James: Bully, Peter. You're a verbal bully.

Pete: Right James. I'm going to say something to you now. I am a verbal bully. You've heard me say it, James. Now will you get of the line and will you not ever ring me again? And will you not listen to my show?

James: I'll tell you what. I will finish with you tonight.

Pete: Please do.

James: I will

Pete: Please do. Please never, ever, ever, ever, ever ring me again. Never speak to me again. And do me a favour, never listen to the show again. Please, James. Promise me. Promise me you'll never ever speak to me again.

James: (Pause) Can I have me say then?

11pm
After a quiet start, the calls start coming in thick and fast. At our busiest, we can be getting 300 a minute.

Jay says sometimes he feels there are two separate phone-ins going on, one in his room, one in mine. He's speaking to them asking what kind of point they're going to make and trying to work out what kind of character they are.

By now he knows what's going to wind me up and wind up other listeners, to make sure the show stays lively. And he knows that on a typical night I don't like too many prank calls, but a few keep me on my toes. So sometimes he'll pretend he doesn't know someone is phoning with a wind-up. Sometimes, of course, he'll know very well. And then there are the nights when we just say: "It's one of those shows – let's have a row," and it's open season.

Pete: See, unfortunately, everybody across the North West – and this is a plea – you know I normally say we don't get calls and it's quiet? Well tonight, I'm telling you, it's absolutely mental. Right? We're mental tonight. With children. Thick, stupid children. And it's a full moon.

I need adults to ring me, please, please. (Despairing) You know, I could be on the ships working doing cabaret – one show a week, earning more money than I'm getting now. Please, just adult conversation. I'm begging you. I'll buy you all a nice tea.

(Screaming) FRIGGING RING ME! Get these crapping kids off my phone.

11.15pm
I start swearing when something goes wrong.

"You've just sworn on air," Jay says to me over the intercom. I panic and press the delay button, which wipes out the last eight seconds.

Then he tells me it was a wind-up. I make a mental note to get him back.

Caller – Rita (a regular who thinks her phone is being tapped): "…I can't tell you on these lines what's going on in my life, because I'm not prepared to put myself to the critical ignoramuses that listen to your phone in. Not all of them – there's a lot of good people listen to your phone in, but I'm not going into it all because I'll be putting myself in danger, don't you understand Pete?

Pete: I think, Rita, you're just an ordinary person, and…

Rita: …No, you don't understand what's going on in my life…

Pete: Rita, I know for a fact you're an ordinary person. I've checked up on you myself. I spoke to your sister.

Rita: She has racist views.

Pete: Rita, you said you'd been tapped.

Rita: We're all being tapped.

Pete: (Wearily) But Rita, who are you? You're nothing. With the greatest respect, you're nothing….

Rita: …I just want to tell you…

Pete: you're nothing Rita. You're delusional. (Sighs) Oh Rita, why would anyone tap your phone? You're just an ordinary lady who rings phone-ins. You're not in a political party.

Rita: I am in a political party, Pete. You don't know.

Pete: Every time you ring up and say you're being tapped, people ring up and say: "The woman's delusional." And it makes a nonsense of your call…

12pm
It's time for the Peaceful Hour. The phone-in has been all right this evening, although many more men than women have been ringing in, and there's the usual truckload of people queuing up to give me homophobic abuse.
One man's rang up with a nice line: "This is sexual discrimination, Pricey. If a man talks dirty to a woman, it's sexual intimidation. But if a woman talks dirty to a man, it's £3.50 a minute."

Caller: I was in Walton Hospital about nine years ago with a chest infection. And I was in there for about five weeks because they couldn't find what'd caused my chest infection. So I was on the antibiotics.

And it was lovely weather, you know, April and May? And I used to sunbathe on the island. You know, Walton Hospital by the clock? And I used to be there in a pair of shorts. And the doctor used to come out, you know with the shot with the antibiotics while I was sunbathing on the Island.

And also we used to go on a pub crawl when I was getting better, on Rice Lane. And we used to take fish 'n' chips back for the nurses and everybody.

Pete: On a pub crawl?

Caller: Yeah.

Pete: You're off your head.

1am
Pat Crawford comes on for our weekly chat about the soaps. I ask her how long we've been doing it tonight, and she tells me 18 years – and, congratulations, she's just become a grandmother.

It's one of the features of the show – another one is a weekly call to Angie and Ruth McCartney in Hollywood.

Pat is still a telly addict, but she used to be even worse. When UK Gold came along, her problem got out of control – she'd go away for a week, and ask her friends to tape everything for her. Then she'd have 300 hours to catch up on. I remember once years ago I arranged a tour of the Brookside studios for her birthday.

Caller: If an African Elephant was put in India, and gave birth to an African baby elephant, would that be an Indian elephant because it was born in India? That's an analogy. No, it goes back by your roots Peter. I'm not being racist.

Pete: [starts to laugh]

Caller: No, I'm not, Peter.

2am
The show is over, and we tidy up and get off home. We're talking about summer concerts, and Jay reminds me of this story. A few years ago, Radio City had organised a huge, free open air concert for 40,000 people at the cricket

club in Allerton, with big acts like Ronan Keating playing.

One of the groups, Honeyz, were sitting backstage, moaning about doing the gig. I was due to bring them on wearing a ridiculously over-the-top luminous tracksuit, a joke as I normally slag off people who wear trackies with their socks tucked in.

"Excuse me," one of them said, tapping me on the shoulder. "Excuse me, excuse me."

"Yes?"

She sighed: "Could we have some water on stage, please?"

I looked at her, fuming. "What do you want water for, you're only miming anyway – water?"

Jay and I are knackered, and I get in the car and drive to the Birkenhead tunnel. Another week over.

Sitting in my car, I wonder who was listening tonight.

The show's got some unlikely fans. A couple of years back, Jay told me: "Peter Kay wants to come on the show." "Oh get a life Jay," I said. Obviously I thought it was a wind up, but it was really him.

"No honestly," Jay replied. "He's driving home, after being on the summer pops."

I was amazed. "You're joking. Not Peter Kay."

It turns out Peter loves late-night phone-ins and he can pick up City from Bolton. He's a radio anorak, even making tapes of the show, which bowled me over as, obviously, I'm totally in awe of his stand-up routine.

Then one day he rang to ask if he could use a clip of him on my show as part of his DVD, Live at the Manchester Arena. "Oh alright then", I laughed. I was ecstatic. I thought to myself: Oh my god. Peter Kay wants me on his DVD.

Peter did a send-up of the interview – they're in the back of a limo with our chat playing in the background.

Sally Lindsay from Coronation Street is miming along to

my voice and he's miming along to his. Since then he's been a guest on the show a few times, and it's always great to have him on.

One of my favourite calls, which I now use as a gag in my act, happened on Evening Encounters, a 90s dating show that led to 10 weddings:

Caller: Hello. I'm very lonely.

Pete: Tell me about yourself. Have you got any hobbies?

Caller: (In a weedy voice) Garden gnomes.

Pete: Garden gnomes?

Caller: I've got 43, and they're my friends. And we take them in at night because they get upset if we leave them out.

Pete: All right, you're scaring me now. Can you shut up about the gnomes?

Caller: No – love me, love my gnomes!

Pete: Ok, tell me, what do you look like.

Caller: Well, I'm 5ft 1in...

Pete: (cracking up) Please tell me you haven't got a red hat and a fishing rod?

(Caller hangs up.)

Next caller:
All right Pricey,
That last lad you had on
– do you think
he was a
gnome-a-sexual?

CHAPTER TWENTY EIGHT
the biggest chump on Merseyside

I WAS sitting at home, and the phone started ringing from Australia, Egypt, Canada. Julian Russell from St Tropez. They were all saying the same thing: "Have you seen the banner? Put your telly on."

It was two years ago, and Liverpool FC had reached the final of the Champions' League in Istanbul.

On TV in the crowd was an enormous banner some fans had made, to take to Turkey. It said…well, I'm going to substitute "chump" for what it said from now on, to spare the more sensitive of you. So it said: "Pete Price is a Chump."

Then they'd got it onto the news, and the poor old cameraman had to keep moving position so the reporter's head would cover it up. Except the people holding it kept moving, too. It was hilarious.

Someone found me the mobile number of the guy who made it, and I rang him out of the blue.

"I suppose I'm flattered," I said. "But what made you do it?"

"Well, Pricey," he began, "I'm from Huyton. A group of us were in the pub talking about making a banner, and I asked: 'Who is the biggest chump in Merseyside?'"

He paused. "And everyone said you."

I cracked up. Since then, the "Pete Price is a Chump" banner has followed the team everywhere – all around Europe.

At the age of 61, the strangest thing is happening to me.

I think I'm becoming an institution. I can't remember the first time someone used the word to describe me, but it's a strange feeling – especially when, like me, you try not to act your age.

Turning 60 was horrible. I'd been all right at 50 – in fact we had a fantastic night. I hired out Rupert's and decided to recreate the club as it was 20 years ago. I invited people who'd been important over the years, and didn't tell anyone who else was coming. The Wilsons flew in from Spain to surprise me.

Then I got the same doorman who had been there 20 years ago. I'd got in champagne for everyone, but drinks on the bar were at 1976 prices. All the DJs who had ever worked at Rupert's were there and at the end of the night I did a set. I finished with the Gang Bang, a dance I'd started all those years ago but the people made the night.

But my 60th couldn't have been more different. I went abroad and sulked on my own. I hated the sound of it: "sixty". But I'm over it now.

My 60th birthday card

Look on the website YouTube and you can listen to prank calls teenagers have done on the show, set to music with visuals. They should really be doing their homework instead of spending hours messing around on their computers like that. The forum on my website is always buzzing with debates about whatever's happening that week. And, if you really want, you can have me saying "I'll knock you out!" as your mobile phone ringtone. You have to text KO to a number to get it, as in knock out, which doesn't seem too complicated. Except one bright spark texted "Kay Oh" instead.

When I go into nightclubs with friends these days, all the kids seem to want pictures on their phone with me. It always takes me by surprise, although I'd be lying if I said I didn't love the attention. That's what I've worked for!

Last autumn a 20-year dream came true for me. Out of the blue Alastair Machray, the editor of the Liverpool Echo, offered me a column in the paper.

Ali may be as nice a journalist as you could hope to meet, but he wasn't giving it to me out of the goodness of his heart. The Echo team had done some research among their readers and I was the person the public wanted. "I told you so," I thought. Editor after editor had knocked me back for that column. But I think I'm in a pretty good position to write it – how many other columnists spend 20 hours a week listening to what's bugging ordinary people in the region?

In the first one I defended Wayne and Coleen, and since then I've written about all my pet hates, told stories and slagged off people who get on my nerves. That means people who eat in the cinema, girls who spend all day wandering the streets in their pyjamas, scroungers who take the mickey at work Christmas dos, grooms who give wedding DJs lists of what they want playing and people who go too far at hen nights. After years of doing my regular Friday night Karaoke gig at Rubber Soul, I wrote an article about the worst sort of singer who turns up, hogging the mike, getting competitive and always singing the same songs. The headline in the Echo read: "My Way or the highway."

The first time I had a go at Jordan, though, I made the mistake of putting a photo of me grinning next to her underneath the article. All week people were phoning me up and asking why I was slagging her off then posing with her.

I didn't really have an answer.

Underneath each article, I give my personal mobile number, in case anyone wants to phone up – just like I do on my show. It's usually a mix of people giving me an earful and saying "good on you", but the balance depends on what I've written about that week.

I've stayed in the same flat since I bought it all those years ago, and recently I achieved a long-standing ambition and bought another property – the flat next door. Imagine the price difference. Now, though, I've no idea what to do with it. I suppose I'm just too used to having everything where it is, but I'll sort it out eventually.

The other day I was asked to give a talk on the Wirral for visiting dignitaries. They asked to see what I was going to say. I thought: "I've lived here all my life, and I've been giving people guided tours for 40-odd years." I loved doing it (not least because the pay was brilliant).

It gets better. Twice now, I've been to dinner with Merseyside's Chief Constable, Bernard Hogan Howe, whom I get on with like a house on fire. Sitting between him and Ali Machray at one of the fancy functions, I did a double-take.

When did the big-mouthed, screamingly camp compere from the Shakespeare become so respectable?

It hasn't been a bad year for parties, even if I say so myself. At Christmas, I went to Ozzy and Sharon's bash. Everyone from Elton John down was there – the lads from Little Britain, Paul O'Grady… and Chico, whom I'd slagged off. Sharon introduced him to me, saying: "Say hello to Peter, Chico. Peter tell him what you said about him."

I told him. He gave me a big wet kiss and said: "Peter, people like you are keeping me alive." Sharon even let me get round the camera ban at the end and take a couple of pictures.

Then there was Coleen McLoughlin's 21st birthday party at Thornton Manor. People were ringing me up offering me thousands for my ticket to that one. Inside it was pink vintage Champagne all night, food from around the world and music from the Sugababes. Afterwards one of the special cupcakes with her face on sold on eBay for a huge sum of money.

But what made it really special was that it was just a traditional party, as only Scousers know how to throw. Coleen had just published her book, which has become a massive hit – goodness knows what that girl will do next. When I see how successful both her and Wayne have been, I say it's down to their families and they are so in love.

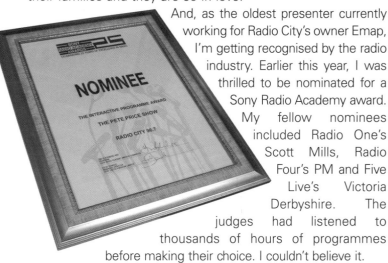

And, as the oldest presenter currently working for Radio City's owner Emap, I'm getting recognised by the radio industry. Earlier this year, I was thrilled to be nominated for a Sony Radio Academy award. My fellow nominees included Radio One's Scott Mills, Radio Four's PM and Five Live's Victoria Derbyshire. The judges had listened to thousands of hours of programmes before making their choice. I couldn't believe it.

At the show, someone interviewing me for another station tried to set me up, sneering: "Do people in Liverpool make a lot of crank calls, then?"

I held my ground and told him all the stories in here, about the power of radio to make a difference to people's lives. Terry Wogan made a joke about my direct phone to the listeners. He said: "What a strange man, a phone to the listeners?" I didn't win, but I'll keep entering.

I'd been preparing for the 29th anniversary of mum's death. Then, a few days before, someone pointed out it was actually the 30th – a milestone. I told you I was rubbish with dates. It's always hard, but this year I felt I'd coped better.

Maybe getting everything down about her on paper has helped but, God I still miss her.

The next 12 months are looking like the most exciting for a long time. As I finish this book, City are finishing their plans for an all-talk radio station, which I'll be involved in. They're trying out new presenters, and I know it's going to be a big hit.

After we finished this year's pantomime, Stan Boardman said it was great how I was helping keep the tradition alive. He paid me a huge compliment by adding I was becoming Mr Panto for Liverpool. I've been signed up for Cinderella at the Royal Court for December 2007, working with Jane again. I can't wait to get

the script, and start trying, and failing, to learn my lines.

Then we're into 2008, Liverpool's big year. Maybe I'll be back at the New Brighton theatre?

When will I retire, people ask me? I always say: "Hopefully never." I want to go on working until I collapse on stage – if I die in the same manner as Tommy Cooper, I'll be delighted. My job on radio should be safe while I'm still pulling in big ratings and, if I can fit it in, I'll still travel anywhere in the world for a gig.

Sisters, sisters, there were never more two devoted sisters (Jane Joseph)

I hear of big-name comics cancelling tours because they don't feel like going onstage and I go mad. How can they not want to work packed theatres, making people laugh? It's the best job on earth.

Getting my picture taken with a star still gives me as much of a thrill as when I was snapped with Sandie Shaw all those years ago.

A card from a friend performing halfway across the world still makes my day. And the thing about show business is everyone is travelling round so much, you can just pick up friendships where they left off.

The other day I met Lenny Henry for the first time in 20 years and he threw his arms round me and sang the opening number to my act, word for word, from all those years ago. I wish I had a memory like that.

And finally, for the past two years, the banner's been going strong. Alan, who made it, rang me just before Liverpool went to Athens for the 2007 Champion's League final.

"Well, Pricey, it's that time of year again."

I sighed. "What's it going to say this time?"

He wasn't sure. A lot of fans had turned on Liverpool Chief Executive Rick Parry over match tickets, so he was thinking about "Rick Parry is an even bigger chump than Pete Price." But in the end, they decided to keep it simple, and go with: "After two years, Pete Price is still a chump.'"

Which leaves me with only one reaction, and that's to say the same thing I've said at the end of my act for the past 35 years.

"Thank you very much, ladies and gentlemen. You've been a challenge – and you've won."

It's official – my show is the best in the world!
As this book goes to press, I am over the
moon to announce that I have won gold in
the New York Radio Festival Awards 2007
– the Oscars of the radio world – for Talk
Show of the Year.

CHAPTER TWENTY NINE

I told you a lie

IT'S a weekday afternoon in April and my head's spinning from another clear out of old photos for the book.

I knock on the door of the house in South Liverpool I've been secretly visiting all these years, and my real mother – the elderly woman whose name I can't give – opens the door. Her face brightens when she sees it's me.

She tells me she's proud of my column in the Echo and cuts each one out to keep.

"I'm so sorry I gave you away" she's said to me a hundred times; "You'll never know how hard it was." She remarried, but never had children.

We chat about the usual sorts of things. And then, out of the blue, she tells me more than she has ever told me before.

But I'm jumping ahead of myself. This last part of the story really begins in 1997. It's years since mum died and I'd found my real mother living in South Liverpool. I had been trying to trace my birth father for years, and the search had got nowhere. I had hired a private detective in America to look for him. Could the badges on his shoulder narrow it down by saying what regiment he was in? Could they work out who would have been in that part of England at that time? Nothing had worked yet. Who was this Polish-American GI with the good head of hair and the face, like mine, older than his years? She'd kept the photo all those years.

I decided to get the media involved. I was in talks with Oprah Winfrey's people to go on the show and put an appeal out. I had written to newspapers aimed at America's Polish community. Then I contacted a production company in Britain. It was making a show with Esther Rantzen about war babies, called Lovechild. We arranged to go on and we filmed the show.

I rang up my birth mother to warn her I was doing this.

"Don't watch TV," I said. "I think it might upset you." I told her about the show, saying I wouldn't give her identity away but I needed to know who this man was and if he was still alive.

She broke down over the phone. "I'm so sorry," she said. "I told you a lie."

"What?"

"It's about your father."

"What about him?"

"He's not a Polish GI."

I was gobsmacked. "What do you mean? I've had detectives looking for him, I've written to all these people." She carried on crying.

"Don't get upset," I said. "Just tell me who my father is."

Then she told me: he wasn't a Polish American GI – he was on the other side. He was an Italian prisoner of war, originally from Sicily.

My birth mother had been stationed at the camp in Burtonwood, near Warrington, and they had got involved with each other towards the end of the war. It was a one-night stand.

He had left, not even knowing that she was pregnant – she had been whisked off to Wrexham in North Wales to have me so no one would know.

The first thing that popped into my head was: "That's where the nose came from." Then I thought how much I liked pizza and pasta. There I had been for all these years, looking at a picture and thinking it was a completely different person.

I decided not to start the search all over again. It might be unfair, but I'm not sure what a traditional Sicilian family would really make of me. He might be alive or might not, but he'll never know I exist. I went there on holiday and gave my birth mother the fright of her life by ringing her from Palermo as a surprise and said: "I've found my dad." She dropped the phone. It was good to know where my roots were. How many more Italians about my age are there running around Cheshire and Wirral – and how many Brits in Germany?

A lot of people are more naïve than you think about having children. Once, I had a woman on my show who was giving birth and didn't know where it was coming from. We managed to get her help in time.

So anyway, there I was round at her house in April. And this time, she told me the full story of how she gave me up for adoption – the story I'd never known. I'd spent my life telling the story about the £300 fur coat.

She had been a corporal in the RAF over here, she said, and her superior officers had shipped her off to Wrexham in North Wales to have the baby. It was all hushed up, as what she'd done was considered a disgrace. She said she was in her early 20s and it was the hardest thing to do.

I nearly grew up knowing her, she told me. Her sister had just adopted a baby herself and told her if I had been born a bit earlier, she would have adopted me.

The day she gave me away is still clear in her mind, she said. She came down with her sister, and they met mum and my auntie. "I couldn't understand why your dad wasn't there," she told me.

Then, when it was all over, she had confessed to her own mother – my birth grandmother. She was very frail and it had broken her heart.

"You realise," she had told her daughter, "You'll never see him again. That will be the hardest part. And I will never hold him."

A month had passed and Hilda had let her come to see me once, even though she wasn't supposed to.

She went up to my bedroom and took a look at her son with the blond curls. Then, there was no contact until Paul knocked on her door all those years later. She told me her stomach had been in knots when she saw me for the first time. She couldn't believe how similar we were, she said. Oddly, she probably met Auntie Mac's husband many times, as they both worked for the same person around the same time. Typical Liverpool.

Things aren't easy with my birth mother, but we're trying to make it work. All her life she had never told anyone about me. When I went to visit her in hospital recently, I was amazed to find out she had told a total stranger in the next bed who I was.

She reads all my Echo columns and keeps them. It made me think of Hazel Collinge's words when mum died: "She was very proud of you Peter, and that is the greatest gift a son can give to his mother."

"I'm so sorry I gave you away," she says to me yet again. "We'll have to all have a meal soon, so you can meet the whole family and I will tell them one day," she says. I'd like to meet them, but I don't want to push her.

And that's another visit.

I wish her goodbye, kiss her on the cheek and get into my car.

I turn my phone off, look at my watch
and think about whether the tide will be out far
enough to walk across the sand to Hilbre Island.

About
Adrian Butler

Adrian Butler is an award-winning journalist on the Liverpool Echo. This is his first book, and he hopes Pete will now stop phoning him at all hours with stories that have just popped into his mind.